Children

WHO BREAK THE LAW

or

EVERYBODY DOES IT

Sarah Curtis has been a youth court and family court magistrate since 1978. She began her career in journalism on *The Times Educational Supplement* and *The Times*, going on to edit *Adoption & Fostering* (journal of British Agencies for Adoption and Fostering), and the *RSA Journal* (journal of the Royal Society of Arts). She has worked in community relations and was co-author of a pioneering series of strip-cartoon stories for teenagers about health and social issues. Her 1989 book, *Juvenile Offending: Prevention Through Intermediate Treatment*, was highly praised. She reviews novels regularly for *The Times Literary Supplement* and is editing the *Journals of Woodrow Wyatt*, the first volume of which appeared in 1998.

Children Who Break the Law
or Everybody Does It

Published 1999 by
WATERSIDE PRESS
Domum Road
Winchester SO23 9NN
Telephone or Fax 01962 855567
INTERNET:106025.1020@compuserve.com

ISBN Paperback 1 872 870 76 7

Cataloguing-in-Publication Data A catalogue record for this book can be obtained from the British Library.

Printing and binding Antony Rowe Ltd, Chippenham.

Cover design The back cover incorporates sections from a Thinkstrip entitled 'Laws' from the series *It's Your Life* by Gillian Crampton Smith and Sarah Curtis.

Children

WHO BREAK THE LAW

or

EVERYBODY DOES IT

Sarah Curtis

WATERSIDE PRESS
WINCHESTER

Children Who Break the Law

CONTENTS

For my grandchildren

Acknowledgements

My first thanks go to the young people and their parents who talked to me about their lives, often recounting painful experiences. This book could not have been written without them or without the help of the youth justice and social workers who put me in touch with them. None of these people can be named but they will see the book and know they have contributed to a greater understanding of what can go wrong for young people and what could help them in future.

I should like to thank many other people for information, advice and the time they spent explaining their work. They include: Ann Crisp (NACRO); Mark Perfect and Dr Judy Renshaw (Audit Commission); Jon Bright (Demos); John Harding (Chief Probation Officer, Inner London Probation Service); Lesley James (RSA: Royal Society for the encouragement of Arts, Manufactures and Commerce); Sue Bokes (Health Visitors' Association); Ann Jenkins Hansen (National NEWPIN); the late Carolyn Douglas (Exploring Parenthood); Lynn Hawes and Lorraine Lawson (London Borough of Hammersmith and Fulham); Ena Fry (National Foster Care Association); Carol Clarke (RAILS); Sheila Paget (Family Friends); Beulah Coombs (Lambeth College); Anita Dell (College of North West London); Liz Jones (Lennox Lewis College); Paul Bellamy and Pat Squires (City of Westminster College); Bob Le Vaillant (Stepney Children's Fund); Brenda Shaw and Ian Wetherell.

I am most grateful to Annabella Scott, chairman of the Inner London Youth Panel 1994-1997, now a member of the Youth Justice Board of England and Wales, for reading the first draft and many helpful discussions. Needless to say, the views and any errors are mine.

On a personal level I should like to thank Hilary Rubinstein for his interest in this project; and my husband Anthony Curtis and my son Quentin—not only for commenting helpfully on drafts but for their understanding of why I believe the issues raised in this book are so important.

Sarah Curtis
April 1999

Part One

The Superpredators

"Invasion of the Superpredators" was the banner headline of a page in the *Sunday Times*. A dramatic picture showed a group of young boys in anoraks, with scarves masking the lower part of their faces, defiantly facing the camera. The story continued:

> They're young, brutal and remorseless. They commit crimes by the dozen and get away with most of them. What can be done to combat the new generation of child gangsters dubbed 'superpredators'?

The article went on to report the activities of a self-styled "Young Firm" on a council estate in Salford, Greater Manchester. The gang was "notorious for the scale and bravado of its crimes, which include scores of robberies, burglaries and thefts". The previous week the police investigating the crash of a stolen car discovered a boy of eight inside. According to the local police 80 per cent of burglaries and car crimes in the area were committed by "a handful of kids".

Anyone reading that story would be horrified by the crimes of these children—so many crimes and by such young children—but they might also be appalled by the way the story was told. Time and again the offenders are called superpredators. The "lair" of the Young Firm is the housing estate, its "hunting ground" extends from surrounding roads, the leaders of the "pack" are in their mid teens, young criminals are like a "cancer" on the community. They are distanced, cast as an alien species. The language, the use of metaphor throughout, suggests they are wild beasts, not human beings, and certainly not the children of ordinary people. There may have been some sick logic in the tabloids calling a young boy who used heating ducts on an estate in Newcastle-upon-Tyne as hide-outs "Rat Boy" but this was a serious Sunday newspaper fuelling a sense of panic in its readers.

This kind of feature is not unusual in the broadsheet press. Three weeks after the *Sunday Times* article of 16 February 1997 the *Observer*, a newspaper which usually takes a progressive line on penal matters, carried its version. It was called "The Trouble with Children" and the big print read: "Lee can rip out your car stereo in 25 seconds flat. He's been charged with 64 offences since Christmas. And he's still only ten. Can anything stop this pocket crime wave?" The leader in the same issue called for "an attack on social disintegration at its roots" but the article which caught the reader's attention painted a horrific picture of chaos and despair.

Fear of crime has a rational basis: one in three people in England and Wales report they have been the victim of a crime. Anger about crime by young people is rational, too: a quarter of known offenders in 1997 were under the age of 18. The under 18s commit about seven million offences a year against individuals, retailers and manufacturers. It is right for citizens to be outraged that two of the Young Firm in the *Sunday Times* article passed "much of the day smoking cannabis and loitering on the street with friends" and "devote the evening to stealing a car and attempting to outmanoeuvre the police". Yet beyond the fear, the anger and the outrage there are some unemotional questions to be asked.

Why were the Young Firm not in school? If they were truanting what were the reasons? If they had been excluded from school because of disruptive behaviour why were they not being taught elsewhere? If it was the school holidays what alternative places and activities were there for them in the area? If everyone knew about their criminal activities, why had there been no intervention in their lives, help for their parents to support and discipline them? Above all, were these young offenders different in kind from others who did not get into trouble? Where, when, how and why did they go wrong?

The questions asked in the press are rarely about what is done to prevent crime, to support families or divert young people from crime at an early stage. The hue and cry—to continue the hunting metaphor of the *Sunday Times*—is about what should be done to punish the current offenders. There was general satisfaction when Rat Boy was sentenced in the Crown Court to four years' youth custody for two burglaries, one of the home of an 84-year-old man. He had committed more than a hundred offences from the age of ten. "Now the people here will feel safer in the knowledge that he is inside for so long", said a chief inspector from Northumbria police, reflecting the general feeling of relief. A respite from his activities. Out of sight, out of mind. But would they crack his valium habit in the young offender institution? ("When arrested he told the police he could not remember the break-in because he had taken 30 to 50 valium tablets.") Would he learn a skill there and get a job when he came out? Or would he be one of the 80 per cent of those who left young offender institutions and reoffended within two years? The attention is focused on the here and now instead of long-term planning for change.

Separate courts of justice for children and young people were established in 1908 but there has never been consensus about how the law should treat these juveniles, there has always been tension between punishing them for their crimes and meeting their needs, between immediate action to stem offences and concern to prevent crime for the future . A youth court in England and Wales has to "have regard to the welfare of the child or young person" but the fine phrase "have regard to the welfare" is undefined. Its significance for sentencing purposes has varied according to the political climate. As a magistrate since 1978, first in the juvenile courts which dealt with children in need of protection as well as young offenders, and now in the youth courts and the family proceedings courts, I have seen the pendulum swing to and fro about how to deal with young offenders and legislation following the swing.

The arguments for early intervention through the courts were strong when I first joined the bench. In Inner London, juvenile court magistrates were then appointed directly by the Lord Chancellor to serve in juvenile courts without having to be attached first to an adult court as elsewhere in the country. Like all magistrates we were there to administer the law according to the judicial oath we swore, to "do right to all manner of people after the laws and usages of this realm without fear or favour, affection or illwill", but we were specialists, appointed partly for our knowledge of the young, and so our focus was wide, encompassing prevention as well as punishment. Today those appointed to the youth courts in Inner London, like their counterparts in the rest of England and Wales who are selected for this work by their colleagues on the bench, have to serve first in the adult courts. There has been a subtle shift of emphasis. I wish the Lord Chancellor's department had pushed the balance the other way, ensuring specialist youth benches throughout the country and emphasising that young people are different from adults, immature and more open to change.

In the 1970s and early 1980s whenever the courts had concerns about a young offender they asked for reports from the local social services or probation teams, including school reports. An education welfare officer was often in court to give details of school attendance. At the least, the call for reports alerted those responsible for supporting children at risk that a family might need help. Parents usually agreed that it would be useful to talk to an outsider about their problems. But the pendulum started to swing against such early intervention. One good reason was that allegations in reports might be unfounded. A teacher might write, "Gary has stolen football kit from the cloakroom and is a playground bully" without any substantiation. Guidelines were drawn up in the 1980s for writing education reports that contained only verified facts. But then there was anxiety about "widening the net". It was said that however much young people needed guidance, the court gave them a criminal record by making a supervision order for a first offence and made it likely that they would receive harsher punishment "up the tariff" if they reoffended. It was argued that intervention by a court of law in the name of justice should be strictly proportionate to the crime committed.

The principle of "just deserts" finally became enshrined in the Criminal Justice Act 1991 which laid down that the penalty must be decided in strict correspondence to the seriousness of the crime. There was to be no community intervention for a child who had just started offending but whose offences were comparatively trivial. You had to do a lot of stealing to get either help or punishment. To subject a 12-year-old to supervision because he was beginning to truant from school and keep bad company was said not to be just if he was *only* guilty of vandalising a telephone box. The youth court was a criminal court. It was implied that the wider needs of young offenders should be met elsewhere but there was no formal mechanism to ensure that they would be. The measures in the Crime and Disorder Act 1998 for youth offending teams (known as 'YOTs') to consider drawing up programmes to help children who receive a reprimand from the police, before they even reach court, are a welcome reversal of the trend away from intervention but the idea is not as new as heralded.

The "just deserts" view of sentencing encompassed a degree of scepticism about the effectiveness of the helping hand. Unfortunately, such scepticism is still shared by many today, anxious for immediate, punitive action and fuelled by press reports like "Out of control boy is sent on £4,400 boat trip". The 13-year-old in this news item was due to appear in court for sentencing on charges of assault and criminal damage. The charity which organized his canal trip explained that the expedition had clear reformative aims. It was not a holiday or soft option for the young offender. But to add to the contention, the social services department, which paid for the boy, was the same local authority which had sent another persistent young offender on a safari holiday which did not prevent subsequent offending. "It spoiled him rotten," the boy's mother told the press, "and didn't prepare him for real life. Mark was better off in prison than he ever was in the social services' care." In his speech to the 1993 Conservative Party Conference in which he declared "Prison works", Michael Howard as Home Secretary summed up the popular view: "Yobs who break the law shouldn't be taken on holidays abroad—they should be clearing up their own communities at home. Let's get them picking up litter and scrubbing off graffiti".

The apparent *largesse* of local authorities in funding "treats" has disguised the general dearth of funds for more mundane, continuing work in the community by youth justice teams to ensure that the young offenders understand the effects of their criminal acts and have constructive outlets for their energies. In a book I wrote in 1989 about preventing juvenile offending I described schemes for young offenders as "like a patchwork quilt" with no common pattern. But until 1991 there was general agreement, not least among politicians, that custody should be a last resort for young people. Prison for them did not work, was too expensive and stored up trouble for the future. The Conservative Government's white paper under the aegis of Douglas Hurd as Home Secretary and John Patten preceded the 1991 Act. It said: "Nobody now regards imprisonment, in itself, as an effective means of reforming most prisoners. The prospects for reforming offenders are usually much better if they stay in the community, providing the public is properly protected."

As we enter the twenty-first century reforming offenders remains lower on the political agenda than punishing them. New Labour promised in its manifesto before the 1997 general election to be "Tough on crime and the causes of crime" but the Crime and Disorder Act 1998 with its tough measures on youth crime preceded proposals to address the causes of crime. On major issues—parental responsibility orders (New Labour) or parental control orders (Conservative), youth offending teams (New Labour) or child crime teams (Conservative), tagging, curfews, secure training centres for 12 to 14-year-olds, community safety orders, trips abroad, even "naming and shaming" young offenders—the 1997 election manifestos and subsequent pronouncements of the Labour and Conservative parties have been curiously alike. So is their rhetoric. Who in June 1997 talked about "young thugs" and "one-boy crime-waves causing mayhem on estates"? Not Michael Howard or John Major but the new Prime Minister Tony Blair in the first of his public question and answer sessions. Many of the provisions in the 1998 Act, especially the emphasis on early intervention and reparation, are eminently sensible but the language in which they have been announced is not. By adopting the whirling words of populist fury New Labour has endorsed the emphasis on the here and now and once again obscured the need for long-term changes over a wide field for effective prevention of law-breaking by young people.

This book has two related aims. First, by reporting what a handful of young offenders say about their lives I hope to show such young people as they are rather than as they are portrayed. Their lives are complex and so is the task of stopping them offending. A great deal is said about the parents of young offenders and we have new laws to "make" parents exercise their responsibilities. I decided to talk when possible to the parents of the young people and see what kind of people they were and what were their views. These interviews obviously do not form a statistically sound sample of the offending population but it is valid to look at what the young people say about their lives and to see if they are typical young offenders and if they come from typical families. I cannot prove that they told the truth to me, did not exaggerate or conceal relevant facts about themselves, but I found nothing to contradict what they said and they had no reason to dissemble.

My second overarching aim is to describe how we can in the long-term prevent young people from falling into offending, ruining their own lives and damaging those of others. I want to change the direction of the anger and frustration about juvenile offending from the obsession with dealing with those who have offended to an equal passion for stopping them from ever becoming offenders. This is the only way to protect the public and the only way for a civilised nation to act.

Let us now turn to the young offenders I met: Tyrrell was a joy-rider of stolen cars, Jason a burglar at 12, Jacquie a consummate shop-lifter, Daniel had robbed a building society, Stephen was being punished for robberies and assaults, Mark had stolen cars and robbed, Josiah had committed robberies, Matthew had assaults and burglaries to his name, Robert and Cliff (identical twins) were car thieves, and Luke had been party to a robbery which left the victim crippled for life.

Tyrrell and His Mother

The first time I saw Tyrrell he was playing pool with his youth justice worker at the youth justice centre. He was winning but it was one of those slow, protracted games which neither player seems able to end. Finally Tyrrell did win, to his obvious pleasure, but his reaction was measured, a silent smile rather than the gleeful roar you would expect from a more boisterous character. He was a black young man of slender build, medium height and looked younger than his 17 years. He wore a baseball cap the right way round, jeans, a blue top, and trainers, blending into the scene rather than making a statement through his clothes. Although in contact with his family, Tyrrell had been in the care of the local authority — 'accommodated', to use legal language — since he was about 14.

Tyrrell's court appearances went back for over two years, starting with theft, including burglary and criminal damage, but culminating in a series of convictions for stealing and driving cars without qualifications or insurance, and aggravated vehicle taking which meant he had been a danger to all on the roads. In that comparatively short time he had received the gamut of youth court penalties, from conditional discharges and fines to an attendance centre order to occupy his Saturday afternoons, and supervision. When I met him he was on a supervision order as an alternative to custody, with as full a programme as the youth justice team could provide. If he offended again during the year the order lasted, he would go straight to a young offender institution. The year was nearly over and so far he had kept out of trouble.

He spoke, as he moved, slowly and softly. This is his story.

TYRRELL

I've had the idea of my own car business since I was very young, since eleven upwards. It's been a dream, ambition. When they said at school 'Do you want to be a fireman, do you want to be like your Dad in construction,' I'd always be saying I wanted to be a car mechanic, not working for anybody, working for myself. I hope I shall succeed by the time I'm 25—that's my ambition.

My uncle influenced me. He took like a father role to me. That's where my inspiration comes from. I did in fact live with him for a lot of my life. I moved into his place for a considerable period. My primary school was down by his area. He died tragically. *He died.* He was stabbed in a club. It was a racially motivated attack. The guy was caught . . . he ran straight into the hands of the police. There wasn't a problem about that. He got about 40 years in prison, mandatory life with an extra ten years for something else. It was a very exclusive wine bar which has a membership [fee] of about £100 to £300 and the bottles of champagne over £100 a head. I don't know for sure about all the circumstances, whether he knew the man who killed him.

I was devastated. Before his children came along I was like the child. I loved his wife. *I* didn't lose touch with *her*. After he died she didn't want me around. The last day I actually saw her I came to the house and had some lunch, spaghetti bolognese. I left the house and never saw her again in my life. I came back to her house and was told by one of her friends who took over the place that she'd gone with her children.

My parents weren't together when I was born. I see my Dad from time to time. He doesn't have a job, basically. My Mum has a very good job. She's a secretary, works in a big building, full-time, and drives a car, an up-to-date model. She hasn't a partner. People tend to use her, my family say, and I agree. She goes to a pub, maybe picks up a bloke and then he may stay there, three months or so. He'll be sitting down on the floor one day when I come back. He'll be on the phone all day, lying on the bed, you know. He may take her car and crash it. She's just that generous. She ends having to fork out a lot of money. She's not poor. Even my Dad says, "Why don't you live with your Mum—she's rich."

I've got one brother, he's just coming up to eleven. He's not my father's son. My father has lots of other children but not with my Mum. I stayed with my grandparents, my mother's parents, for a time, while I was at primary school. They came originally from the West Indies. My father's mother is actually Chinese I think.

I quite liked primary school—I can't really remember it much—but then I was in a military school. It was a very strict school. You have to walk at a certain pace round the school, something like three steps a second, and when you stop and talk to teachers you have to put your hands behind your back, feet together, speak and then march off. The only good part, we all loved, was every Friday we used to go boating. That was fabulous.

I still wonder how my mother got me into that school. She shocked me by the look on her face when she told me about it, that that's where I was going to be going in September. I was very, very keen. It seemed very upmarket, not the common, everyday kind of school. My mother knew a boy who went there. His mother used to play dominoes and my Mum was a very good friend of his Mum. There used to be trips where they'd go away, like to Wales, to Sheffield, and play other dominoes people. They used to take their sons with them on these coach trips. We used to have a great time. It used to be like a party when they'd finished playing dominoes, that started at about 12 o'clock and went till six o'clock in the morning. The driver would be sleeping. He'd wake up about six o'clock and then head straight home and we'd be back about 12 o'clock.

I was like the class clown, yeah, the class clown, very disruptive. I had child guidance from a very young age, about eleven, and there was the school psychologist but they couldn't do much. Certain classes weren't much of a help to me, like geography classes. I would skip a lesson to have a fag, things like that. When it was time to do work I would work but at a very slow pace—I think I was a very slow child. I'd draw on the blackboard, do all sorts of stupid things to impress my friends. As soon as the teacher came in all the children in the class would say, "Tyrrell's just done that," and I'd be sent straight down to the headmaster and have to stand outside and be in a hell of a lot of trouble every single day and I'd be sent home—which wasn't very nice at all.

A lot of things were piling up at that time. In the end the last thing that rounded it all off was that a friend told a teacher I urinated in the drama cupboard. It was automatic. Straight to the headmaster to tell me, "We don't want you any more and I'm phoning your mother". She came down and said, "Look, put it this way. You're not going to chuck him out, I'm going to take him out because it's not good on the record to say he's been chucked out of schools." So that's what she did, and found me another school to go to.

My education went wrong down the line at the next school. I got in with the wrong crowd, older boys than myself. All the boys in my class did what I did. To get in you've got to be like the joker, one of the rich ones. That's where it all went wrong. The second school was a very open state school, a mixed school, and there wasn't that area of discipline.

In the district of my first school there wasn't much mucking around, kids breaking into shops and the like, but back in the other area it was very derelict compared with the one where there were millionaires travelling in on the trains, suits only. At that time I was moving with that crowd and I never thought there would be anything stopping my getting there—my Mum always had a very good job. I'd steal an ice-pole from a shop because all my friends was doing it—it'd be summer time—a very cheap one. I wouldn't go for an expensive one. The whole of our class would be there, 50 of us. That's why they wouldn't allow us, more than three people or two, in the shop.

I was living with my Mum at that time. Living with my Nan played a very big part in my life, the first few years of growing up. She taught me a hell of a lot of things which are very competent and handy. Something as silly and stupid as having a bucket in my room to go to the loo in. Instead of me getting up and rushing round the house, if you had a thing in your room and throw it away in the morning, it wouldn't affect anyone—little things like that come in handy.

Another thing was living in a very big house. My Nan had an over ten bedroomed house, it could hold all her kids—she had 18. All of them were grown up, the youngest would have been nineteen. My uncle of about 45 was there and some other kids, my little cousin and my little brother moved in so she was looking after three of us. She cooked for everyone, poor soul. There was about nine of us in that house. It was very big so stuff like having a shower wasn't a problem. Living in a big house like that you could feel the same vibrations of living in your own flat.

My mother's flat is compact and very small. It's only two bedroomed. I shared a room with my little brother. My curfew time was about 10 p.m., with 10.30 p.m. as a luxury. I started trying to make her go to 12. I'd be out with my friends, I'd come back at three in the morning and find that things weren't exactly working out. I never worried about dangers but I was shaken up when a boy got killed on an estate, sexually abused by a black man. When I heard that one on the *Crimewatch* show I was very upset to think that wasn't very far away from me. They showed a reconstruction of what happened. It was at about a quarter to 12 at night and those were the sorts of times I started roaming the streets. It shook me up when I heard it but it didn't stop me. I wasn't really worried it would happen to me.

When I was 14 my Mum threw my stuff off the balcony. That wasn't very nice for me. I was coming in late. So what I did was I went down to one of my friend's houses. My friend told me I could stay so I used to stay down there quite often. Then one day he chucked me out so I went up by the social services department and they took me into accommodation.

At that point I saw myself as being a very grown adult. I thought I was round 18 years old and my point of view was that I was a grown chap. Obviously I wasn't. When I was out I'd hang around corners with my friends, maybe have a cigarette. It wasn't cannabis at that point.

I don't exactly have any friends now. I may go down to where my Mum lives to see someone but I don't walk out of my front door here and see friends here and all that.

The first time I got into trouble with the police I took the day off school. I had a bus pass because of getting to school. I went to the biggest toyshop there is, a superstore. I was eleven. One of my friends had said you can get marbles there and he took me up one day when we took a day off school. From that I went back on my own and started having a look at more of the toys. I may have gone back twice and then I got caught. I wasn't thinking at that time that someone might have to pay the cost of them. What was on my mind at that point was whether I'm going to get this toy and whether I can play with these things. I didn't think about the consequences. My uncle was very upset. He didn't like that kind of thing.

I had one of those pouches you keep money in. I walked round the superstore and picked up a £30 game. I slipped it into my pouch. Then I was surrounded by all these people. I was terrified. They took me back into the store and said they were calling the police. I was begging them not to. Anyway the police came. We went down to the police station and they took me down to the cells. They started ringing my Mum at work and asking her to come down but she never came. This had a lot of meaning to me, that's why it was all so memorable.

I committed the offence at 10 a.m. in the morning and I had to stay in there till nearly one o'clock at night, *and that was at eleven years of age*, in a police cell, waiting for my Mum to come. My Mum refused. My uncle (who had the garages and was like my father) was the one who made her come and collect me. She said, "I wouldn't have come and picked you up. I'd have let social services collect you if your uncle didn't force me to come and collect you". I had done similar things before but I suppose more naughty behaviour. It just got on her nerves so much. She basically doesn't like that sort of thing.

Can you imagine how terrified I was? I was sitting down there thinking 'I'm going to get out quite soon, after half an hour', but there I was, those stone walls. You realise you can't get out of there, you've not got the key. I didn't steal for a year after that because I was so terrified. I was cautioned—it was the first time. Then temptation set me going again. Stealing was wrong, it was, it was.

My first appearance in court was for burglary. I saw scaffolding up on the flats near where I lived and the window was open. I knew the people. We tried to take the video. I got one or two friends involved. We ended up with the stereo. I don't remember my Mum telling me when I was young that stealing was wrong. I never heard about that. Nor at school. Stealing and things I don't think about now. I've grown out of that.

It was at the children's home in the country where social services sent me to live that I started smoking [cannabis]. At the weekend we got our pocket money and our smokes. Everyone smoked. You couldn't not. You got more and more involved. It was about £1.50 a smoke. We used Ecstasy but heroin I never heard of. It's not the case of being frightened, it's just never been my scene.

They told us about safe sex there. They introduced condoms. You could come down to a cabinet and take some. I don't really like them, I don't enjoy myself with them. I'm not sure if my girlfriend was on the pill or not. I actually got two girls pregnant for an abortion in two different homes. Children don't worry me. I like children. I'm happy that I've got one of my own. My girlfriend doesn't want me at the moment. We were in fact very close. The baby's with her in care. I want to see the baby but I have to ask social services to see her. My girlfriend wants me to get some education. I want to be able to give my daughter a job some day so she won't steal. She'll have the things.

It was boys coming down to the home in stolen cars to see their girlfriends that started me off on stealing cars. The home was in the country— it was a private home, maybe a charity. The managers took me once to stay in Jamaica with their family. My Mum contributed. It was wonderful. When I started taking cars it was excitement for me, very, very exciting. The first time I didn't know what to do but they showed me. Then on the way back from school I'd say I'd seen a car, "It's very nice, it's got alloy trimmed wheels on it." We'd go back and drive them away.

I didn't think I was dangerous driving. I was thinking of myself more as a very skilled driver. The one danger I actually was came when I picked up speed to 70 or 80 miles an hour with about 14 police cars chasing me, so many of them, all very angry. I was looking in my little mirror and could see ten at least, trailing me round corners and all the rest. I was going very fast.

I'm on a motor car project now. Joe who runs it is a very good mechanic, a specialist in motor bikes too. He says I'm his best assistant. He's got a car for me which we've fixed and I'll have when I've passed my test. I'll go to college in it. I'm enrolled on a course for September. I've been for my interview. The course should last five years for the BTech. I'll have section 24 funding at first because I'm in care. By the end I'll have to start forking out money, money I can't really afford. I don't want a part-time job—it's not my ambition to work for anybody to gain an extra few pounds.

I thought once about a paper round. I saw an advertisement. I told my Mum. She said, "Well, have a go. I'd be prepared to let you do it." I went to the shop and the guy told me it was something like £10 a week. I'd have to post something like four roads so it works out about £1 a day which wasn't at all what I expected. I said "No, I'm not having that."

Seventy to 80 per cent is theory on my course. It's definitely worth striving for. I'm prepared to put six years with the college and that's what I've told them. It's an option to take the skills course first to get on the HND course. It's not something I'm particularly keen on because it'll put me back a year but not a lot of people have my motivation. They turn round at 25 and say "Jesus! What am I doing?" It hits them in the face. They take the dole and their friends start to reject them because of this drugs atmosphere. I want to go to college now.

I know that one day I will succeed. To get the capital to start, that's where the bank comes involved. You can go to loan sharks, people who will give you a big loan under certain circumstances. I'm hoping that by my status at that time I could go to the bank and show them me with a degree and say, "Look, I've just come from university. Could I borrow £10,000 to £15,000 or so," the most they'd give me. They'd see my status as a highly trained mechanic in this field with an HNV degree and management skills. I'd say, "Would you be prepared to give me a head start?" You know the difference between a bank and a loan shark? With a loan shark, if you don't give it back, then maybe there are personal vendettas and things like that. In a bank they borrow you the money at very low rates and if you don't take it back, you suffer the consequences in a jail sentence and there's a certain procedure it goes through.

I'd love to know how my uncle managed. He owned various car businesses throughout his life. I'm not sure if he had qualifications but he was very highly motivated in that area. I think he went to college. Those are the steps I'm trying to take. I don't think I could go to the bank now and ask for a loan, when I'm 18, and not a scrap of anything behind me. It's like me saying, "I want to set up a mobile shop and employ people to take it over for me". Wouldn't everyone be doing that?

I haven't taken cars for a long time, since I've been at youth justice, just coming up to over a year. I couldn't. I've never stolen a car since I've been away from my girlfriend and since she's had a baby. She wouldn't get in a car. She'd be frightened of losing her baby over a car. She doesn't like being arrested. She's had a lavish life-style by stealing clothes all the time and then selling them and so forth. She's finished with all of that and she'd never risk stealing again. Maybe, on the drugs sector, I wouldn't put it past her that she'd have a smoke.

I'm hoping to move into one of the flats for semi-independent living attached to where I live now. There's a curfew of 12 o'clock now. I go to a skills course one day, see my youth justice worker another day, the motor project another day. I prefer having something. I sleep quite late but the cleaners like you out by eleven or so. They're quite nice and will make you a sandwich for lunch, cheese or something (not salami— they're on a tight budget). I've outgrown it. I'll get the skills for looking after myself, cooking and cleaning.

I haven't stolen a car for a year. I'm mixed up in this banger project now. I think I'm racing on Saturday. I'm quite keen on that because I can actually win a trophy—so that will be quite interesting.

TYRRELL'S MOTHER

Tyrrell's mother, opened her flat door with a large smile and the offer of a cup of tea or coffee. A plump, relaxed-looking lady, she unlocked the sitting room for us to talk undisturbed by her eleven-year-old son who was dashing in and out of the other rooms with a friend. It was a hot day and her feet were bare. She sat back on the comfortably dented leather settee. The room felt lived-in. The only new-looking thing I noticed was an elaborately stacked hi-fi sound system. The rest was unselfconsciously worn and untidy. The front door was missing its knocker and scuffed, in contrast to the neat appearance of the other front door on the balcony landing. A photograph of Tyrrell at about his brother's age smiled happily at us from the fireplace. This is what she told me.

Tyrrell booked himself into care. I couldn't get him the expensive things in life he wanted, trainers costing £90 to £100. He said, "Right, I'm going to use social services." He decided that at 14. He was bunking off all the time from school. Then he started going round with a certain group of people and was always running off. He only got caught by the police once at first. It was usually a case of bringing him home and sorting him out. There wasn't much on record.

I'm a secretary. The primary school I went to, Tyrrell went to. He was with my mother then, so they were there for him when he got back from school. The secondary school Tyrrell went to at first was much better than the one I went to but he dropped out, went to another school, it didn't work out there and that was it. I just went to a normal secondary school. I had no qualifications when I left school apart from a typing certificate. I worked myself up. I got a government job and ended up as a secretary.

I was about 19 when I had Tyrrell. Tyrrell's Dad has never been around apart from coming and making promises about what he's going to buy him for his birthday. He came down and saw Tyrrell but he never took any responsibility for him. He never treated him like a son; he treated him like a mate, a buddy. Times they'd be sitting there, arguing, and I'd say, "He's got no respect for you. Look at the way he talks to you. He won't talk to me like that. You will treat him like a friend, won't you? What do you expect?" Tyrrell's taken the role of wanting to look after his Dad, seeing that he's got a drug problem now, the last couple of years. He goes down there and seeing the state he's got himself into he feels he needs to look after him. I think it puts him off drugs. He'll phone, "Mum, Dad wants you to come down." I think: "What's the matter with him now, what's he after?" "He wants you to keep him company, he probably feels lonely." Tyrrell feels he should be with him whereas I don't because he wasn't there for Tyrrell as a child.

I supported Tyrrell myself. I've worked since he was ten months old. My social worker helped me get the nursery and helped me sort out myself about getting a job and a roof over my head. She got everything for me and then once she'd left that was it, there was nobody else. She was the very best. Her husband got a job somewhere out in the country and she gave up being a social worker. I was just left on my own.

Tyrrell was in nursery at ten months right till the age of five when he started school. He was a very bright child. He was walking and talking before the age of one, and when I say talking, you could have a conversation with him. He was reciting the alphabet before he was two.

The problems actually started when he started primary school because all what he's learnt at nursery they were repeating again at primary school at the age of five. They labelled him as a disruptive child because he said he was bored, he'd done it already. They said that, just because he'd gone to nursery, "the world doesn't stop for Tyrrell", the other kids had to be talking. If he's not getting any stimulation from his work, he starts getting fidgety and doesn't know what to do with himself. The next thing he's disruptive. It just never worked out from day one. I tried to get help then and there was nobody. He was probably about eight or nine when he first saw an educational psychologist. He's a bright child. I felt he was held back. There was no one to help me push him. He was just labelled as disruptive.

If you get to talk to anybody, they'll make a note of it, say they'll get in contact with who they've got to get in contact with, but then it stops: nothing was ever taken forward again. It was just left. I tried him with cubs when he was younger and that lasted a little while but his problems really started at secondary school. I reckon Tyrrell had a rough deal through his school life. Everyone said they were going to do this and that for him and then it just stopped dead on paperwork.

Tyrrell was about seven when my other son was born. The other boy's father never lived with me. Tyrrell has had a much better life than my younger one. When my brother was alive they went everywhere together—holidays to the Isle of Wight, they were always out and about. Every weekend my brother had him. He adored him. He'd be down at the garage with him, he'd teach him the ropes of being a mechanic. When he'd done well in school, my brother was the sort of person that'd give him a little treat or say, "We'll go away for the weekend" or whatever.

His business was doing well, he worked hard, he was all right money-wise. His ambition was first to get a nice car, then a nice house and after that, the kids. It didn't work out like that. He got the nice car—then the kids. He didn't get to have the house yet. They were still in their Council property when he died. He was always getting Tyrrell games and what have you, and then when he died, the case is [I said] that "there is no more to get, he's gone now".

My brother and his partner had always had Tyrrell. When she had her kids they still had Tyrrell. Then, when he died, it was a case of don't want to know. She just took the kids and took off; they live somewhere far away. She cut herself off totally. To me, that's the worst thing you could do to kids. He thinks of them as brothers and sisters and they loved him. If they didn't see Tyrrell they'd be crying "I want Tyrrell, I want Tyrrell" and she'd be on the phone saying, "Tyrrell, get down here."

Everyone had Tyrrell, everyone made a fuss of Tyrrell from day one. Even in nursery one of the staff would say, "Can I take him away for the weekend with me?", and he'd say "I wanna go, I wanna go". There were always people who loved him and wanted to show him off and take him away on holiday. I'm just surprised the way he turned out. Tyrrell was wanted, right, left and centre. He had the best; he had no reason to behave that way. He had anything he wanted— computers, a TV in his room, stereo in his room, he had everything. The more stuff he had, the more he wanted.

I wanted Tyrrell here but Tyrrell didn't want to come home. He doesn't like the restrictions I lay down on him. To me, if you're at school, you're in here at a reasonable hour. You don't disappear for days and come knocking on my door at three or four o'clock in the morning and expect me to get up when I have another child to get to school and I have to go to work. I won't have it. The younger boy's different. He's never bunked off school. Although Tyrrell was a much brighter child, he's not that way inclined, a completely different child.

I don't think they should have taken him into care. They should have sent him back home. They gave him the things I couldn't. We're not church people, except for christening. Tyrrell was christened as a Roman Catholic like me and I told him what was right. When I had him here, he wasn't really in that great deal of trouble, it was just the odd occasion. I remember when he got arrested at the toy store. I wasn't going to run and fetch him. As far as I was concerned he should have been at school, not thieving at the toy store. I had my job to do, I was tired. I wanted to teach him a lesson, frighten him off. I told the police they could have roughed him up a bit to show him. Now, since he's been with them, he must have quite a long record. Next time he gets into trouble, that's it, he's gone to prison.

Tyrrell's always wanted to get into the car business. As I keep telling him, you have to work hard for it. You don't just sit on your backside and it comes to you. If you want things enough, you go out and earn it.

Tyrrell likes being noticed. He needs one hundred per cent attention and he's prepared to do anything to get it. I had no one to go to when he first started truanting. The school knew he was truanting. They don't bother to phone you. It's just by chance you get to find out about it. To me the schools don't feed you in straightaway about what's going wrong. It's a long time after and it's really going back. I would have liked to have known from the first day, not to be told that your child hasn't been going to school for the last few weeks. You get him up, he's got his school uniform on, he's got his books and he's gone. As far as I'm concerned he is in school.

That all started at secondary school. The teachers called him the class clown. I think he was still clever but he was trying to fit in with everybody else. You don't want to be too clever in case your friends start ridiculing you about it. He just messed around to get attention. I thought at the time that that school, discipline-wise, was right for him. It was run by men. There was nothing boys could do to pull the wool over their eyes [I thought], they'd know how to deal with it. And I was just so wrong because for silly little, petty things they'd be phoning me at work to come and remove him from the school. I thought, "Oh! What has he done?" He'd written on the walls, something rude. I said, "Well, can't you just give him a bucket and a mop and tell him to clean it up?"

He'd be in the classroom and he'd put up his hand wanting to go the toilet. No, they said, so he went in a corner. Please remove him from the school. So what do you do? They're supposed to be teachers. If a child wants to go, he wants to go. But I guess having him down as the school clown, he decides to go in the corner, they don't want him there, he's disruptive. He didn't settle at the next school. The group of boys he met in there was roaming the streets all the time. So he got in with them and didn't want to go at all. He just left. He walked out and never went back.

I don't enjoy working but I need to survive. I do get satisfaction sometimes but I'm really tired, I need a break. I just don't understand what makes a child these days turn to crime, especially a child that was loved.

Tyrrell asked his Dad if he would see me but it proved impossible."He didn't seem to understand," Tyrrell told me."He said he'd only see you if you paid him £200".

Jason and His Parents

The social services office where I met Jason was housed in a tower block. Two young boys were playing around the grass verge at its base. One looked at me closely but said nothing. I smiled at him, wondering if he might be Jason. His social worker fetched him up on my arrival, a slim 13-year-old with a broad-browed oval face, olive skin, very short hair and a scar at the corner of one eyebrow. He was smartly dressed in grey-blue trousers and a bright green pullover with a designer name across the front. The points of the collar of a window-check shirt showed neatly at the neck.

Jason had a string of convictions for theft, criminal damage and burglary and had already appeared in the Crown Court. He was given a conditional discharge there for his part in a serious burglary which took place at night with the owners of the property in bed asleep. The adults with him were imprisoned.

Jason's family had received support from social services for some years, from the time his older step-brother was young. We began by discussing his interests, slowly.

JASON

I like football and bike-riding. I ride a bike quite a lot. It's not my bike, it's my friend's. In the holidays I usually wake up early, about half eight, nine, it depends. I get up, then I take out the dog. Then I come back home, I have something to eat, watch telly, get changed, then go out to my friend's house. My mate's called Jason, too. He was outside. He's been my mate since primary school. He goes to the same school as me. I go the Centre, ITC [Individual Tuition Centre]. He's not been in trouble, I don't know why.

I don't remember when I first did something. I thought I'd get away. When I first got arrested, it was burglary. It wasn't round here. I won't shit on my own doorstep. I won't 'cos you'd just get known, wouldn't you? If you do it in another area, you come back to your own area and everything'll be nice and normal. I prefer it to be nice and normal.

I take systems and all them valuable things. I keep them, sell them. There's always people around who'll buy them. My Mum wouldn't know, my Dad wouldn't know. I never think about the people when I do burglaries. My most precious things are my system and my clothes. If they got nicked I'd go out and look for the people. If I found them I'd get my stuff back. I wouldn't tell the police. It ain't worth it. They don't do nothing.

It's just something to do. I'm just bored. The most exciting thing I've ever done is bike-riding. The sports centre down there has tennis, snooker, swimming. Swimming ain't me. Youth clubs are rubbish, boring—too young.

I've got lots of brothers and sisters. The two oldest ones are sisters. They've not been in trouble. When they heard I'd got into trouble they hit me. They hit me hard to try and stop me from thieving. It stopped a little while but not for long. I stopped but then I'm off again. I can't stop, I'm used to it, I can't just stop it that easy. I don't know, *nobody* knows how to stop stealing. You do think about your saying you'd not do it again when you do it but not really. Old people may not do it but all the youths round here do it, all the youth from the age of nine.

It depends who's there whether I do it alone or not. Most people do it. People you wouldn't think would do it. You know what it's like when you ain't got no money in your pocket. You know what it's like. I'd like to have a job, any kind, when I grow up. My Dad's a cleaner. My Mum's a cleaner too.

When I'm arrested they come down to the police station. They hit me up to try and stop me. People all round here, they have to get hit to learn. You can't tell them. You have to fill before you spill. *Telling* ain't no use, I'm telling you. If my children got into trouble I'd hit them. I'd get them what I got. To stop them getting into trouble I wouldn't let them out. My Mum can keep me in for as long as a year—I'd stay. It's better than going out there and getting arrested. I don't like that.

It does worry me about upsetting them [my parents]. Prison doesn't worry me. I know about it. People around here go to prison and say about it. It doesn't stop them. Prison's only a little slap on the wrist.

I'd never nick a handbag—no way. Never, never, in the whole of my life. I just wouldn't. It's too . . . It's not good to do that, to run and just take it off her. It would be understandable perhaps if you're not looking to take it. People get hurt, people get hurt taking people's handbags. Only crack-heads run and take handbags and beat her up. They just want crack and it's the easiest way to get it. I don't smoke cannabis. The furthest I've got to smoking is a bloody cigarette.

What's the point of doing cracking? Say the police come and there's a time for you to run: you've been smoking—you'll collapse, especially if you're smoking cannabis. It makes you just high, when you don't know what you're doing, turning round and hitting. When you wake up next morning you think, "Oh my! I don't know what I did".

Nobody gave me the idea. You just go and do it. I started stealing from sweet shops, then clothes. These jeans cost about £300. These jeans, they're velvet. See this belt? [*Jason lifted up his pullover and showed me a black leather belt with a big, bright, gold buckle. It looked to me rather large for him, with the end beyond the buckle tucked in*]. This belt is money, money. I know a lot about money. I tell my Mum I bought them from a friend. I got them from a shop. I didn't *nick* them. [*He laughed, as if he'd read my thoughts suspecting him*]. I paid £348.99 for them. I got these when they first came out. No one ain't got these—they're warm and they're thick. I sold something to get them.

So how long do I go on with this talking? [*We fixed another ten minutes and Jason resumed*]. The police don't know anything about this area. They think they know everything but they don't because they only catch the low criminals. There are high ups, higher ones. They do anything—big armed blags. They have pistols. It doesn't worry me that they might kill someone. That's *them*. Whoever gets in the way get's blown. I'm not going to die because everyone round here knows I'm smart. *No* one's using me, *no* way.

I remember nursery. It was all right. At school I like art and that's it—and PE. I like painting. I hate reading 'cos it's slow. I never in my whole life bunked off school. I got excluded for fighting and that's it—not doing the lesson, play fighting and real fighting. I was never bullied. I wouldn't stand no one bullying me. I've never bullied no one. I was bored. I didn't like any of the teachers. The lessons were boring. They could have made them more interesting, played some music. Lots were excluded.

It's all right where I am now [*at the Individual Tuition Centre for ten hours a week*]. I go there when I'm meant to. I've no idea what I'd like to do when I leave school. I've never bought a bike because I want clothes to get big. I get excited by all that top stuff in clothes. If you'd get me a paper-round job, I'd do it every day. It'd just be good, running round on my bike, doing what you have to do, like a job.

JASON'S FATHER

The plan was to meet Marilyn and Tyrone, Jason's parents, together. I confirmed the time with Marilyn the evening before but she forgot to tell Tyrone and forgot to come herself. She was out when I rang to see what had happened but luckily Tyrone was at home. He was able to come over straight away to talk to me and we fixed another time for Marilyn.

Tyrone was a slight West Indian man, with a gentle manner, looking younger than his 56 years, only just beginning to go grey. He wore neat jeans, a black bomber-style cloth jacket and a pale blue peaked baseball cap. I asked him first about his family as Jason had said he had "lots of brothers and sisters".

Jason has two older sisters—one is nearly 16, one is 14—two younger sisters who are 12 and five and there are two boys of ten and eight. He's got an older brother as well of 19 who is Marilyn's son, not mine. He doesn't live with us—he comes and goes, you know. We've been together about 18 years, something like that. We've never married—I think she was married already. I'm 56, she's 40.

We've a council flat—only three bedrooms. Jason sleeps with his brothers. They sleep anywhere they can really. We make like a bedroom under the stairs. We take carpet there and put a little bed inside there. I have a cleaning job for a private firm. Marilyn has no work at the moment.

I helped bring up Jim, the eldest. His schooling was all right for a time and then things just changed. I don't really know why. I used to take him to school that time because I was working there in the kitchen—I used to deliver the school meals. They used to put him in there, you know, and then he'd go out the other door. [*Tyrone laughed*] He used to get into trouble, he used to run away a lot. He's all right now. He's not working at the moment. He lives with his girlfriend— she works. He isn't in trouble now as far as I know.

With Jason, it all started going wrong at infants' school when he was about seven. Somebody dared him "that you don't trip over the teacher" and he did. He got excluded rightaway. The new head teacher had come there and she threw him out rightaway. I think she wanted to make an example. He goes to the centre [*Individual Tuition Centre*] now every day, sometimes in the morning and sometimes in the afternoon, not long hours. The oldest girl is at the centre too. He go to the centre before and then he went back to school. When he was eleven and went to secondary school, he didn't truant, he got disruptive. He never talk about it, you know what I mean.

A few times they'd write from school and then I'd have a word with the teachers and so on, you know, but things didn't change. They said he can't concentrate for long. No one said how I could help him concentrate. We could only talk to him but he could be all right and then the next minute he'd just change, just like that. He started getting into trouble after he'd been thrown out of school. He started mixing with other kids, the bigger boys I mean, not his age. They were about 16 or 17.

He can't read properly. He is very good at art. We couldn't really help him at home. His sisters did try. The bigger one, she used to read with him but that didn't last for long. It ended up arguing. If there's something he can't quite spell, he'll get annoyed. The teachers, they say, "Well, he could be all right but give him something he can't do, he won't make the effort. He don't have the patience." I think that's the root of his problem. Those are the things he's not interested in. If he's interested in something he'll stick to it, but then again he won't be interested for long.

He's very good at coming in on time. Now he can stay out until nine o'clock. Most of his shop-lifting was daytime and his burglaries during the day. We never knew. He didn't tell us. He don't talk much, you can't get that out of him. He would more tell his mother but he wouldn't tell me. [*To punish him*] I'll tell him he's grounded, he can't go out. They get a smack now and again but not regular. The trouble is, most of the time he's been getting away with it and he must have got to realise, "Well, I can do this and get away with it", so he continues doing it.

What could stop him? Well, that's a very good question. I don't know what would stop him. I speak to him about it but he gets very, very rude to people, not to us at home but to people in the street. The slightest little thing—I don't know if he shows off. Yesterday I had to give him a slap in the street because he abused two women outside there and he didn't realise that these women, the one did know me. She come and complain to me and I see him coming down the road so I call him and he try to say nothing. I hit him in front of the woman. I don't know if it will do any good.

The last time of telling him he's grounded, he'd been rude to another woman, a neighbour. He tried to say not and the woman said, "Yes, it's you." I tell him he's grounded and he decide—well, he's come and telling me he's going to run away. And he disappeared for the night. I think he went by his brother. The brother's trying to talk to him but it don't seem to make no difference. He could be all right and suddenly he just change, just like that.

I don't know the reasons. We've only ever seen the social worker. When he was young they tried to see if he was deaf but when they tested him there was nothing wrong with him, it was all right.

The people who did the big burglary with him live on the estate—they're his older brother's friends. They used him. They took him some place to put his hand through the letter-box and the police was watching them. We didn't know because he went to bed about half past nine and the police came about five o'clock in the morning and they were ringing the bell. We didn't hear and then they phone up and they say: "We've got two policemen waiting to come in. I'm sorry to say we've got your son at the police station." My daughter gets up, she went downstairs and open the door for them. They come and say, "You'll come this way." Marilyn says, "What for?" "For your son." She turn and say, "He don't live here". "Jason don't live here?" "*Jason* live here. He's in bed." Then we go downstairs. It was empty. He climbed over the balcony. We live next to the road and he sometimes comes in through there.

When he came back, what could I say when he came back? He doesn't understand about doing wrong to people. I think they should have sent him to see a psychiatrist, or something like that, to find out what's wrong with him when he was young, seven or eight. I personally think something is wrong with him because he'll just change in a flash. He's very, very good inside the house. Some mornings, you know, h e used to get up and make tea and all this sort of thing, and he'd bring i t and give it to you—and the next couple of days he'd just change. The older boy's not a good influence on him because he's been in trouble and he seems to look up to him and what *he* does is right.

Jason don't be interested in nothing for long. That's why I said something must be wrong with him. When he was going to the football club [*a famous premier league club*], they tried him out, he came home feeling so good like 'Oh, he's done this and he done that' and the next day they threw him out. He go there and he's in a different mood. He got funny with the man who's training them. He was so happy because there was so much boys and they all liked to be goalkeeper. The next day he was back home. "So what happened?" "I be thrown out." He said the man tell him this and he didn't feel like doing it. I go down there to see the man, like talk to him man to man, and the man say no, he be very rude and the thing is the kids be glad to see the back of him as well. So he must be very, very bad.

The lady at the centre is very strict. She seems to like him and she said his report was very good. He seems to like it. He don't stay away from there, he goes. I don't think he'll get back into ordinary school again. We've not been told anything.

The younger ones are all right—no trouble from them yet. [*Tyrone laughed*]. I would have liked more help if I'd been given it because I think something's missing. I don't know how the system work. All we know is the social services. Nobody else to turn to. They can only try to do their best. Then again you can't be looking to them all the time.

JASON'S MOTHER

I would never have guessed that Marilyn was the mother of eight children. With crimped, auburn hair framing her head and shoulders, bright blue eyes and slim as any fashionable young girl, she did not look her age. She wore white jeans and a purple shirt which admirably set off her pale skin, giving her an almost pre-Raphaelite air. Round her neck were a few thin gold necklaces. She was embarrassingly apologetic for having forgotten our appointment. It happened to have been for the first day of the school term, the first day of comparative freedom for her after the long summer holidays. It was easy to see why she forgot. She gave the impression of being friendly, capable and if necessary tough.

I wasn't actually born in this area but I came here when I was about 13. I never liked school. I actually got excluded from school when I was about eleven—that was a few years ago! Jason is like me in such a way when I was small. But I wasn't a thief, wasn't a burglar—Jason is. I can see me in him ever so much, not in everything, I mean, but his attitude, his schooling.

He's fantastic at art, really, really good. He wants to be so many things but he starts off and after a while he gets these complications and he can't be bothered. It's his lack of concentration—only three or four minutes, maybe five. He was OK with you because he was warned.

He was a terrible baby, he was a horrible child. I was told he was hyperactive. He just cried. I wasn't helped with him much. I was told not to give him this and what food I shouldn't feed him but I wasn't actually given enough help with him, his behaviour. When he started school, obviously they realised something *was* wrong because he was just very, very disruptive. They did think at one time he was deaf, or partly deaf, and that turned out to be that he wasn't. It was just that he constantly had colds and the fluid was going down into his ears, what they call glue ear now which we didn't know anything about. That put him back because he wasn't able to hear what the people said. Unless you looked him into the face of the person he was talking to, he didn't really hear.

His tantrums were never in front of me and his Dad. They were always in front of people like teachers, nursery even. Not in front of me and his Dad because although he's a handful, he's still got the respect there for me and his Dad. But it doesn't stop it. As soon as we let him out of our sight, he just wanders off. He's *so easily led*.

I was nearly 20 when I had Jim. I split up with his Dad and met up with Tyrone. He brought Jim up from when he was six months old. Jim was never treated differently from the rest of the children. The only difference is that Tyrone's black and he's white, a big difference. Jim does look up to Tyrone. He's getting older now, he's not really around so much but he does respect Tyrone and he doesn't do things in my house when he comes round which he'd probably do in his own house. He wouldn't smoke, not in no way.

Jim was worse than Jason because he was running away for weeks on end. We were terrified at the time. Jason doesn't run away to stay out. He runs off but he always come back. Jim's OK now, he's almost 20 now, he's more of an adult. He's got his girlfriend and she has a nice little home and that part of it's going out of phase. I can't speak for Jim. I don't know if he were faced with that sort of situation whether he'd do it but I think he thinks twice about things now and before he never used to care. He was very disruptive at school, too, but he decided he didn't want to go to school. His friends didn't want to go to school so he decided he wasn't going to go. Jason just couldn't cope with school, he just couldn't cope with it. He is so, so behind. He can hardly read and spell—I think my five-year-old can do better than him.

My eldest girl was excluded from school but for a fight. It was quite a serious fight which ended up in Crown Court. They had no option but to exclude her from the school. She had been in fights a few times. She is—I'm not praising—a very, very clever girl. She's doing so well over there at ITC [*Individual Tuition Centre*] with computers and whatever.

Round here, if you don't stand up for yourself, you tend to get trodden on and then people use and abuse you whenever they feel to do so. So I think really for this area you have to do something about it. These days you've only got to look at the kids sideways and they want to kill you anyway. They're very, very aggressive and I think the girls are worse than the boys.

My daughter did get caught shop-lifting once but it never got to court or anything like that. It was during school-time; she went during dinner-time and did something with a friend of hers. The police brought her back to school and that was it, we never heard no more. And it stopped.

From the time Jason started thieving, since he was seven or eight, it's very rare that he doesn't get caught. At first it was petty, silly things, you know, shop-lifting. He'd go and get silly, stupid things, pencils, pens that he wouldn't even use. Now he's gone on to bigger things. He's been going for robbery, a residential, big robbery. That was him and two older boys. I don't say that he was influenced by the two older boys because it was during the night that this happened. He actually sneaked out of my house. When the police came and said "We've got your son," I thought, "Oh my God! Jim's gone and done something." When they said "It's your son *Jason*," I went to the bedroom and expected to see Jason in bed with the other kids but he wasn't there: he was at the police station.

You can wind Jason round your little finger he's so easily led—it's unbelievable. If he thinks he's going to be a star or, you know what I mean, he's doing something that he thinks is really, really clever, you don't have to ask Jason twice, he will go. And I don't say that these two boys led him on at all really because he knew exactly what he was doing because he got up out of his bed. He was in bed asleep when I went to bed—at least I thought he was asleep—so therefore he obviously has this plan down to go out and do what he was going to do.

He was 12, they were 19 and 21. We knew them. One lives on our estate. Actually I'm quite friendly with his mother. They were our eldest son's friends. They went with him to school. Jim's now out of that area. They've carried on with their games, Jim's grown out of them. I think Jim's a good influence on Jason and he doesn't have a bit of trouble with him.

It was a residential burglary with two people actually sleeping in the house which made it very bad. What we did was try to explain to Jason that [*Marilyn paused*] it's wrong, you shouldn't have been there in the first place, but to actually go into somebody's house when they're sleeping, you could actually lose your life over it. Because, I mean, if you find someone in your house, you ain't going to ask no questions first, you're going to lash out. It's bad enough stealing from shops or any stealing but to go into somebody's house when they're there!

His Dad was so upset and so was I about it—he was really annoyed —because Jason was the one that went into the house, not them, they were outside. Jason gained access. They went in afterwards. So Jason could have been hurt, really hurt. I tried to explain to him that it's just not on, not on at all.

In my house, if someone touches something of his or if it goes missing, it's World War III, yet if he takes something from one of the other kids it doesn't seem to bother him. He doesn't have that understanding—you can't just go round taking people's things.

It's no good hitting Jason. We tried that. I don't think it does prove at all. Kids have to be smacked now and then, I do believe, especially when you have a lot like I have and you're trying to maintain a standard. There are rules and regulations and they have to obey them in my house, it's as simple as that. But grounding Jason is the worst thing [*for him*]—he *hates* staying in. He likes his freedom. He gets like claustrophobic—he can't be in one space. If that door were locked, he'd try his best to break that door down. He doesn't like being in a cell which the police will more than tell you.

If he gets in trouble with the police or something's happened, he has to come in every two hours. He can go back out but he still has to come home to check with us all he's done. He doesn't really go anywhere. All he's doing is with his friends—half the time they're probably up to no good. If there's a bad one there, he'll find them. He says, "Oh, Mum, I went here," but he's just around here, hanging round the street, making a nuisance of himself sometimes. The other Jason is a schoolfriend of his but he's much smarter than Jason. My Jason goes in front, Jason's at the back. My Jason doesn't stop to think. He just steams into something. We make him come in at nine o'clock at night-time which he's very good at. If he has to be in at a time, he's there on time, if not before.

He did once run off. He runs, he comes here to social services and they say, "Jason, phone your Mum up, you're going back home". He has had a spell in care. He was on remand for something, some offences, and he ran away. He hated it at the assessment centre. They put him there as an emergency placing because they didn't have anywhere else for him to go. The kids tried to set his hair alight. They used to bully him rotten. He was even, I think, committing crimes with some of the boys there. He has been to a foster carer—that lasted one night. He had to be physically restrained because he went beserk, smashing things, because he was caught smoking and he couldn't handle that. He does smoke cigarettes but he's not that much of a smoker.

They won't take him back at the football. He goes somewhere with a good heart and someone says something he doesn't like or tells him to do something he doesn't like, and that's it. There's no, "Oh yeah, I'll stop" or "I won't do this." Jason can't handle being told to do things. It is from an early age. The younger ones are not like that. The girls can be very pushy but they do as they're told. I'll not say that they're doing fantastic at school but they're doing just as good as any other.

It embarrasses him that some of the younger children are spelling better and doing a lot more work than he could. That's why he doesn't do a lot of writing or reading—he can't read, anyway. When he was at school he'd bring home his reading folder, things you'd expect to do with a child anyway. You did as much as you can but you just couldn't get through to Jason. You'd be sitting there and it would be me reading the book and he'd want to be elsewhere. You'd say "Jason, Jason, Jason". He just wanders off, loses concentration, can't be bothered.

He likes the centre but then we're stuck again. They can't put him in a mainstream school because he can't cope with being in a big group of people. He needs one to one, or two at the very most. It's just impossible, impossible. But somewhere there's a nice kid. He'd go full-time to the centre if he could—he'd have no choice. If he were sent to school, he'd have to go to school. If we found out he hadn't gone to school or gone off from school, then we'd have to know why so he'd have to answer to me which he doesn't like at all. He gets into trouble and he's a handful but he knows the consequences.

They have opened up a club now which they go down to of the evenings. I don't say he goes there regularly but he goes there quite a few times with two of his sisters. They're mixing records and tapes and all this business which he probably enjoys and he's very good at it.

Jason used to go away for ten days in the summer holidays which gave me a break, to a children's country holiday. He used to love that because he'd be out in the fields, you know what I mean, and could run for miles. I had no trouble, only one year, and that was a few years ago. The family he went to was a police officer's and of course that didn't go down too well with Jason.

There was no holiday this year. We went with the play centre on day trips to places like GreatYarmouth. He's fine on them. I like to sit with him because I wouldn't like to be embarrassed. He actually enjoys it, acting like a kid and not trying to put on this image which doesn't suit him at all.

I give him so much pocket money a day. If I have any extra money, or his Dad has extra money, then we'd give him some but I don't like Jason to have too much money at one time. I fear that he'd go out and they'd all muck in and buy drugs with it which I'm not going to encourage at all so I limit myself. He has £1 a day. I think that's quite sufficient. Every now and then I might give him a fiver but I don't make a regular habit if it.

We get his clothes and then he might appear and you think, "Oh! Where did that come from, Jason?", and he says "My friend gave it to me". Of course you ask the friend and he says, "Oh yes." [*Marilyn laughed*]. He has gone through a phase of selling *our* clothes. I gave him a bloody good hiding because it takes me a long time to save the money to keep my kids dressed to a standard of where they want to be because we said we might have a large family but it doesn't mean to say your kids have to go around like tramps. I do try my best.

The kids round here, they all want to outbid each other. Everyone's got to wear this and that one's got that and they all want to just make themselves better than that other person. They want money in their pockets all the time which is impossible for me to have, let alone them to have.

This social services is fantastic. The ones before were sad, not useful at all. If these can do something, they do it. When they say they can't, then they mean they can't. It's the *family* who has a social worker. He's a fantastic man, he really is. He is really caring and he's seen the things that happen. But help from social services really goes nowhere, not through their fault. The places where Jason's been haven't worked out or haven't been the right places in the first place. Apart from that there's nothing. Nobody's really said, "Well, I can help Jason" or "I'm going to help Jason". Nobody's really taken him on. Or they will take him until something happens.

There was no plan at nursery, nothing even really at school. It was actually *left* until it was beyond repair. I've always been very good with the schools and the nurseries, said, "If my children do anything wrong, phone me and let me know. Don't leave it until it's too late. Phone me and let me know." With Jason I suppose it was so many occasions when he was doing things, they just thought, "We can't keep phoning her up like that." At the school they never used to phone me. They might give me the occasional letter home. The next thing I knew it was exclusion and that was it.

He was—is it estimated?—no, *statemented*—when he got excluded from primary school and they actually told me that they couldn't find nothing wrong with him. Your child got excluded from school, got sent to see someone, have them examined, and that was it: end of story.

I've always praised him when he does things and I've always had a 'please' and 'thank you' from him as well, you know. But then he just gets—not fits—but these days when he don't care, when he can't be bothered. I don't know if he's had a rough night or whatever. There's no reason with him.

We tried to put Jason in a boarding school. It's never, ever come. He knows about boarding school, that it would be 52 weeks a year and weekend visits. I think it's a conversation we've got to sit down and talk to him about because he can't keep going and doing this because eventually he's going to end up in prison. He's getting older and the rules are changing. I've always said that unless Jason does do a term in prison or they send him to some place where he is locked up and confined and he can't go where he wants to go and do what he wants to do, I don't think he'll be stopped. It's like he gets a buzz out of it or something.

What bothers me and really does worry me is that his offending is getting more serious. It was petty before, it's getting worse. He's up now for having hit some man over the head with a bottle. He says he didn't do it. It's got to be proved but if he did do it, the thing is that's a very, very serious charge, for his age and the size of him as well—he's not exactly ten foot tall, you know what I mean.

I wouldn't like to think he would have mugged anyone in the street because I've seen people get mugged and I don't like that. I think it's very, very sad and there's so much of it outside here, anywhere round here. The muggings are unbelievable.

You don't want your children to make the mistakes you made. You do try and teach them right and wrong but what can you do but try? You can only do so much and if they're not willing to listen to you, there's not much more you can do, is there?

Jacquie and Her Mother

I didn't notice Jacquie come into the room but there she was in front of me, saying hello, a slim white girl of 17, with a small, pale face and pert short hair. She was wearing smart white trousers with narrow black stripes, a fitted white leather jacket, big white trainers and big gold earrings. She looked lovely. She went straight to the point.

JAQUIE

When I first started shop-lifting it seemed like fun, it seemed like really the best thing that I could be doing at the time. It was so easy. I could just go anywhere and take what I wanted. I could keep it for myself if I wanted to or sell it and make money from it. My Mum couldn't afford to support me so I had to go and do it myself and that was the only way I could. It seemed a lot easier to shop-lift when I first started.

I was 15, a couple of months after my birthday. I never *loved* school but I didn't hate it like some people. I didn't leave but I wasn't going any more. I missed a lot. I could have done my exams. I was growing up and there was a lot of pressure. Ask anyone round here. I just got dragged in really, not into a bad crowd but they was doing shop-lifting for making their money.

I usually go with my friends. I have gone on my own, I've been arrested on my own as well, but usually I am with friends. It makes it a little bit easier, to look out for each other. You work together. It just happened really. I didn't used to be a thief when I was little. I used to be scared to steal things from shops. I wouldn't steal from somebody's house.

My Mum knew. She did know but she didn't know what she could do to stop me doing it. I suppose it was the easiest thing I could do. It was fun, I enjoyed doing it, I liked doing it—not no more I don't because it went too far. But when you *are* shop-lifting it's fun, it's a game. It's like you're in competition: who can steal the most expensive things, who's got the nicest clothes, who's got the most perfume, who can go into this shop and steal, who can go into that shop to steal.

Last summer I'd go into a Versace shop where it was very difficult to steal trousers. People find out I've done it and they'll go and do it and get their pair of trousers. It's like: "Why are you doing that? I've done that first," and then you go out and get an even better pair. You see what I mean? It's a thing of 'Who's the best at it, who's got the most guts to go and do this?' Even though, when you're together with a person, you'll steal together and you'll work as a team, when you're separate from that person it's like they're always watching what you've got and how you got it.

When you go into a big store like Marks & Spencer's, if you go in there and you're stealing, you wouldn't even think twice about it. You'd think, "Imagine how many stores they've got all over this country and how much money they're taking in." It doesn't even seem like you're taking anything. You think to yourself, "They're not going to miss it, they're not going to starve because of it." Get what I mean? I didn't see it like to ask, "What would happen if everyone did it?" because not everybody does do it (even though quite a lot of people do, you don't realise how much). I just used to see I was getting so much money from it. It dragged me in eventually and before I knew it I couldn't stop.

Anybody will buy anything off you. I know you yourself probably, if I knocked on your door and said, "Do you want to buy something off me?", you wouldn't buy but mainly everybody I could think of would. People ask you for something, say a T-shirt, maybe extra large, a couple of bottles of champagne for someone who's getting married—I'll get that for her. Anything you can sell: at Easter I can sell Easter eggs, the really nice ones. Any time of year you can sell alcohol, clothes. People always want them, they're so essential.

When I steal, even though it's bad to steal, I'm not greedy with my things. People I know get very greedy. I'll give most of it away. I'll sell it cheap to people who haven't got no money. The woman who lives next door has three children—four children—and she has to survive on social security so every now and again I used to go and get her kids a whole load of new clothes, same as my auntie's as well. Yes, sometimes I do think I'm being followed around all day and they're watching where you go. It's a paranoia that you get after a little while but you know you're just being stupid.

For my friend's house I stole wallpaper and paint and decorated the whole of their house. It needed decorating badly and her Mum didn't have the money. How it started was with my friend's room. I said, "When you need that paint I can get it for you," and then I forgot all about it. Then she said, "Can you get that wallpaper you said you'd get?" It was my friend saying, "Yeah, yeah, let's do it, let's do it." Her Mum knew I was doing it. She'd say, "Please don't, please. I know I need my home decorating but please don't get yourself caught." Then, when that room'd got done, her Mum's husband said, "Could you do my room?" And it was his birthday so I got it for his room.

I was going to the same wallpaper shop all the time. It was feeling like I was supposed to be doing it. Where it was old and everything, with all this new wallpaper and paint it was like a palace when we'd finished. It got like a good thing I was doing rather than a bad; even though it was wrong because I was stealing the stuff; it was like I was making up for it because of what I was doing with it. A lot of people would look at that house and say even though it was stolen, that doesn't matter, it was a good thing that it was done there. I don't think my friend's Mum would have let her do it if *she* was stealing the wallpaper. If *I* was stealing, it was different.

The first time I got arrested was when my friend—she was older—stole a bottle of wine. I wasn't 'arrested' but I got taken into custody for my own welfare because I was young and I was on my own. It was quite late in the evening and my Mum had to come and get me. The first time I got caught, after a couple of years, when I was properly doing it, I went into Tesco's with loads and loads of stuff from Marks & Spencer's and all over the place. We went into Tesco's on the way back to steal some litle bits and bobs. They just given me a caution on the spot when I come back out of the cell. I was in there two or three hours at the most.

Now I've been arrested 17 or 18 times at least. It was like an experience at first. It wasn't like, "Oh no, I'm scared." It was, "Wow! This is something new." My Mum, she didn't even know that time. I phoned my aunty's house and she came and got me. My friend was in a children's home. My aunty bailed both of us out—if you're a juvenile, you've got to get an adult to bail you out. Boys don't really shop-lift at all. They do car crimes, robbery, things like that. I've *seen* boys but they've been younger.

When I was going to court I was getting conditional discharges, ten pound fines and fines for not attending on the right day. They've got a girls' group at youth justice here, every Monday or Tuesday. If you've been in trouble with the law you come here. You don't have to but I did use to come. Then last summer the courts ended up giving me a supervision order to last for one year. I didn't come at all until I had to go back to court for breach of my supervision. My workers at youth justice said they'd take me back here and give me another try. I didn't use to come at first but I started coming in about February or March and I usually attend regularly but sometimes I might miss it. I haven't been arrested since last year. [*Our talk was in July*]

A lot of time I did use to do it not for drugs, not for crack cocaine, not Ecstasy, things like that, but cannabis most of the time. That's what I was doing it for. Even though I couldn't smoke cannabis and then go shop-lifting, I had to go shop-lifting so that I had that drawer always full, sitting there at night. I had to have it there every single day. So many people do it; it's so easy to buy; it just seems like smoking cigarettes; it doesn't matter. Every youngster tries nearly everything there is, that's how much it's round this area. It's not a normal thing but you have to try it just to have that experience.

When I started shop-lifting was when I started smoking cannabis. It's all around you, everywhere you go, if you socialise with somebody. Maybe when you come here you'll bring this grapes and strawberries for us to eat, for refreshing because we're sitting here talking. My friend comes out to my house and what we'll have there is a drawer, Rizla [*papers for smoking*], cigarettes, a lighter and we sit down and smoke. Do you understand what I mean?

It's after it's over and you're addicted to it that you realise it's messing up your head. All you can do really is just sit there. If I'd have smoked cannabis before I came here today, I wouldn't have been able to sit here and talk to you. I'd be sort of paranoid, like in a little bit of confusion, you wouldn't really be there. I'd just end up not knowing what to do. At first it makes you relax but it gets the better of you.

When I was in secondary school, because my Mum and Dad was arguing, fighting, my family was very unstable. I had one teacher who was head of my year, she used to help me a little bit. It was many different reasons added up to me doing what I did do. It wasn't one little thing, it was a whole load of things in my life. I'd be sitting down thinking and feeling depressed, I just wanted to go out and do something. By going out and stealing I'd be taking my mind off my family life at home and my problems and everything because all I'd be thinking of was: "Is anybody watching me, is anybody watching me?" And then I'd be thinking as well, "Yeah, as soon as I get back home I'm going to sell this stuff and have my cannabis."

I was 12 when my Mum and Dad was splitting up. After my Dad left I went to live with my auntie, though she chucked me out a few times. She got a new boyfriend and I didn't like him. Then I lived with my Dad in his flat. Then I went back to my auntie's, then she chucked me out. Last Christmas she chucked me out for a couple of months. I'm back there now. She lives a couple of doors away from my house. She has three children but they're young, eight and younger. She lets me take her children with me shop-lifting. She doesn't stop me. I know it probably sounds disgusting to you. I wouldn't take them with me if they knew what I was doing—just the little one, he's two, in a push-chair. If I were just going to do a couple of things, I'd take him with me. Same as my next-door neighbour. She lets me take her children as well.

I haven't got a role-model, but I've got a really good girlfriend who knows what she's doing and we sort of keep each other going. I'm the kind of person who might end up shop-lifting again and she's the kind that'll get lazy so we sort of help each other out. I'm on the track now but it's hard to keep yourself on it.

Basically, I just come into youth justice and speak to my worker for half an hour or so once a week. I don't know how to explain it really. What they do here is really good. Being here rather than going into custody is a lot better and it is some form of justice that you do get. But they don't properly understand what's going on. Don't get me wrong—they're very good people but when they're not doing it themselves, it's hard for them to connect properly, to be able to understand.

I have driving lessons. I think it's a brilliant idea. It's giving young people opportunities they wouldn't be able to afford otherwise (unless they went stealing to get the money—and then you couldn't rely on it). There's a lot of activities going on, there at the motor project, but I don't usually do them—jet-skiing, scrambling on motor bikes, things like that. It doesn't interest me.

If I've got something to do, I can get up at any time, early. Like today, I got up at eleven o'clock, I got washed and dressed by twelve o'clock to get to the project for a driving lesson and come here for two. If I weren't doing anything, I'd probably get up at about 12, just lounge about doing nothing, maybe go to the library or the DSS, read my books. I like Virginia Andrews books and Stephen King books as well. Stephen King sometimes is horrid, a bit deep for me to understand. At the moment I'm reading *Misery* by Stephen King. It is a film and everyone's seen it but I want to read the book because it's really good. The best Virginia Andrews I've ever read is *Heaven*. That's really good.

I've been going to a little place which gets you up to scratch on the English and maths before you go to college. It's finished now but they taught me how to write a letter properly, how to space it out, all the different steps. I didn't do typing at school. At this place we did lots of application forms for jobs and we did punctuation: commas, exclamation marks, question marks, capital letters, those things that if you haven't been in education for a long time, you forget quite easily. I tried the other day to get a job. They sent me an application form and I sent it back. They sent me a letter saying that I was unsuccessful in my application. They didn't say what reason. I did something wrong. The record was on my application form or something. I did try.

I've put in for a Health and Social Counselling Course at college. I'll do two weeks of health and social studies, two weeks' business studies, two weeks' computer course and then I decide what one I want to do—I can do two if I like—and I still have maths and English. Then I carry on to do it for the rest of the year. It's full-time. That's good—but if I come out at five o'clock, I could still go out shop-lifting at five o'clock.

A lot of the time it boils down to if I'm with friends who don't steal, I won't steal, but if I'm with friends who do, it's hard not to. I'd go into shops and see people who used to be in my school looking at me, a little bit embarrassed, and I'd think I'd rather be in a shop working than being followed around by security guards. In this area, it works in a weird way. You're a better person if you go out and steal than if you've got a good job. Giving it up is easy to say but it's hard to do. Even with the project and things to do, it's still hard to stop myself. When I do shop-lift it makes me feel like I've become a little kid, like I couldn't grow up and go out into the big world. It sort of holds you back.

Whatever had happened, I think I would still have ended up doing the same thing. If my Mum had been more stricter with me, guided me more with the right and wrong way, then maybe I'd have thought twice. When I was younger my friends stopped because they had their Mums telling them "this is wrong, this is wrong, this is wrong". My Mum never really cared as long as I wasn't telling her I had to go up to this police station or police stations in far-off places. She's got to work all day and then go up there in the evenings . . . We don't talk much. I'm a bit distant from her, now that I'm getting older. Whatever my mother was saying to me didn't mean nothing. She was just wasting her breath. It's easier to work with other people's children, to guide them more than your own children.

I think my Dad knows. It was nothing to do with them getting divorced. He was never there when I was getting arrested. It was a couple of years later that I started properly going and stealing.

Seriously, it's not worth all the trouble what you get yourself into. You don't realise when you go for a job—I applied for a job the other day, for a chamber-maid person, and even on that they asked me "did I have a criminal record or any previous convictions", on the application form. It's all right when you're getting out of the police station, you're forgetting about it, but that record you've got stays on your back, whatever you try to do. I've got friends that are 19 that have criminal records that are quite long, and that's never going to go.

When they were telling me at youth justice that at 18 you go to the magistrates' court, I was realising that if I don't stop now I'm never going to be able to get a proper job and I'll just be useless really unless I could do something dodgy—and I'll have to be doing it for the rest of my life. I know that if I get caught, stealing or something, that's it, I'm going to have a proper criminal record. They have told me. I want to pull my life together now and I'm lucky that I realise it before it's too late.

The police tell you but they're not as powerful as the judge who makes the decision. They're just the ones who take you in, write it all down and then it's up to the courts to deal with. The police laugh and joke about things. They're not as strict as they could be. They do lock you up in a cell for a long time but they're laughing at you through the little window thing. They make you feel you've done wrong by the long time you've been in there but it's not really that bad. It's only when you're in court that it seems like you've done something wrong. You've got to be polite and quiet, even though you're sitting there thinking "but you don't really know what goes on, why I have to do it".

The only thing that would have stopped me, after the first time I got caught, from doing it a second time, the only thing, would be if they'd put me in prison. If they'd put me in prison and not just given me bail, I'd have never, ever done it again. It's easy to say that and it might have made things even worse but—I've said it to the youth justice workers—it's the only thing I can see for keeping people from just going on and on. If you just get a smack on the wrist, then of course you're going to do it again.

If I had kids of my own I'd tell them that it's not worth it. You think it is at the time but in the long run it's not. I couldn't tell them it's wrong because of my record behind me. I probably would say "You shouldn't". I'd explain a couple of things and then if someone just tried shop-lifting, I'd tell them, "Yeah, it's the wrong thing to do, ra ra ra" but I'd probably just end up telling them what shops are the best shops to steal from so they wouldn't get caught if they were going to carry on doing it. Understand what I mean? Rather than "Don't do it!". I don't think I would tell them it was wrong, even though it is, but there is no way I would let my children do it. No way.

Every school tells you that it's wrong to steal, but not that much they don't. In primary school they used to teach you things like "Don't go away with strangers!" "Don't run out in the road and get hit by a car!" "If there's a fire, this is what to do!" They don't really teach you "Don't steal!", though when I was younger I used to be scared. As I grew up it just became part of my life really, an automatic thing.

I've got three brothers. One's 13, one's eight nearly nine and one's 18. He's got a baby. He used to live with me but now he lives with his girlfriend. They've got a flat, a nice flat. None has ever been in trouble with the law. My younger brothers go to school. One has a job in the market after school, packing things away, and on Saturdays. He gets about £20 a week. He used to have a paper round as well but that didn't last very long because he had to get up extra early and he had to get to school on time. My older brother works in a factory a couple of days a week.

I wish I hadn't done shop-lifting because of the record that I've got but I'm glad I did it for the experience that it's the wrong thing to do— and it's addictive, like cigarettes, like cannabis, like alcohol. You don't realise but it is addictive. I could easily fall back again.

JACQUIE'S MOTHER

I met Pat, Jacquie's mother, during her lunch hour at the multi-racial, multi-lingual community centre where she works. The activities advertised on the board ranged from "Keep fit for (mainly) Spanish (mainly) over 50s" to a sewing circle, sessions of board games and a computer club. There was a playground outside and nursery-age children ran in and out of the reception area where we talked. "What you got for your dinner, Pat?" "What you doing, Pat?" "Hi, Pat!" Pat responded with a smile, calling each child by name. She looked attractive and competent in navy blouse and tracksuit trousers. Her dark blond hair was drawn tightly back from her face. She wore no make-up but lots of bracelets and rings, and she had a huge bunch of keys which people kept coming to borrow. Jacquie ressembled her.

I've been here just seven years. I work in the playgroup and three and a half years ago we started up an out-of-school care scheme so I work here full-time now. I'm a trained nursery nurse. I got my qualifications in 1974. I did it straight from school.

This is a voluntary organization. It's a PPA [*Preschool Play Association*] playgroup. The council gives some money for it and we fundraise a little bit more to keep it going. For the care scheme we fundraise the whole lot of money. We get some from City Challenge, some from local charities, places like that. I came to work here through living in the area.

Jacquie's my second child. Tom is my oldest. He's 19, nearly 20. He's working in a bookmaker's. He's got a flat with his girlfriend and they've got a little girl. My youngest boy who's eight comes here with me in the holidays and the 12-year-old does sports and goes to clubs or friends. There's plenty of activities for those who want them. Jacquie never wanted to go.

I was married before we had a child and my husband lived with us up until 1992. I wasn't really surprised about Jacquie. I've got four children and out of the four she's always been the one that caused the trouble, if you know what I mean. She was the one that had the tantrums when she was little, when she was a toddler. She was the one who would be difficult when she was wrong, more than the boys . . . You sort of get to know their personalities, so I wasn't *that* surprised—if you know what I mean. I suppose you're always shocked, to know that your child has done something like that.

It all came from when we had the break-up in the family, my husband and myself. He's an alcoholic and from about 1990-92 we had a very difficult two years. I'd sort of decided I wanted the relationship to finish and he wasn't agreeing to it. In the end I went to social services. I had bruises on me and when I talked to them about it they decided the children were in emotional abuse and put them on the At Risk Register. I had to take him to court to get him to move out of the flat. Of all the family Jacquie was the one that backed him and was very against me in what I was trying to do. She was about 12. She always thought it was my fault the family broke up. And even though deep down inside she knows it wasn't, she blames me . . . I don't understand the psychological side.

I first heard about her stealing when the police came to the house to get me to go to the police station one time when they arrested her. She was very sneaky about it in the beginning. I think she was using the money for things like smoking so that I wouldn't actually see things that she had. She'd *spend* the money. Do you see what I mean? I wasn't walking round finding expensive things in the house or anything like that. I knew she smoked cigarettes but I didn't know she was smoking like marihuana. She wouldn't be smoking in the house.

At first I was really, really angry. I expected it to be just like something else your child does. You just say, "Well that's it—you're not doing it any more", and I sort of expected her to stop, but she didn't stop. I used to talk to her about it, explain how bad it was, she mustn't do it, and stuff like that. It's hard to remember exactly but I think I was more saying, "OK. You made a mistake. That's it. We'll forget about it. You must never do it again." But that wasn't the end of it.

When we broke up, for a year she lived with me and then she was like being so difficult in the house, in our relationship, that I told her she should go and stay with her Dad. She went to stay with him for about eight months and then she realised, I think, she saw his personality for how he was, because she was at the receiving end of it. She came back and for a period of time she was sort of between aunties. He's got lots of sisters. She'd stay with them and with her friends. When she got with youth justice she started to calm down a bit and then she moved back properly.

She knows it's wrong but she's the sort of person that doesn't really care about consequences. She'll like flaunt the consequences of everything, all kinds of things. For example, I had lots of trouble about getting her to do things in the house, like to do her own washing-up, or to do *some* washing-up. The consequence of that is that I'm going to be angry or that there'll be an argument. Whereas my sons would say, "OK, I don't want an argument", she'd say, "Well, what could happen? So what!" Do you understand what I mean? That's her attitude to everything.

I could see what she finds exciting about shop-lifting but I don't think we've ever had a conversation about it. She doesn't seem to like talking to me at all but my older son and I would have lots of long conversations about all kinds of things. Jacquie doesn't. She wants to be very private . . . She's still got a lot of antagonism towards me so we haven't got a good relationship to talk about things. The only times we've really talked about it is if we've sort of been in a situation when we've *had* to be together because, say, we're sitting there in a police station waiting and we've had to sit there and I've tried to talk about why she should do it, things like that.

The first court appearance didn't seem to bother her at all. I was more upset and embarrassed than she was. After, she just shrugged her shoulders and walked off. Me, I was really shaking and upset. She doesn't like being locked up at police stations but it's an *inconvenience*. With Jacquie it's just [*imitates*], "Oh, they made me sit there." She'd be rude to the police and be making comments like, "They've made me stay all that time . . . broohaha, broohaha . . . Who do they think they are?" She really embarrassed me. I said, "Sh . . . Just shut up—you're the one that's in the wrong." I'd just want to die and in the end, and after this one time when she was really saying things, I said "I'm not coming with you any more. That's it." And the next time I said to them they'll have to get the social worker to act as the appropriate adult.

I think youth justice have helped her to realise the consequences. I don't know how they've done that but they've really made her see what's going to happen to her if she carries on down that road. They've helped her because she'll trust them more than she'll trust me, I think. Also, she's got a couple of very sensible friends and they've been telling her similar things. She's said to me, "I'm not going to do it any more" because they've told her that the next time she gets arrested they're going to send her to Holloway. So that was the ultimate thing and that was what stopped her.

It's funny. To be quite honest it kind of wears you down. When she first did it I wouldn't have anything to do with it and I wouldn't let her bring things into the house or anything. Now, a couple of years down the line, sometimes I'm tempted and I'll say "Oh!" and I'll give her money for things because you think everybody does it. It's like all around you. Everybody you know is saying to you, "I've got a job the nights and I sign on" or "My boyfriend's robbed this, done that". People you would never think. In this area it's very, very prevalent. Everybody does something illegal, when you actually talk to people.

It was in the third or fourth year of secondary school that she started not going. That was her way of rebelling and showing she was sort of emotionally having a lot of trouble with the break up and the things that were going on in the family. At the beginning of the fifth year they said that she hadn't done enough course-work but she could still take her GCSEs and she'd probably pass a few of the subjects. They were very good in encouraging her and trying to get her to do them but they weren't that good in a practical sense. I said, "Well, if you could give me a list of the pieces of course-work that she needs to do, I'll like try to get her to do them in the holidays." They never did come up with that so in one way they were good but in another way they weren't. They didn't tell me the moment she started truanting. I think it was a little time before I found out.

My son Tom had the same problem. He was very depressed and also because my husband was hitting me and stuff like that he had this thing where he didn't want to leave the house in case something happened to me. It kind of caused depression and he used to sleep and couldn't wake up. He actually did drop out of school as well, at about the same time, the beginning of the fifth year. So she'd seen that as well—you know what I mean—I couldn't force him, I couldn't physically lift him and take him, so I suppose she knew that she could get away with it. We'd argue but the bottom line was that I couldn't actually do anything.

With Jacquie the education welfare people didn't do a lot. She'd go one day a week, she kept going enough so that they didn't see it as a big problem. I don't remember having a meeting with them about her although I know I had them about Tom. She had friends that were doing the same kind of thing and I think it was them that got her into shop-lifting.

My son didn't need to be qualified for the job that he's doing. His girlfriend's got quite a lot of influence over him and she's sort of got him into good ways, if you know what I mean. Because he had a child he had to straighten himself out.

Jacquie's not really got boyfriends. She had one very good friend, a boy that I think she liked in that way. He got run over, he was killed, and she was really sad about that. I think he'd been on a bit of a thing, partying all night and taking Es, the weekend before the accident, and if he'd been a bit more alert, it wouldn't have happened. That shocked them all out of it.

At first I was optimistic about the course at college in September because her friend was doing a similar thing but they put her into an Access Course. She just has to go two days a week, to do English and maths, and she's missed out loads of it. I said to her, "If you can't go two afternoons a week, how are you going to go to a full-time course?" But she's one of those people, if she sets her mind to something, she can do anything. Like now, she's set her mind, because the youth justice people have given her driving lessons, she wants to be able to have some money put away to buy a car—so she's decided she's going to work in the summer. She got a job last week and she did some chamber-maiding for a couple of days. It's really bad pay but she got a feel of what it was like and she's found out about another place and she's going for an interview. I think it's today.

So if she sets her mind to do this course, she could do it. She's very, very determined . . . She's so happy about the driving. She loves it. I think it's terribly, you know, [*Pat laughed nervously*] unfair that kids that've been in trouble get to do nice things like that and other kids who've sat and studied and done all their exams, don't get anything, but there you go. I'm pleased for her she's getting an opportunity but it doesn't seem fair really. Also, you've got to have something the kids like to do to make them actually attend. She'll get up and go to that because she loves it so much whereas if it was just a meeting or something like that, she wouldn't. So it's making her get a routine and making her focus on things. I think it has lots of benefits but it just seems an unfair world when kids that have done wrong get the good things.

We went to family therapy a couple of times. She didn't really want to go. I mean none of us really wanted to go but it was suggested for her more than for the rest of us and we kind of talked her into it. I don't know if it was really helpful at all because there was a lot of us—we were all there, not my husband but the four children and myself. I think we had to go from the social services because of them being on the At Risk Register. I didn't find it that helpful and I don't think she did either.

I think a lot of it [*generally speaking*] is that the Conservatives have been in all of this time. All they're doing is telling people, "You're out for yourself, you're out for yourself" and "Don't worry about how bettering yourself affects other people". They've given that feeling to the poor people as well as the rich people. Do you know what I mean? A place like this, they get their funding cut. In the old days people would be arguing. They just wouldn't have been able to cut back. In the voluntary sector all kinds of jobs are being cut . . . There's not like the sharing and caring attitude there was 20 years ago.

I think prison would shake Jacquie up a bit. She'd do anything not to go back there because she would hate it. I know she would hate it. If that happened to me, I'd like grit my teeth and I'd be all right. I'd find good in it, you know. I'd say, "I'm going to study these books and make friends with people." She would just hate it and every second would be dreadful. I think the system lets them get away with too much. I don't know about the research about prison but I say why don't they just *do* something, even if they lock her up for only a week or a month, to say you've got to stop and this is what it's like. I really believe it would stop them.

The same thing happened to her Dad. When he was young, he was really like into trouble all of his teenage time. He'd been to loads of youth detention places by the time he was 17. Then he had this court appearance and they put him into The Scrubs for three months and that was it. It was 1968 and he never offended again. He said, "It was just horrible and that was it. I said to myself, 'Never again am I going to do anything.'" I met him after that and he already had a job. He'd seriously sorted himself out. He doesn't have a job now. He went on booze and then he went downhill again—but maybe destroying himself and not society, you know what I mean.

It's not something I've ever talked about with Jacquie. I don't know if he talks with her because I don't have any contact with him at all.

After we'd turned off the tape recorder and I was on my way out, Pat told me that when Jacquie was born, "I never let myself totally bond with her like I did with the boys." She'd wanted a girl and she felt "that lucky" because she'd had one. But her husband had a daughter before they married who told her she'd had a sister who'd died in a cot death. That affected Pat. She had post-natal depression and couldn't ". . . let go that last little bit to love her" because she was afraid she was going to die. "Whether she sensed that," Pat said, "and was insecure, felt I was going to leave her because I felt she was going to leave me . . . "

Jacquie asked her Dad if he would see me but "He didn't want to know".

Daniel

Daniel lumbered in to meet me at his youth justice centre, looking sad and lost and sullen, a large black boy of 16. He wore a baseball cap, a dark, anorak-type jacket and off-white tracksuit trousers in some soft, knitted fabric which looked comfortable but not the height of any fashion. He spoke very slowly, with a minimum of words, rarely elaborating any statement. He was polite but looked as if he'd rather not be there—or anywhere.

I'm on a two years' supervision order with 60 days specified activities. I come here three times a week. I fill out some forms. They ask you like "Why was you doing this criminal stuff?" Asking questions about your life. It's all right. I've been here since June or September, I'm not sure.

It was a building society robbery with my other friends, three other boys. We ran in there, jumped over the counter, took the money and run off, run to the car. First we was going to another place but we just saw this one and we went there. We got £4,000. The police found it. It was the first time I done it. I went to prison, I was on remand for four months. They remanded me into custody for the Crown Court. [*The youth court must have declined jurisdiction in the case, because it involved a 'grave crime', or Daniel must have been accused with adults of a joint offence.*]

I'd been in trouble for fighting on the bus and that when I used to go to school. The bus driver was arguing with us about like we can't all come on the bus. I go to school now but first I went to one school, then another school and then I went to some special school. I still go to a special school now. I've got dys . . . dyslexia. I was fighting on the bus when I was in the first and second year of my first school.

The school I'm at is helping me now. They don't do GCSEs. They do some other thing but you get a certificate. I thought that's good enough. And I work at my Dad's shop. It's a record shop. He pays me £40 a week. That helps a lot. I save £15 a week to buy clothes, when I need a new tracksuit or trainers or things like that. I don't give my Mum anything. I spend the rest. I work from five to seven every day, not weekends. He deals in black and American music, reggae and that. He plays music. I sell the records to the customer.

I want to try and be a computer engineer. I don't know if I can do that. I'm going to try to go to college.

Since the building society I've got arrested for burglaries. The police know my face, some of the police I know, and they stop me all the time. They try stitching me up for some robbery that I've never even done. They arrested me. I was at my house asleep. I have done things, sometimes, burglaries and that. I haven't done no [more] building societies. I don't think £40 is enough money. I can't buy anything I want with that.

I can't think about the people [affected]. I won't do it if I think about them. I don't care about that. It's their business. People do what they want to do. If my stuff gets taken, it just gets taken—that's how it goes.

I live with my Mum. My Dad left a few years ago, four or five. I still see him. I've two sisters and one brother—one big sister. They've not been in trouble. My Mum's a school teacher in a junior school. They were angry about my fighting on the bus. That's all that happened. They were angry about the building society but they came and visited me in prison, definitely. They were angry but it just happened.

I don't have to be in at any time [at night] but I don't take liberties like coming in early in the morning or no late time. I come in at a decent time like ten o'clock at night. I'll tell her what time I'm coming in. I have meals with my family. My Mum wants me to go to college. I don't know. I go to college on Wednesdays with my school. They say that I must apply. I don't know what will happen if I don't get into college. I go to school regularly, every day. I've been there today and then I came here. It's not a big school, just a little school.

Me and my friends just hang round on the blocks. We don't really do much—play with computer, go out, sometimes we go out when there's a rave. There's a big drug scene. People sell drugs around here a lot but not everyone does it. It's up to you if you want to do it, in't it? I don't mind. That's people's business, in't it? If they want to make their money that way, that's their business—I don't care. It messes them up. I don't do it —only small weed and that. My Mum smokes cigarettes. No one drinks. My Dad's a drugman, a Rasta – no drink.

I had to come in for supervision for that fighting. Before that I had no social workers. The school tested me when I was 14 and transferred me to my present school. I always used to be behind. I didn't like primary school. My Mum used to give me help all the time because she used to know about my reading. She used to let me read and that every day.

Most of my friends are in prison for the building society. The other boys were older than me and they had too much on their previous record. One of them had an outstanding bank case. Prison ain't a good place. If I have to go back, then I'll have to go back. The screws and that, they drive you mad. Sometimes when it's association [*recreation time when prisoners are allowed out of their cells to mix with others*] they don't let you out of your cell. I used to go to school there but school wasn't school. You play games and do drawings and that. You don't learn much.

I was like in court every week. I was getting remanded back into custody because it had to go through committal and all that. If you're in a cell with someone and you go to court, another person might go in that cell and you might go to a different wing or something or a different cell. You might be in your own cell or you might be in a cell with someone or you might be in a cell with three other people. Most of my friends were in there, weren't they, so I had no problems with bullying.

I used to get beaten when I was little. It didn't stop me. I didn't care. If they were really bad I'd beat my children. I wouldn't beat them for little things. I doubt if I'd beat my kids. I don't know about getting married. I've got a girlfriend. She don't want me to do them things. I listen to her but I don't know. I'll be nice to people if people'll be nice to me.

Daniel was not sure about whether he wanted me to meet his Mum and I did not think it right to press him.

Stephen

It was a bright but chilly autumn day when I met Stephen. He was wearing a yellow string singlet and plaid trousers, with white trainers and a baseball cap. He had a stud in one ear, a nose ring and a thick, catarrhal cold. A white boy, he seemed young for his 17 years, plump and laid-back rather than a macho trend-setter, despite his gear. We started talking about his present circumstances.

I live by myself, in a bed-and-breakfast hotel at the moment. I'm waiting for a flat. My parents live down the road. I've been there for about three months. Before that I was in another hotel but I got kicked out of that. The man was rude to my Mum so I had an argument. I'd been there for about three months.

I was about 15 when I left home. I was living right over in [a nearby town] with my girlfriend who came from there. I didn't tell my parents I was going away, I just left. They were very worried. I was gone for about a year. I was sometimes in touch. I was in touch with social services there but under a different name. When I got arrested there I said I was from there and had no fixed abode.

I got arrested for all sorts of things: offensive weapons, three robberies, assault, things like that—ABH (Actual Bodily Harm). Before I left home I wasn't like that. Then I went up to the centre of town, hanging around and that with the wrong people and it started happening.

At home there was a lot of work for me. My Mum's got ten kids. I just left. I just met my girlfriend, I don't know where. I got a job fixing tills and cleaning them—cash registers. I went looking for a job every day and then I went into a shop one time and the man said, "Yes, come in for an interview." It was easy at first. All they wanted me to do was clean tills and that, give out stickers to the shops.

I didn't give my girlfriend rent. She was 18 or 19. She never knew I was 15. I still see her sometimes but I'm not going out with her no more. I still see her on a friendly basis.

I've been staying at my Mum's for the last week. Mondays, Tuesdays, Thursdays and Fridays I have to come here [the youth justice centre] so Wednesday is the only day I've got off. At the hotel, I sleep there and then I get up and go to my Mum's or to [the town] where I've got a lot of friends up there. There's room for me at home and I can stay there when I want but I like to do my own thing.

I'm an MC. I'm taking it further because I should be going to college soon, doing a music course. I've been for an interview already and I'm just waiting for them to get in touch with me. My keyworker suggested that—I wanted to do it but my keyworker just pushed me ahead. Before I went to another college but that was for something I didn't really want to do, Art and Design, and I didn't really stick to it. I will stick to this.

I'm doing 60 hours community service, I've got a £25 fine, 40 days of IT [intermediate treatment] plus a year's probation for three robberies, attempted robbery, ABH, assault, offensive weapons plus abusive language. Two of the robberies wasn't even robberies; it was fights but it turned out it seemed like a robbery. I was in town with two friends. It was raining. We was all walking and this one man, he beat up my biggest friend and my friend knocked this man to the ground. We all got arrested and because the man had a car stereo in his hand, the man thought we was going to rob him for the stereo so we all got arrested for robbery.

None of us was drunk. My friends only smoke weed. I'd never met violence like that before I left home. I'm a person—the only violence I use is in defending myself. When I left home I started seeing things different. I was part of the robbery because I was there. There was one of them where I was there and I took the boy's chain. That was the only time I actually done something. The ABH was self-defence to me. I went to the amusement place in the centre of town and the security guard didn't want me in there so he threw me to the wall and I bust my hand so I punched him. He said that I'd hit him.

I had fun in the centre of town at first till every police officer got to know me. I got into a lot of trouble, arguing and fighting and stupid stuff like that. I'd be up there all night with a couple of my friends, messing around, going to clubs, talking to girls, hanging around, from Saturday night to Sunday morning and then go home. I wasn't actually thinking about doing anything else then.

I lived with my girlfriend for about four months. Then I lived in an hotel and they [the court] banned me from the centre of town. Then they put me in a children's home, not in a secure unit but I wasn't allowed out by myself at all. But I kept going into town and I got caught.

I've been in prison on remand. I don't like it. It's the lack of freedom, in't it? I wasn't bullied. I keep myself to myself in those places, not arguing with no-one. But I saw it happen. When I was there I promised myself I wouldn't get involved with nothing again because I realised what it was to be in there. You wake up early and when one day comes it's the same as every day because it's in a cell, 23 hours. You come out for one hour, then you're back for 23 hours. I was only there for a month. My social worker, my sister and my girlfriend came to see me. My Mum didn't know I was in there because I didn't tell her.

I left school when I was 15. I was good at school but I was not good as well. There was some days I'd go in, you know, and I just wasn't in the mood to work. Some days I'd go in and I'd work good. I'd be on report just to make sure I'd get my work done. Sometimes I'd be lazy and I wouldn't do nothing. I got expelled quite a few times, you know how it goes. I did exams my first, second, third and fourth years but not after. At this IT place now I'm getting education again. If I had the chance I'd start all again. I regret messing about—it gets you nowhere.

I'm the eldest in the family. All the younger ones are OK and my Dad works and everything. There's a lot of kids. When you go there, the noise! My Mum had a baby three weeks ago. My parents were strict enough. You couldn't get away with bad stuff. My Mum liked the house clean all the time. If you spilled anything on the floor, you had to pick it up. You can't just leave it there. We was allowed out, we got pocket money and everything, had curfews and everything and got grounded. Mum didn't really hit us. If you was rude, you got grounded or got no money, or if you was going on a school trip she'd stop that, stuff like that.

When I was young I was slow. I didn't really want to listen. My Dad spent a lot of time with me reading but not with my sisters. They're fast learners. I was that slow so my Dad had to spend more of time with me, reading books and music and things like that.

I want to become involved in music, like producing. It's something I've wanted to do since I was little, from when I was eight, even younger than that. I've always been interested in singing. When I was 14 my Mum bought me a karaoke machine for my birthday. I've got everything like that—records, everything.

I want something to fall back on in case. I'm interested in architecture, drawing, buildings, stuff like that. But if you're going to do that, it'll take a lot of work. I know you need to study a lot for that. If I don't get what I want, I know a lot about painting and decorating. I've been doing it a little while. I'd be prepared to do that for a job if I had to.

I went to see my flat on Monday but I got there a bit late so I missed my social worker. They made a date for the eleventh, tomorrow, ten o'clock. It's sometimes a bit difficult getting up early in the morning if I go to bed late. I watch *Sky* at my Mum's or at my cousins'.

I don't smoke drugs. The only thing I use if I want to sometimes is weed. I can control myself. As a person my friends say I'm very light-headed. If I drink I know how much to drink because one bottle of eight per cent, that's OK. I'm not like people who drink and drink. I can only drink so much and if I drink too much I start to vomit so I don't do too much. I'm aware of the dangers so I don't go too far. I don't take nothing like cocaine or speed or that or tablets but I know people who sell those kind of things. I smoke cigarettes. I know it's bad for you. I started when I was 14. I just followed people. I followed my cousins when I started but then it was a hard thing to stop, you get me.

I don't really talk to the friends I had now because most of them are in prison actually. They're the people in town. The people here are my good friends. A lot of people were trying to rob me before and I was trying to defend myself.

It's seven or eight months since I've been in trouble. I've only done two hours of community service because I can't wake up to go there. The thing is I've got to wake up and get here from quite a way before 9.15. The community service is painting and decorating. I don't really like it. It's an alternative to custody. I know I've got to do it, 58 hours left. I do seven hours every Saturday.

I don't really like it at the bed and breakfast so when I go there I go there late, I go there to sleep. I've got my stuff there, TV, radio, clothes. Most of my other stuff is at my Mum's home. If I could change things in the past, it'd be to behave myself. If I didn't run away I reckon things would have been different. I don't know what would have stopped me. I'm a person, if I make up my mind, I can do something, you get me. If I want to do it, I'll do it.

What I'd say to other people is "Think before you do something". It's hard to get away now. There's no point in stealing money when you can make it. I realise that. There's no point in taking what I can make in a day, if I really want to.

Stephen's parents were not willing to meet me.

Mark

Rhythmic strumming of a piano vibrated cheerfully through the house, a former children's home, used by the youth justice team who introduced me to Mark. A slim, blond young man of 17, he wore blue jeans, a bright petrol blue shirt, gym shoes and an engaging, open smile. He had two rings on his fingers and no cap. He seemed eager to talk.

I've only been here three weeks. The order was for 90 days. It's an alternative to custody. It was either this or prison. It goes back for a long while like I was getting into trouble with the police, hanging round with the wrong people, mixing with the wrong crowd, from about the age of ten. I'm 17 now.

I think it was being part of the gang really, being part of the crowd, that's how I think you really get into things, one of the lads you know, being in trouble, nicking cars. You don't think about it being dangerous, them sort of things, when you're with the boys. My parents didn't really know till I got arrested that I was doing that sort of things, taking cars. At first, when I was younger, I used to do shop-lifting as well. Then, as I got older, it was nicking motor bikes for a couple of years, then it was cars. Then one night I was drunk, got into a row, got done for attempted robbery. That's why I was sent here cos it was an alternative to custody and thank God these people were here. If they weren't here you know, they'd just lock you up and throw away the key.

I've been done for robbery before. I wasn't drunk then but that was all blown out of proportion. It was someone of my own age. I think it's aggression more than anything, anger. I dunno—you just sometimes get depressed and that, it just makes you angry about all sorts of things: friends, people. They say "count ten" but I never paid attention to that.

Didn't you know I've been in a boarding school since I was ten till I was 15 for behaviour problems? You'd be at school Monday to Friday, in the country, then you'd come home weekends. I didn't ever go to a secondary school. I would like to have stayed in normal school. I went from primary school to boarding school and then from boarding school to a centre and then from the centre I was doing college one day a week but then I was just at home all day, nothing to do, bored, no money. I had to make money elsewhere. But I started offending before I went to boarding school.

It was a brilliant school but unfortunately it was closed down when I was about 15. The education was brilliant and the staff were all brilliant. I'd have done my exams. They had a policy where you could stay on and they'd pay for your college and all that. They closed it before I had a chance of that. After that I was out of school for seven months before they put me in that centre.

I've been like that all my life, basically a little villain [*Mark laughed*], a little tearaway. I live at home with Mum. I've a younger sister. I'm the eldest. My parents split up when I was very little. I do see my Dad. He has a girlfriend and his girlfriend has a little boy and they have another son. That's it, basically. I don't think he's interested—I never see him hardly. I'll ring him now and again; if I go up there, I'll see the baby, know what I mean. I don't bother ringing him all the time because he don't bother ringing me so why should I make the effort?

My mother knows what he's like. She doesn't work. My sister's ten —she's my half-sister but I call her my sister. My step-Dad lived with us for a while. He was all right, treated me fair, gave me money, bought me presents. He and my Mum split up.

My Mum can't control me. It's a matter over years. It's not just a two-week thing, a three-week or a year thing, it's over the years that I've been bad, you know what I mean. It could be from when I was a child or something like that so that's why they sent me to boarding school. When I first went there I didn't like it, I hated it, I wanted to be at home, I ran away a few times but in the finish I got to like it. It was brilliant there. We used to go out, go on holidays, do woodwork, art, play football, basketball.

I want to be an electrician. I'm waiting for a college course now, a three-year course. They'll pay me £98.42 a week for the first year. I don't know how much after that. The course has work experience in it. It's like an apprenticeship but it's not an actual apprenticeship. It's like YTS [Youth Training Scheme] but it's not YTS. On YTS you only get £30 a week. On this you do City and Guilds, NVQs and all that

I'm on the verge of leaving home. I don't get on with my Mum— behaviour problems again [*Mark grinned*]. I play music loud, late at night, you know, all that sort of stuff: bang doors, open cupboards, always come in too late at night. My Mum doesn't like it because she has to get up to get my sister to school in the morning. I won't be lonely in my flat. I'll have my girlfriend. She'll probably move in with me. She works. She's my age.

My keyworker's sorting it out. I want to try and go and make something on my own. I want a little bit of help off somebody and I've found the help here. These people are very helpful, you know. It's a good thing there are these sort of places. For young kids, if you've been in trouble with the police, it's just throw away the key. Locking them up, if you do something, it's like paying the price—but I think these places do brilliantly.

I went on a motor car project voluntarily. At the time I was on probation that I got from the courts for two years. My probation officer thought it'd be good if I could try this project because I was doing nothing in the day anyway. So I went in for a while, a couple of weeks. It was good. You smash up motors, fix them up and then come banger racing on Saturdays.

As you get older you come to realise, know what I mean, that you shouldn't do it, it's not worth it. I didn't realise before about insurance, running someone over, but I weren't one of those crazy ones, you know. I can drive properly. I ain't not getting into a car and going Brrwhrrbrrrrrrrrrrr [*Mark made extremely loud and realistic car revving noises*] 90 miles round the corner and all that. I drive like a proper driver. Fair enough, you think [*he interpreted my thoughts rightly*] "they all say that" but you know, most people in a car, they go speeding. That's what joyriding is all about. For me it weren't like that. For me it was more getting used to being in a car and driving the car. I'll take my test now, I'm learning, and then I'll probably buy a car.

I'm going on the victim compensation programme here. It's brilliant. It's a good thing. I mean, you can't be a criminal all your life. It's not worth it. All these big villains that've been on the run for years, they come back to England and they've been caught, haven't they? It's not worth it. I've only missed coming here once. You can't miss here anyway—if you don't turn up, you're out unless you've a reasonable excuse. If you ring up and say you can't come in because you're ill, they need a doctor's certificate, so you can't lie, basically.

It's hard getting back on the straight and narrow. Here they've got house rules. You have to abide by them, sign an agreement. There is rules at home but I break them. Sounds silly. Bang doors . . . I love my Mum but I've had problems all over my life, it's not easy [*Mark raised his voice, as if indignant*]. People have different upbringings, do you understand. Some people are different towards their mums from others, know what I mean—so there you go [*and he seemed to relax again*].

At home I got smacked [*Mark giggled*] when I was naughty. I used to like have squabbles with the teachers at boarding school. They used to grab your arms and put you down like, hold you down, because you were so young and active, effing this and effing that. It quietened a lot of people down. If you'd have known me seven years ago, you'd see the difference to now, you know, how much it had changed me.

At primary school I was one young kid out of control. As soon as I got to the boarding school I noticed the change between primary staff and people at boarding school plus like they could handle you if you tried to fight them or run out or threw a fit or something, you know what I mean. They could handle you, hold you down, keep you quiet whatever, you knocking or punching them. And they didn't let you get away with things like normal primary staff do because they're not so in control, are they, because they've got a class of 30 people to look after so it wasn't easy for them with one villain like me.

I couldn't tell you what made me play up at school. I'm quite smart. I've got some end-of-term reports in my bag here, reports from the centre where I went. I used to swim a lot, for a club. They arranged all the sport at my boarding school. Have a read of these if you like, if you wish.

Mark opened a fashionable black nylon briefcase he'd put beside him and pulled out a sheaf of precious papers. There were certificates and badges for swimming, life-saving and ice-skating along with his Record of Achievement from the Individual Tuition Centre and football programmes. He was delighted by my admiration of them.

I've never been in custody, prison. This is like on the verge, alternative, and I'd sooner do this any day then go to prison. Nothing frightens me about prison but it's—I'd like to say a word but I won't say it. It's a dump, it's a crap-hole. Someone would try to bully me there, give me a punch or something, order me around but I wouldn't stand for it anyway. I'm not that kind of person, never matter how big they are. The bigger they are, the harder I'd fight.

There are drugs everywhere. I used to puff. It's always available, anywhere you go, no matter where you go. It's easy. The cost depends on what you take. It doesn't solve anything. Basically, that's why most youngsters take drugs, because they think it solves their problems. It doesn't. I've just seen so many people just go, down the grave, dead; it's killed them off. It kills them. I've had loads of friends die from drugs. It's digging a grave.

Some people are strong-minded and won't. If someone said to me, "Stick your head in the oven", I'd say, "No. You bloody stick your head in the oven". If I don't want to, I won't take it, I can guarantee you that. I've stopped cars now. I say, "Go on then, see you later. On your bike, pal, see you later." You just tell them "no", tell them straight. They can't force you. If they try to force you, then tell them "no". No one can make you do something you don't want to do, not unless you've got a gun against your head.

Of course I've seen guns. It's not specifically here but there's armed robberies. I've seen them. It's not my scene. I mean, if you can't use your fists, you're a mug. That's the end of it.

I don't get on with the police. It was quite funny the other night. I was on the way to my girlfriend's about half 12 and this coloured fellow had locked his keys in his car and he's trying to get into his car with this coat-hanger and I'm standing there. I'm not trying to help him and this police officer stops, gets out of his car and he says, "I know you from somewhere, don't I? I've nicked you for TDA" [*Taking and Driving Away a vehicle: actually now taking a vehicle without consent, or 'TWC'*]. Then he said, "Come and help us get in this". I told him how to do it, gave him a bit of advice, bent the door back, pulled it up. Otherwise he would have had to break his window to get in the car.

Four months ago I got done for burglary. I had a video recorder in my bedroom. The police got in because they thought it was there and they found this video recorder in my bedroom which had been from a burglary the previous day before. Now I bought this video off somebody, you know, and they charged me for burglary. But when it was brought to court I put me hand up and pleaded stolen goods [*handling stolen goods*] because I knew it was stolen—see what I mean—but *I* didn't steal it.

The same geezer, after nicking me for that, two or three weeks back I was with my mate and he said, "I'm arresting you for suspicion of burglary." I said, "You're having a bloody laugh". He goes, "If you never did it, you've got nothing to worry about." I said, "If you do, I'm going to do you for wrongful arrest" (that's what they talk about at the nick). He interviewed me and I told him the full story. He said I done it on the Saturday afternoon between three and four and I was definitely described. I turned round and said to him, "It can't be me, mate. I was at a wedding in [a nearby town] with me girlfriend, you know—which I was, with about 50 other people." Then he asked me to bring the video down to prove where I was. So I brought the video down and proved where I was. I was on the video at the time and the date. I wasn't here.

That's the kind of thing they try and do. If you're known to the police, they will always pull you up, even if you keep out of trouble for 30 years. Once you're known by the police, that's it. They will never leave off your back, no matter what. You could be going 100 per cent straight and the police would come round and bribe you, bribe you, to ask you information about other people. Many's the time they've asked me for information. I've said, "No, it's all right." There's a big blow-up in the papers to pay grasses and all that. But that's their job, in't it, at the end of the day.

You can't make yourself stop, you can only stop yourself. You've just got to stop and think, basically. It's like anything, you've got to think before you move. Think before you move and you'll always make a wise move. See yer!

On that note Mark started to pack up but then he suddenly picked up the tape-recorder again and gave the following unsolicited testimonial to the work of the youth justice centre.

This place is an alternative to custody which I'm on and I think this place is brilliant because you got your victim compensation. Victim compensation is brilliant because it gives you a chance to go and do work on estates and that for the community, basically like community service. You go over there, get your overalls on, go to the estate, do something like gardening, or something in the local playground, work in a flat, filling in the walls, painting. It's good stuff. It's like experience.

Your lunch money is three quid and they give you £12 a day, £6 when you go home and the other £6 goes to your victims, which is pretty good bacause it's a way of giving back. You can't give back something what you've done but at least you're giving something back. You're not just taking. I thought places like that would send you round and make you do it for nothing but they do give you something, like stipe you know, which is good.

And then there's your education which is brilliant. I've got it this afternoon, education. You go out there and do stuff like reading, writing and spelling, which is pretty good. The staff are very friendly and they're firm as well. That's what I like: they're firm, you know. They won't tolerate for any bad behaviour or any stuff like that, so it's good.

You've got a piano, pool table, music, television there, food and drink. Then there's Offenders' Behaviour Group on Monday but I haven't started that yet. My programmes's four days a week. It's pretty good really. I think more of these kind of places should be open for young offenders.

Mark's mother did not want to be interviewed.

Josiah

I had been told quite a lot about Josiah (a black young man of 16) before I eventually met him. He had been difficult to supervise. For the first six months of his order he had not attended as instructed, had failed to meet all appointments until he was 'breached' and brought back to court. The court gave him the alternative of attending as instructed or custody. He decided to attend but still did not always do so regularly, as my experience showed. He missed the first two meetings we had arranged at the youth justice centre, despite having fixed the first with me himself on the telephone. But as his social worker forecast, once you met him it was impossible not to like him: "His personality enables him to get away with a lot", was her verdict. We had been worried about his whereabouts as he had also missed his routine appointments with his social worker and there was no reply when she had visited his Dad's home but he was all smiles when we met. It was a very cold day and his outfit would have graced the ski slopes: padded jacket, big trainers and a hood pulled over a woollen hat. He told me:

The last time I was meant to come it completely slipped my mind. I've been at my friend's house. That's why my social worker couldn't find me. I sleep and eat there. My Dad doesn't worry. He knows I'm safe. It was my cousin who was with me just now when I came. I've got seven uncles and lots of cousins.

I go to college now, regularly four days a week. The rest of the time I see friends, play on computers, borrow computer games. I don't go to college on Fridays which is why I'm here now. I'm doing a computer course, GNVQs in IT. What I really want to do is a course in brick-laying and then get a proper job on a site, not just a labouring job, so that I can earn good money. I wanted to do a brick-laying course but there weren't no brick-laying courses open. I was interested in computers too but I'm not now. I went down to the careers office and they told me I could do a three months course and get a certificate.

I've been in a lot of trouble these last two or three years. I wanted money for things like smoking and clothes. Everything's expensive and parents aren't going to buy you what you want. You've got to get it yourself. It's not your friends telling you. You just need to look good in the public. See what I'm wearing now. It's all Moschino—about £150 my jeans, £150 my jumper, £110 my shirt. It's the Italian, in't it? Sometimes my Dad gives me pocket money but at the moment my foster parents do.

I've stopped doing a lot of things now. I was just getting caught too much and I see prison coming soon. If you go once to prison you always go back. Bound to, aren't you? It's easier to steal than to work.

I live with my Dad. I've lived with him since I was two years old. I haven't seen my Mum since I was seven. She used to come and see me Christmas and birthdays. I had a little brother born on New Year's Eve and I've got a little sister too. They have different mums. My Mum used to drink so my Dad got legal custody of me. He had a steady job. He's a draughtsman, in architecture. He's—what do you call it?—a freelance now. People come to him to plan their houses in Jamaica. He's fully qualified. He's had no trouble with the police except when he was about 18. He had a knife. He's 37 or 38 now. He's from Jamaica. He talks posh and wears suits. He's Nation of Islam so he wears a black suit, white shirt and red tie. I've grown up not eating pork.

He had a drug problem as well. I never confronted him about drugs. I went to live with foster parents while he sorted himself out. I was 13 or 14 years old. That's when all the offending started. The foster parents aren't strict enough on you because they're not your parents so they can't tell you. I'd be back after ten and they wouldn't open the door to me. I'd wait outside or go and stay with a friend. I told my social worker but she didn't do anything. My foster parents didn't trust me to give me a key. They were elderly black people. He was all right but his wife always told him what to do. They had their own older kids of about 27 and 28 and someone else was there too. It was near here. My Dad visited.

I smoke weed but I don't do crack and those other things. I still smoke weed but I don't do it till I'm out of my head. One spliff and it'll make me go to sleep. I don't smoke cigarettes no more—they're bad for you.

I used to do shoplifting, mainly bottles of champagne and brandy. Sometimes I'd rob kids on the road. They were my age, not young kids or old people. That's sick, robbing old people. I wouldn't do that. I'd take more from places that are insured. The government pays when they're insured . . . well if the government doesn't the managers then. One or two shops I know would take the bottles. They probably did know they were stolen but it was going cheap—I'd charge less than £10 a bottle.

I quite enjoyed it too. It's like acting. I'm not bragging but I'm quite a good actor. I'd put a bottle in the bottom of my trouser leg, talk to the security guard for a bit and then walk out. My foster parents used to come to the police station for a bit when I was arrested and then social services. I first went into foster care when I was arrested for robbery and they put me in local authority accommodation till the first court date.

I went to the Individual Tuition Centre when I was with my foster parents. I was expelled from my last school. What happened was that someone was getting bullied. I wasn't doing the bullying but someone passing who wanted to stop the bullying grabbed me. I pushed them away and they fell against a car that was passing. They weren't hurt much at all but it was a big issue at school. At my previous school I did bully people. It was to show off, impress people. I'm getting older now and it's all changing for me. We used to just take the Mickey out of the teacher. The teachers would send you to the head and you'd go into other classes along the corridor causing trouble in them.

I used to be top of the class. Dad would pressure me when I was at school. He'd help me with my homework. When I was in trouble I'd throw away the letter they gave me for him and just go home. Or in the morning I'd put on my uniform as usual, pick up the letter from the letter-box as I went out and bunk off with my friends. Of course it ends up worser if you do that. Dad didn't really beat me. He just grounded me when he found out, stopped my pocket money.

Now I don't get arrested. At least I have been arrested recently but it used to be twice a week. Now I get arrested for old cases I forgot the date of and didn't go to court.

I'm into girls—*Josiah laughed*—but I've not got a steady. In five years I see myself working on a site and earning nice wages. In ten years – I can't imagine ten years – but maybe I'll have a family by then and I'll be working.

I finish my supervision in May [*five months later*] and I'll have been supervised for two years. I was 12 when I first went to court. It was then I first went into foster care like I told you. The case was prolonged because I pleaded not guilty. They said I snatched a woman's handbag over a footbridge. They said I was wearing multi-coloured jeans but I had no multi-coloured jeans. I knew who did do it but I didn't do it. I got my first supervision order then. It was upsetting.

Before that me and my friends, it was raining and we were in an empty house three doors away from where I lived. We were playing cards and having a laugh. We were arrested for burglary. It was a basement flat, empty, but they said we'd take the light screws. It got thrown out of court. There were nine of us.

From that day on the police have harassed me. They all know me. "Come here. I want to search you. Name check." Some are all right. I'm not saying all policemen are bad but some will nick you for anything if they have a chance. I was arrested recently for a case I'd already had. They kept me at the station overnight. It was "a misunderstanding", they said. They let me go. I wanted compensation but my solicitors say I can't do legal aid for that.

This is the only interview which is not a verbatim transcription of what was said but reconstructed from my full notes. The tape-recorder Josiah held stopped recording after the first few minutes of the interview. Thus, although the record is accurate, I may have missed some of the nuances of Josiah's expressions.

Josiah was willing for me to talk to his Dad and his foster parents but his social worker did not think it appropriate.

Matthew and His Mother

Matthew was a tall, good-looking, black boy of 16, in a blue track suit top with a white and red ribbon running down the shoulders and sleeves. His trousers were yellow but the general effect, topped by the standard baseball cap, was lively rather than garish. He was clear about why he had got into trouble and was attending a youth justice centre under a court supervision order.

MATTHEW

I got into a bad crowd. I'm from an upper middle class family. I don't live down here really. I got mixed up with the wrong crowd and I got sent down here to my uncle. I used to go to a private school when I was living at home. I just wasted it.

I've always been a curious kind of person, wanting to know what's underneath the sheets or what's behind the covers, things like that. I don't know my Dad. I never knew him, even when I was a little boy. My Mum, she works: she's the manager of home care up where we live. My Mum never said I was bad, she never said I was a bad person. It's just that the people who . . . I'm a very friendly person, I make friends. I have good friends and I have bad friends. I don't think of the bad friends as bad friends. I just know them but they get up to a lot of silly things, getting into trouble, getting me into trouble.

My good friends don't get into trouble. They go to college, they have a job, they work. I'm at college. I did have a job but it didn't work out. It was for a company that looks at the walls of a house for cracks that need processing. I did that for something like two months. It was getting in the way of my college work so I quit the job and I went back to college. At the college at the moment I'm doing the RSA core skills course in computing, maths and English. It's to brush up and help you on things that you've missed.

I lived in Holland for a year when I was 13. My life story's pretty big at the moment. My Mum sent me over there to a private school. I speak a bit of Dutch as well. I speak a bit of French, a bit of German. I went to a boarding school—my Mum paid for it. It was supposed to be a good education. I was living in the countryside. It was nice there. I wouldn't say no to going again.

I started getting mixed up with bad friends when I was about 14 or 15 after I came back. My trouble's been nothing big, nothing big at all. For the latest one I've just got the case acquitted because of lack of evidence for handling of stolen goods. It was credit cards but I found the credit cards on a bus. I had another case for assault and I got a £50 fine for that.

What happened was I went to an off-licence shop selling drinks. The man said, "Are you buying anything?". I said I was just looking. The man said, "Come out of the shop because we don't like you boys inside the shop." I said, "There's no need for that." He said, "Get out." The man pushed me out of the shop. At the time I was with friends. He pushed me out of the shop. He said, "We don't like you kind of people being in the shop." I said, "What do you mean?" Then it clicked and I thought, "Ah! He's talking about different race." So I picked up a stone and flicked it through the window. He called the police and the police came and arrested me.

They took me down to the police station and they looked through my pockets and found the credit cards in there. So I got the fine for smashing the guy's window and assault. The handling of stolen goods, I got that dropped. It was also because the case had been going on for nine months. I've got no more cases now outstanding.

That was all fair but I don't think it was fair [when they charged me] for attempted burglary at the hospital. It was something stupid, just one of those silly things the police try and pick me up on. It was on a Friday. Me and my friends were just sitting around, a group of boys and girls. We were all just talking there, making jokes and having a little to drink. One of the girls was bouncing up and down to the music and then she slipped. It was in my friend's house. She dropped down and a piece of metal went straight through her temple. So we had to rush her to the hospital.

We took her in and she was seeing the doctor. One of my friends said, "Is there a shop?" I said "Why?" He said, "I'm a bit hungry and I want to buy some food." So I said, "OK. Let's take a look, see if there's a cafeteria, if it's open." At the time it was about 12 o'clock. I didn't realise the time. I thought it was about a quarter to eleven. I went round to the shop kind of bit—it's got a newspaper shop and some other shops. I was looking round there. Like I said, I told you at the beginning I'm always a curious person to look what's behind the bars.

I picked up a stick and started banging it on the shop shutters. I was just making up a beat and my friends started singing and then the security guard—he must have heard the banging—he run round and he goes "Oi!". Through the shock of it I dropped the stick through the gap because there was a gap between the shop and the desk. He jumped on me and said, "What are you doing?" I said I was banging it and he said, "No you're not. You're trying to get the stick to reach the sweets." I said, "What are you talking about? How can I put a stick in there to reach the sweets when the sweets are so far away?" He goes "Right" and he calls a back-up and then the police and the police nicked me for attempted burglary.

It's silly things like that. Even though I wasn't guilty for that, I pleaded guilty for that because the trial was going to take so long. I couldn't take the trial. I was just banging it, making a beat.

I'll keep clear now. In five years' time I know I won't be poor. I won't have to do anything bad, I know. At home now I save my money, every little money I get. On a Friday my aunt gives me £40. I just put £10 aside or £20 and keep the rest in my pocket and I have to budget that to last me the week. I don't have any trouble with that. I want to become a computer manager or work in computers. I'm quite good at maths.

My aunt and uncle both work and they have children. I come from a big family. All my family scorn me because none of the members of my family have got into trouble with the police or the law. I am the only one in the whole of my family that's got into trouble with the police and the law. My uncles, my aunts, my older cousins all have big jobs, driving big cars, enjoying life. My uncle is a scientist, another uncle is a chauffeur, I've an uncle who is a computer manager with IBM. My family is always willing to help me. I don't know if all families do that. Mine does.

I play basketball. Last year my uncle took me windsurfing and I got my windsurfing licence. I stay at home now, read all sorts of books—action, *The novel of the Ghost* by Smith Williams, Malcolm X . . .

At this point there was the ring of a telephone from somewhere inside Matthew's jacket. He pulled out a mobile 'phone.

This is my aunty's—she bought it. Not many of my friends have them. She bought it for me to keep in touch with her, so that she can call up and say, "What are you doing now? Come home for lunch or whatever." I have a curfew. I have to be in at 10.30 p.m. at night.

At the moment I live with foster parents. I've been with them about eight months. We get on well. Basically I wanted to give my family a break. I wanted to clear things up for myself, I only wanted to do it by myself. I did it myself. I went to the social workers. I want to go back and live with my Mum eventually but I want to finish my education here as well. She was on holiday in the West Indies over Christmas so I haven't seen her for about a month. I went to my aunt's on Christmas Day and New Year's Day.

My grandmother lives with my Mum. I've got family and aunties and cousins in the West Indies. I've cousins in America as well. It's St Kitts. My Mum met my Dad there. He's American. My Mum's never really talked about him. She says she hasn't his address.

Yes, I suppose they're helpful here, at the youth justice. They ask me questions. I fill in forms . . . I shouldn't be here. I shouldn't have got into trouble.

Matthew gave me his aunt's telephone number and she confirmed what a supportive, successful family he came from. He was "privileged", as she put it, adding that maybe too much was expected of him. His troubles had begun at a school which perhaps did not know how to stimulate him properly. He switched off learning and started truanting. His mother, her sister, had found the school in Holland which offered a one-to-one approach for disturbed children and Matthew did better for a time after his return. But then he fell in with a bad crowd and was expelled from his well-known private school. Her sister sent him to live with their brother, to see if a fresh start would help.

"He's got to the stage now when he doesn't recognise the truth," she said. "It's difficult for him to distinguish between reality and fantasy. That's the thing that stresses the family out. I mind his lying to me continually. He could have stayed with me, I've plenty of room, but h e didn't want to stay with me because I'm too strict. I think children should be responsible for their actions and know that every action has a consequence. I'd be totally irresponsible if I let him stay out all night, for instance."

She said she had not given him a mobile 'phone and was perturbed that he had one. He was not old enough to own one and if any of the family saw him with it they'd tell him so.

In her view part of Matthew's problem was that "He's so gullible. He won't analyse the situation. He'll just be swept along with the tide." Her main worry was that he'd become part of a gang and get enmeshed in a criminal culture. They were Christians and he'd been brought up not to drink, smoke or take stimulants, even tea and coffee. Most of the family were vegetarians but Matthew ate chicken.

She thought girls were easier to guide. "For a boy it's his honour," she said, "his pride. They have too much pressure on them."

You can't choose for children, she concluded, but you can always encourage them on the right path.

MATTHEW'S MOTHER

Matthew's mother found it painful to talk about her son but was willing to do so on the telephone if it would help others. She spoke fast and fluently, appearing to be glad to make her points to a sympathetic outsider but angry about what she saw as an impossible situation.

Normally children who go into crime come from broken, poor homes and deprived families. I'm a single parent, yes, but I worked hard to get my degree and all my family are professionals in their own right. It was a disgrace the way Matthew behaved at the private school I paid for here. He made his own decision to be the way he is. He had two weeks running wild in London as a means of spiting the family.

I have two children and there's been no difference in the way they've been brought up. My daughter's seven and a half and she's fine. This is a Christian home. I teach them values, how to survive in life and the norm in terms of what a youngster should do. If he did wrong as a small boy, I'd speak to him, tell him the consequences of his actions. When he became a teenager, about 13 and a half or 14, he said he wanted to make his own decisions and that I didn't fit his values. He wanted to be part of his group, wear earrings. He said he was a teenager, not a robot. But he's not a man. My Mum, who lives with me, and I make the decisions here. I won't have my children ruling me. If you're part of a family you have to be part of that family and obey its rules. I had to abide by the laws in society and I had to work.

As a child Matthew was caring and helpful, just the opposite of what he is now. My friends and family can't believe he's turned out as he has. There were no problems at his early schools. I sent him to Holland because I wanted him to go to that particular Christian school but he was homesick so I brought him back.

Matthew can't say I've neglected him. I could have had many men in my single life but I kept myself to myself for my children. I sacrificed myself for my children. I stayed in a lower paid job so that I could spend all of the evenings and holidays with them. We always went out, did swimming and activities together as a family.

This is the first year he didn't come on holiday with us. I'd said I'd take him home [*to St Kitts*] for his sixteenth birthday but he was in care and couldn't leave the country. There were too many cases outstanding against him for him to come. I've only just got back. He's missed out on so much. Going home he'd have seen black people in such a positive light—my daughter has had that experience now but not him. Our people there have moved on from nothing, from cotton picking a generation ago to becoming professionals running their own businesses and hotels.

As a Christian all I can say is this: I know there is only one person you have to serve. There is a good spirit and an evil force in everyone. If you don't ask divine power to overcome the evil within you, then evil will take over. Matthew has chosen not to go to church. That's a choice for him to make but it doesn't mean he should have no values. He's totally caught up in his own world, wants to impress his friends that he's tough. I always said, "You're a Christian. You weren't trained to steal or tell lies so if you do you'll be caught. You're an amateur so you'll just get caught."

Now he's regretting what he did. He says he's finished. I'm praying for him every day that he'll see the light. One of the hardest things to think of for any child of 15 or 16 is that he's not here at home. I still can't come to terms with that, with the thought that his room is empty every night.

The Twins and Their Mother

Robert and Cliff were identical twins, white youths aged 17. Both had the same very short hairstyle but the day I met them their dress could not have been more different. Robert had an earring in one ear and was wearing casual clothes: baggy white trousers, a big puffer-type jacket and trainers. His twin wore a smart black quilted jacket over a black formal suit, white shirt, narrow black tie and was the only young man I interviewed who wore ordinary shoes — and they were well polished. If they had been dressed the same, it would have been difficult to tell them apart, as many in authority had found in the past. Both had a regional accent but I found Cliff easier to follow and he offered more eye-contact, fixing me with a firm, almost gimlet gaze. I talked to Robert first while Cliff was with his social worker, discussing the content of a report for the youth court where he was due to appear on offences connected with cars and criminal damage. Robert was on licence for three months after a spell in a young offender institution.

ROBERT

It's good being a brother but he is a pain in the arse sometimes. We'll go out, and sometimes he's with his girlfriend and I'm with my girlfriend, but all day, all night, mostly we're together.

We started off together at school but then I got kicked out and went to another school. I was there nine months, ten months. I didn't like school, I didn't like the teachers. The teachers' work I didn't want to know. I wanted to know about driving, mechanics, things I was more interested in, really practical work, anything on a car. I just wanted to know all about screenwork, complete work on the body, servicing, brakes, clutch, gear box, tuning the engine, all that's possible for a mechanic's work, anything on an engine. I've learnt about it by working with other people, learning like with them.

The only thing I wanted to do at school was just maths, that was my subject I wanted all the time. There was a policy that you've got to do science, PE, English and all that. I'd bunk off after lunch or I'd just sit there and go to sleep. Cliff was all right, he did well. My reading's not bad. I could go back to college and relearn it. I got in with a bad lot of people and I started driving.

At this point Robert rose from his chair, walked slowly over to a waste-paper bin at the other end of the room and carefully removed a large glob of chewing gum from his mouth and put it in the bin.

No, I didn't worry about harming others. I wasn't really bothered. I would have been upset if I'd run over someone but at the time I wasn't bothered. They told me about it but I'd say "Shut up!"

When I went to court for the first time for a driving offence—no driving licence, no insurance, no MOT—I got a fine and some points for my licence. No one was really bothered. It came out of my pocket money so I didn't get any pocket money, to pay my fines. That's what made me, that's what started me going out thieving, to get my pocket money back. I started liking it and I carried on. It started there, shop-lifting like, and then I started going on to like stereos, nicking motor bikes, things like that to sell them. You nick something and you can sell it rightaway.

My Mum didn't know till I started getting arrested. She beat me up. Then I started getting worse and worse and worse. I didn't change. I didn't give a fuck about no one. Nothing would stop me.

Now I've just come out of prison. I'm on parole till April. I just want to settle down with my girlfriend, move out of [this town], go to college, get a job. I'm applying for a flat, going to Birmingham. I've family up there, a friend up there, so I'm going to live up there. My girlfriend doesn't want to go to Birmingham.

I won't go to college full-time because I haven't got the patience. I'll get a job and do something like day-release, night courses, something like that. I ain't got the patience to do full-time. I get bored too easy. It's all written work.

I've been to college once, about two years ago. The teacher did something I knew and he done it wrong. So I put my hand up and said, "That's wrong." He thought I was being patronising and having a go at him and said he was right and I was wrong. Then I showed him how to do it. He knew I was right but he dragged me outside and said I'm putting him down. He started on me saying, "You should have waited till after the class." I said, "You're the teacher. You should have known that. It was pure mechanics. They could have done that to someone's car and fucked it up. Then they would be sued, wouldn't they?" Then he said "Yah" but then he chucked me out of his class. I went back and punched him and walked out. He didn't do nothing—shitted himself, did nothing. It put me off college.

Cliff's my business partner. I do recovery of cars and bikes, repair cars, sell cars, buy cars. We keep them outside my Mum's house or in a friend's driveway. I got some cards printed up and we advertise in shop windows. I tell my mates and all my mates know. They tell their mates. People come to us. Cliff likes doing the driving and lets me do the work. He's like a lazy person. He knows quite a bit about cars but really he don't like to get his hands dirty unless he has to. If he has to, then he'll do it.

I'm on a two-year ban from driving. I've got two "driving whilst being disqualified". I'm just out of prison and I've got loads of previous. I've stopped driving. I wouldn't go back to prison. It wasn't exactly tough but it was boring. Everyone's boasting that "I've been to prison" but it isn't something to boast about and if anyone says it's such a good place to go, I say I've been and I know what it's like and I wouldn't go back. I'd rather go straight if I could.

If there's a car that's been nicked, burnt out or something like that, I'd take it away, you know, destroy it, I'd take it to the shredder. If it'd been parked up, the only condition I'd take it is if no one owns it and it'd been sitting there something like three or six months.

I can't stop driving. Some people are addicted to drugs. Well, I'm addicted to driving. I still drive now and again but I'm careful. The police know me. It's a year and a half still. My brother drives mostly.

If I would travel back time now, I'd have wanted to stay with the girl I was with before. I'd have stayed at college, have the job I had. I was working at a mechanic's garage. I was getting home too late and my girlfriend was getting all pissed up about work. I quit the job and then I went to college. Then I had the row with the college. We were at her Mum's. She was still at school. She comes home, something like half four and I had to be there about four o'clock, half four. I'd come home half past six at night and it got too late. I was with her two years.

At this point Cliff came back and said he had an appointment at half past eleven so I should see him. We had just a few minutes to talk.

CLIFF

Yes, we buy and sell cars. I do the driving and I mainly deal with the financial side, do the books, supervise everything, see the MOTs are done properly. I list the income and the outgoings. We don't pay tax and what we make varies. We have to pay wages—we get a mechanic to do the jobs we can't do.

I'm at college, doing a City and Guilds mechanics course, one full day a week. The exam is at the end of the year, theory and practice.

I first got into trouble when I was about 14 when I was mixed up with the wrong crowd. It was for driving with no licence and a few criminal damages, mainly traffic offences. I didn't know about insurance then but it didn't make any difference—you have the buzz through driving. I always stuck to the speed limits and drove carefully.

Sometimes we'd get take the rap for each other but I mostly have taken the blame for Robert. Everything I've done has been jointly with him but my offences haven't been enough for prison. I passed my driving test first go. It was just before they began the written—people say that's hard.

The business takes most of my time. We went into care when we were 15. We already had our own business then, buying and selling cars and making money. We've lived in bed-and-breakfast, hotels, every kind of placement, fostering . . . we wanted different. We're in a Council flat now.

If I had children I'd give them freedom but not enough to go off the rails. I'd discipline them not by smacking. I'd talk to them.

CORINNE, MOTHER OF THE TWINS

I rang the bell of the house and after a couple of minutes the door opened slowly, not all the way. I said who I was and a quiet, flat voice replied, "Oh yes". Corinne opened the door and welcomed me in, offering me coffee or tea. She looked frail, slight in stature, with a curtain of darkish hair half over her face. She wore an attractive, Aran-type embroidered sweater with jeans, her feet were bare and her toe-nails painted. She didn't look well. Her face was sallow and lined beyond her years. A small, rotund pit terrier jumped at me, barking. She shouted at it "Shut up or I'll smack you" and it went off into the back garden where white sheets were billowing in the breeze, as clean as in an advertisement. We talked in the comfortable dining area adjoining a spotless kitchen. Cut glass sparkled in the dining room cabinet and there were new digital machines in the kitchen but the kitchen ceiling and walls were peeling. "It takes a long time to do the decorating when you're on income support," she said. She smoked while she talked, her voice at times becoming animated as she gave her views, particularly about the education system.

I've got two other boys as well as the twins. One's 23 next week, the other's 20. Nothing was straightforward with them either, not at all. It was mainly the elder one. He was constantly getting arrested, going to prison—he's been twice, the first time it was for burglary. It gave him a shock, he's not the type to be locked up. It was three or four years ago; the younger ones weren't affected.

He seemed to be in court every week, every Wednesday. The police station must have been on average two or three times a week, mainly late at night and you've got three other kids in bed and no one to look after them. I feel that if all first offenders from a very young age were punished differently, we'd have less kids in court now. Whether it's mine or someone else's, mine included, give them a short sharp shock first time. The other way it's going to escalate and escalate so that you've got a mugger on your hands or a robber or worse than that, a rapist or something. You give them a short sharp shock straight off.

But he's turned his life round now, basically by meeting a girl and having a child. It's changed his life. He's studying at college to be a solicitor. He's just coming to the end of the first year and it's all fine. He goes on to university next.

My boys are all pretty honest with me about what they do. I tried a mixture of things with them. I talked to them, slapped them, threatened to throw them out, disown them, and at the end of it, I stand by them, I'm their mother. No one wants their children to get into trouble and get locked up, no one.

I'm the type I sit and talk to my kids. And they know, if they've got any problems, they can come and talk to me, good or bad, and obviously I try and help, the one lifeline, I try and listen and help, that's what I'm here for. Many the times I've told them [off] if they've hit a young kid, you know, or anyone else, the aged . . .

My eldest was 13 when he started and I was on my own with four children. They've all got the same Dad—I divorced him when the twins were three. It wasn't a nice divorce but it was my choice. I couldn't live with him any more, with his life, his womanising. They've never really seen him since, just on/off, once or twice a year. They've lots of family on their Dad's side—he had four brothers—but they don't see them. I stopped taking them down to see the grandmother. If she wants to see them, she knows where I live. My parents are near but they don't bother with me and I don't see my brother and sister. I've got friends here.

It doesn't help when you're saying one thing to a child—you could be accusing him of something, you put your facts out, you know you're right and you're trying to discipline him—and there's someone else saying you're way out of line: no, he hasn't done this. They pick up that. I had that with the eldest one when I found out he was getting into trouble. I got his Dad and he said it was me, I was just being an hysterical female and there was nothing wrong with him really. And then you got his brothers saying, "Don't listen to her, do this or do that". Obviously he looked to them more than what I had to say.

Two of the brothers had been in trouble themselves. My husband was never in trouble, nor was I. I done quite well at school really. They wanted me to go on at school but I wanted to get out earning money. I was a wages clerk. I haven't worked since I had children. I remarried six years ago and I'm sort of still with my husband [*she made a see-saw movement with her hand*]. He's in work and has had no trouble with the law.

Robert's first trouble—I'm not sure if he was driving a car and hit someone's fence or was caught in the Coca-Cola factory with a lot of older kids. The police actually brought him home and said they'd caught him driving. I smacked him across the legs as he was sitting there. I didn't care if the police was there or not.

With mine, if they went out and drove, broke a law or got into a fight or anything like that, they would come and tell me. And obviously if they stole anything, because they knew I'd batter them nothing was ever brought back here and I wasn't told, but at the end I would find out because of the police arresting them.

I've tried battering them. I still do. They have to take it. They don't like it but they have to take it. I've tried everything, from grounding them to stopping their pocket money, to stopping the telly, going out—everything. I find a few slaps—I mean I don't batter them in the sense that I hurt them, you know what I mean, but I do punch them on the leg or the arm, scream at them. I don't really know if it helps more because when I get going and I'm hitting them and that, I won't let them leave the room, I push them to sit down and then I say my piece; they're made to listen. Obviously now that they're a lot older it's harder.

Different kids should be punished differently. I mean, you've got the punishment to fit the crime for a start. Each child reacts differently to different punishments. I mean you can smack one child and it'll work but you can smack another child and it won't because they're the rebellious kind.

My 20-year-old—he lives at home at the moment—I've never had to hit. I've never had to smack him. I just took him away from the telly and made him sit in the kitchen with me and it worked. I've never had to shout at him. I used to talk to him and he would relate and listen and understand. And as a result I've never had to go to court with him. He was in trouble just a couple of times when he was little and broke a boy's nose. In my eyes my one done nothing wrong. He saw this boy lighting a fire and told him to put it out. The other boy said "What's it to do with you?" and gave him a push. He's been easy to discipline and easy to control. He listened to what I had to say. It was my views that counted. And it's paid off.

The twins left home the November before last. Basically, I was out and when I came home my video was missing. They tried to make it look like a burglary but it wasn't. When they came back they denied it all. My other son said, "I'm going to bash you for what you've done to Mum." I was very angry, obviously. They said, "I'm not coming back" and I said, "I don't want you back." They took it literally, you know. Obviously deep down I didn't mean that but I was very angry at what they'd done. They went to social services and things got worse. They come home now all the time.

They were little terrors from the time they were born. My husband was never there. I was on my own. I had home help till the age of six months because of the other two and their ages but that was only temporary help with feeding and that. I still had to do the rounds from school and playschool and all the shopping myself with the two little ones. But you get through it, you know.

It was the school exclusions that started it. When the school sees a problem they want to remove it rather than deal with it. It's the problems that have to be dealt with not just removed for the moment. In fact we took Cliff away from his school because he was wrongly accused of stealing something and at the end of it, when they found out it wasn't Cliff, they basically refused to apologise—which isn't adult standards because to me if that was the other way round, they would have expected an apology off Cliff and it's adults that set the example in my book. And an apology—what are they going to miss? We could see the problems coming so we moved him. He was in his second or third year, about 13.

I couldn't get Robert to school. I used to take him, literally, and as I walked away he would walk off the other way. The education welfare people would say, "Just carry on bringing him so your back's covered." At one stage I used to go and look for him. But where do you look? I mean kids are a bit shrewd, they know where to hide. I thought I'd done all I could do by getting him out of the house, taking him to school. At one stage I volunteered to sit in the classroom with him and the teacher said, "No, that's not necessary." It's hard to stop a youngster walking out of school, it really is. You've [*you teachers have*] got a lot of kids to look after, I can understand that, but I felt that when he used to say to them, "I'm going", I don't think they done their job properly in trying to prevent him from going. Obviously there were times when he just walked out without saying nothing.

The reason he didn't go was basically he didn't want to go to school. Cliff got on better. Robert's hearing's always held him back and intimidated him. Being made to sit in the front of class and have the Mickey taken out of him didn't accord with Robert one little bit. It was easier not to be there. He's been under the hospital for years. They're saying now he's got to be fitted with a hearing aid but he's refusing to wear one. Kids can be cruel. Robert's thinking, "If I wear it, everyone's going to take the Mickey out of me."

My views are—and I've discussed this several times and I'd like to see something happen about it—less classroom work and more work experience from a younger age. Because I think if you could get youngsters to go and do a day or two's work rather than sit in a classroom five days a week, it's obviously going to be more interesting for them; even if they done a mixture of things they're going to realise what they'd really like to do as well. I think two weeks' work experience in the whole of their school life is nothing.

If they have it like more often and if like somewhere along the line they were paid a small amount for doing the work experience, it would again interest kids into going to school. It's not really bribery because in a sense you're giving them a chance to work at something that they want to do when they possibly leave school and getting them a very minimal [*wage*]. I'm talking of 13 or 14-year-olds that you can just give a couple of quid to and they'll be happy with it. You're not talking about large amounts of money.

I know: I've brought this up with my own kids and I've said, "Would you rather be in the classroom five days a week", to which the answer is "no", "or would you rather do two or three days' work experience and then finish off the rest at school and get maybe four or five quid at the end of the week?" and straightaway they said "yes". I think it's more interesting and they're still learning.

There is a drugs problem round here but Cliff and Robert don't take drugs. They drink but they're not too bad, maybe once a week, a couple of pints. They're not the type of kids that *have* to have a drink or anything. They're not interested in sport.

There's nothing for them here. There's no motor project for teenagers here, no option for them to stay off the road. A youth club just a few hours once a week is not really what they want. They want something more regular. You can understand in a way why kids get bored with hanging round the streets, even though I would never let them do that. I had a curfew until they was 14 of seven o'clock and many times I went to go and look for them. They used to hang round with a boy round the corner, in the park. He was no good and led the way for Robert to follow, cars and thieving.

It's mainly driving offences with Robert. You can't keep him from wheels. He had a breach of community service and attendance centre that sent him to prison—there were complications. Cliff does less. I'd like to think it's basically because of the way I've taught him not to break the law and that, or whether he's learnt with his older brother being in prison. Cliff was always the leader—he dominates Robert, still tries to.

Robert's been ever so good though since he's come out of prison. He won't get in a car. I'd like to believe that he's learned his lesson, I really could—I can see he'd like to. If that had been his punishment to start with, he could have had his licence now rather than smacking and money, smacking and money [*that's how he was punished*]. You fine them but none of them bother to pay it. You talk to a lot of youngsters and their reaction [*to fines*] will be, "Oh, I owe £200 but that's only ten days inside."

I think they should have trips to prison from school, at eleven years old. They'd see what it actually looks like, not what it's like on telly. "This is where you'll be sleeping, eating. There's no TV, no computer." Robert's cellmate was in for arson with his step-Dad in the car. They shouldn't mix people who do crimes like that with those in for soft crime. They can learn things they didn't know.

Robert desperately wants a job but he wants to work with cars or electrics (because that's his other hobby, anything to do with wires). I've seen him go through my *Yellow Pages*, phoning garage after garage, actually going in and asking, and by the end of the first day he was getting despondent, and then more despondent because they ask, "What experience have you got, what papers have you got?" Well, how much experience can a seventeen-year-old have? That's my view: unless they've got hands-on work, they're not going to gain that experience.

Robert's knock-back was when the local college refused to accept him a couple of years back. I don't know why—probably on the grounds of how he presented himself at the interview. I don't know, but there it is. Being under age [*for benefits*], how can he go to college now? You have to pay fares, books. That's his concern: he's got to wait now till he's 18 so he'll be looking at September before he could start college. It's how the benefits system works—it works against him.

Being given the right help and, I dunno, the right opportunities really, that's what's needed but at the moment everything is against them either because of their age and because of they'd done something or because they haven't any cash to start them anything.This generation has got a different outlook from what we had when I left school. When I left school I knew I didn't want factory work or anything like that. I wanted office work so I lined up a few interviews before I walked out of school. I ended up with a choice of two jobs. They accepted me and obviously I went for the one I thought was better for me. (I think it was the right one—I was there all the time till I had my first child.) I don't think they've got those opportunities now. There are fewer jobs and the employers are asking for too much: for qualifications. You could honestly go for a job and say, "I've got no qualifications but . . . " and they was willing to give you a try on your ability rather than a piece of paper—how you present yourself, obviously.

A police siren sounded in the distance. Corinne visibly flinched for a second and almost glanced at the window.

The way I see it is that you have kids and they're your responsibility, no one else's. You've got to develop them and bring them up so obviously you do your best, you teach them right from wrong and yet it would be nice to have some help, some support because no one's a robot, you know, to keep on. But at the end of the day they're yours, you don't go running and whinging for help and all that. Obviously, if it's got too bad that you can't cope, it's different. I mean everybody's different anyway.

Some people are lucky. They've got their mothers around them and they help. I don't know if that's one of the problems or not [*that some people haven't family support*]. I certainly don't blame the parents for how kids turn out. I used to think when mine were little that, you know, it might have been the parents, letting their kids do this and do that. My attitude's changed as mine have grown up and I've had screaming kids and I've tried to put mine on the right track, but no, don't blame the parents. Getting the discipline at school is the first problem. That's where they started going wrong. I really do believe that.

It's affected my health a great deal. I'm on tranquillisers. I've got to the stage when if I hear a police siren now I'm—probably you've seen me a minute ago—I think, "Is it mine?", even though it can't possibly be Robert because he's over in town today. If I see a police van coming down the road, I think "Here we go, it's coming to my house." I don't sleep very well. It has affected me.

They've both got nice girlfriends. Robert's girlfriend is still at school. She's in her last year but she's quite firm with Robert and that's good. Cliff's girlfriend, she works and she's got a baby as well, not Cliff's but he idealises that baby and she's very firm with him, very firm. [*Corinne's voice went very quiet here*]. So if they can take over where I've failed, then good luck to them and let's hope it works.

When I left two police vans were parked in the road outside, with several policemen chatting besides them. Corinne said, "Oh my God, I'm locking my doors" and went in. A policeman was shouting through the letter-box of the next house, "Where's your Mum then?"

Luke and His Step-father

Fourteen-year-old Luke was unable to make our first appointment because he had to help his step-Dad's wife look after her small children. He was a sturdy, muscular black boy, already about five foot six inches tall, with a broad face which showed little expression. He looked neat in navy track-suit trousers, a T-shirt and sports singlet, and white training shoes. His demeanour was subdued, even withdrawn, and he was the hardest of the young people I met to engage in conversation. He answered questions gently and politely but rarely ventured more than a sentence or two in reply and did not initiate any topics. He had been released about two months previously from 18 months in secure accommodation to which he had been sentenced for his part when he was 13 years old as onlooker of a robbery which had disastrous consequences for the victim. The only time he smiled was when talking about his little step-brother and step-sister. His face was then transformed and he looked much younger. He began by telling me how he occupied his time now that he was at home again.

LUKE

I spend my time at the moment reading a book at home or maybe I go to the park with my friend who lives in my road. He's 18. I do jogging, running and I lift weights. I look after my step-Mum's little children a lot. I fetch one from school. I like that. I get £5 pocket money. I'm not at school at the moment. We're looking for a new school now. We've already spoke to the headmistress. Maybe I'll be able to go in three weeks. They haven't had room for me. I was never in trouble at my old school but I don't want to go back there because of the incident. I've seen people from my old school since I've been back but no one in my own class. I know how not to talk to them if I meet them. I don't have supervision now but Nigel comes to see me about once a month.

Nigel, his youth justice worker, explained that Luke's period of licence following completion of his sentence was nearly over but he would continue to see him regularly until he was settled in school.

I was good at work when I was at school. I liked science—learning about human bodies, insects, animals and particles—and sports best. Gymnastics and football were my best sports. I want to go to college and be a sports teacher. I did football four times a week when I was locked away but there was no gym. We had lessons every day. The other kids weren't bad. I'd expected bullying, everyone told me about that, but I didn't get any. I expect because I'm tall for my age. The worst thing was just being there. I didn't get no visits, none at all, maybe because transport was difficult. I got letters and I could phone.

The secure accommodation centre where Luke was placed was at the other end of the country from his home. Such is the dearth of secure accommodation for children who have committed serious crimes.

I live with my step-Dad and his wife now. He's an engineer. He married my Mum when I was about five or six. Then they split up after about two years and I stayed with my Grandma. I came from the Cameroons when I was about three with my Grandma. I don't remember my Dad at all. I don't hear from him. I'm not really in touch with him. They speak French in the Cameroons but I don't remember any of that though I started learning a bit of French when I was away. I got a letter from my Mum when I was remanded waiting my trial. It was private. I hardly remember her.

About the robbery. Me and my friend was going through the park to see another friend. It was winter, about nine at night. There was a woman walking past and my friend says he wants some money. She was quite old. He told me he wanted to get her bag. He ran, he snatched the bag. She held on and she fell on her back on some railings. She's still in a wheelchair now. I feel sad. I just wish I hadn't been there. I wasn't sure what to do when he told me. He hadn't been in trouble. He wasn't a violent person or on drugs. I don't know why he did it. I understood what went on in the court. He pleaded guilty because he did it. They told me to say not-guilty because I didn't do it. But he did tell me. They found me guilty. I got two years, more than him. They [*his lawyers*] appealed and they cut it to 18 months.

I've never had lessons about saying 'no' to things. We didn't have lessons about laws and things at school but once the police came and talked about things like knives. I should have known myself not to get involved. Yes, I'm a Christian. We go to church on Sundays. My step-Dad understands about it all. What I'd say to other people is, "Keep out of trouble and if you're going around with friends you can say 'no'. I know it's hard but you can do it."

LUKE'S STEP-FATHER

I met Joshua, Luke's step-father, about two months later in the family home, the top maisonette of a house in a terraced street. Some rubbish was dumped in the small front garden but the house itself was very tidy for one containing four children. An elderly visitor left the sitting room for us to talk and Joshua turned off the television. There were books as well as videos on the shelves in the room, a computer on the table, a hi-fi system and the latest photographs of all the children. I could hear the children playing in the next room. Joshua was a tall, alert-looking man in his thirties, wearing neat slacks and shirt on a very hot day. He talked quietly at first but then more fluently. His demeanour was serious but his face lit up when he smiled, reminding me of Luke, though they were not related by blood. He told me first about his background.

I came here in 1985 to study. I went to high school in the Cameroons and took my degree in computing studies here. I'm a computer programmer now, working on contracts. One has just finished. I'd like to work on my own some day. I'd known Luke's mother back home. We didn't meet here—we come from the same village. Luke never knew his own father. He was about two when we got together and ten or eleven when we separated. His mother went home and she asked me to look after the children till she came back, both Luke and our little girl who is eight now. We were engaged to be married but I'm married now to someone else and we have two little ones.

His mother and I still have very friendly relations. She's working and has her own business now. I'm a resident here and I don't think I'll go back. I haven't adopted Luke and I can't do it. Adoption is not even a word in our language. It's different there.

Regarding this incident, Luke just wants to forget it now. He doesn't want to discuss it any more. He'd never been in trouble before. I think it was because he doesn't know how to say "no". He's easily influenced. If you went to ask him something like, "Do you think we should do this?", he'll say, "Yes". He never says, "No, I don't wish to do it this way" so I came to realise he's a yes-man, that whatever I say he just accepts it. He's easily influenced by his comrades. That's what led him to it. I've never met the other boy. He was the same age, from Africa, at the same school. He got less punishment, 12 months, and Luke got two years before the appeal.

That December my cousin was on a course in Belgium and he came to spend Christmas with us. We lived in a very small apartment and I asked Luke to stay with his Grandma because there was no space, just for the nights but to come home in the morning for the day. That's when this thing happened. Because the grandma couldn't keep proper control, sometimes he was out too late. Nine o'clock at night is too late for a child of his age to be out. If we'd been together, I can't see that happening. I should have paid more attention to the time he went to his granny's—it's not far—but I assumed he went straight there.

On the day it happened, a Sunday, I'd been to a christening party at a friend's house. I'd had a lot to drink. I took a taxi home and was sleeping on the settee and a detective came with a search warrant.

Luke had been arrested at his granny's. I asked, "Do you mind telling me what this is all about?" They told me it was for robbery. I'd heard on the radio that a pensioner had been robbed and received serious injuries but I didn't know it was for that. I went back to the police station in the early hours. They told me what it was. My mind was just with that lady. There was a duty solicitor there. All the time they were questioning Luke. The next day he appeared before the youth court and they remanded him into care, a children's home. It was a nice place.

It was the solicitor's idea for him to plead not guilty. He asked Luke. Luke was trying to please me, to tell me he couldn't do a thing like this, at the police station. I knew he must be involved and I told the solicitor that in my opinion I would like him to plead guilty because I was very certain that he was involved. There was one simple thing. He told me he said to the boy he didn't like it but he was following the boy. I told him that if I were the prosecutor I'd ask, "Why were you following the boy?" He followed him to the scene of the crime. He didn't pull the bag but I told the lawyer he was *there* and that means he was involved. I was really upset. They had to go to a jury, all the expense of the state's money—and he was punished for that. I couldn't say to him, 'You've *got* to plead guilty' and have him say to me later, "Actually, I wasn't guilty." What I said was, "If you know in your own mind that you were involved, you plead guilty." At one stage he told me he was going to do that but he didn't.

He was put [in secure accommodation] a long way from here. I don't call it education what he got there. Education is more than just reading a book and doing some maths. The environment must be where there are other children. You learn from them, too. It was not enough but it was better than if he'd been in a young offender institution.

Nigel, his youth justice worker, has sorted out his new school. He's been there since the end of the summer term. He's doing all right. I've told him, "You got into trouble because of the difficulty you have in saying 'no'. It doesn't mean everybody's bad but if you have a friend and he says 'I want to do this' and you think it's not proper, you can just back out and say 'no'." I've told him, "If you want things, you must earn the money." He's good at maths and English. There's no reason why he shouldn't get to university like I did. I'll encourage him.

In the holidays Luke goes to the park a lot. There are no jobs for 14-year-olds. I don't want to put too much restriction on him. I don't think it would do him any good. I'm able to keep a good eye on him but I can't follow him for 24-four hours a day. He talks to me and we do things together. What has helped is that where we were living, we moved from there. We were going to move out of the area anyway. It wasn't because of that we moved but the whole street knew and I wasn't pleased about that. Nigel has been here all the time, asking how do you feel, how are things going, and he looked for the school.

I think the solicitors could have used their own judgement to advise him how to plead. Maybe they wanted the legal aid, the money. I don't know. I don't see any need for any jury in that case. It wasn't necessary from my point of view but I couldn't see any way how to get him out of that situation. If you look at the cost of the whole trial— two days . . . The victim didn't come but the relatives were there. All that could have been avoided.

Where I come from they don't take these crimes lightly. I don't want to send him back there now because they wouldn't treat him as he should be treated, not now. I can't entirely criticise the system here. It's a better system for children. He'd be in jail in my country. The lady was crippled—it was a very serious crime.

I saw Luke for a moment or two when I left. He seemed more relaxed at home, cheerful and friendly. He looked much younger, an ordinary 14-year-old.

Typical Young Offenders

The young people I interviewed were selected for the number and seriousness of the crimes they had committed. I asked various local authority youth justice teams in urban areas if they could put me in touch with young people under the age of 18 who were deeply into trouble. I made no specification about their family circumstances, their race, or whether or not they were at school. All that mattered was that they would be willing to talk to me about their lives in general, not just their offences. The local authority asked the parents for permission for me to talk to their children. I then asked the young people if I might approach their parents.

There have been many studies of the characteristics of young offenders both here and in the United States—or rather of those who have been caught offending. Whenever we consider the figures for those convicted we have to remember that there are other young people who break the law whose particulars are not recorded because they are not officially cautioned by the police or convicted in the youth court. If the figures of crimes not reported to the police are taken into consideration as well as those crimes reported but not solved, the amount of crime committed by young people is staggering. The Audit Commission in its 1996 report *Misspent Youth*, a disinterested and hard-headed examination of the youth justice system, found that only three per cent of the estimated seven million offences committed by those aged ten to 17 each year resulted in arrests and action by the criminal justice system. The police in many areas suggest that a hard core of persistent young offenders is responsible for some of this crime—three per cent for 25 per cent of offences—but nevertheless the number of those who break the law is huge.

The most daunting and shaming statistic about crime is that in England and Wales one in three men by the age of 30 has a criminal conviction—and that does not include motoring offences like speeding. This figure makes one wonder about an element of hypocrisy in the public outcry against youth crime. With that kind of collective record why do people hark back to a golden age of innocence—which history shows never existed? The amount of crime by young people is shocking but current levels are not unusual. In proportion to the population the level is about the same as in the early nineteenth century. Fear about crime and obsession with short-term punishment may be understandable but they are fuelled by fallacies.

For the record, over 80 per cent of crimes committed by young people are "property-related"—handling stolen goods, stealing from shops, cars or schools, burglary. There is not much violent crime by young people. For obvious reasons mugging, snatching handbags and Rolex watches, and horrendous rapes or murders are more often reported in the press than crimes against property, with the result that they appear to occur more frequently. But young people are more likely to be victims of personal crime than adults. It is not so much the little old lady who should go in fear of being mugged as older teenagers since it is they who have the highest risk of being assaulted. The pain and psychological distress caused by crimes to property are real and serious, especially for the victims of burglaries and repeated burglaries. The national charity Victim Support assists a million people every year and its case histories are perturbing to read. A central argument of this book is that in the long term the most effective way to support the victims of crime is to take steps to prevent crime by young people and thus to reduce the crime rate.

The most recent Home Office research, some of it quoted in *Misspent Youth*, gives a menu of 'indicative' factors which predispose children to delinquency. The first set revolves round their relationship with their parents. Young people who get into trouble often have poor relationships with their parents. Their parents may quarrel a lot and quarrel violently. They may be separated and they may themselves have a criminal record. In bringing up their children they may supervise them loosely and give them vague and conflicting rules. On the other hand, they are often prescriptive and punitive.

The second set of factors is centred on the children's performance and behaviour at school. Those most likely to offend do badly academically, are influenced by other trouble-makers, truant at an early age with their absences at first unreported, and often end by being excluded from school. In addition, young people over school-leaving age who are not in a job or training, who drink heavily and who use drugs are particularly at risk of becoming offenders.

Few people will be surprised by this list but the evidence it provides is important because it shows the points at which things start going wrong for children and indicates where there could be intervention to stop the rot. This book is not a research study which aims to generalise from a large random sample but it is clear that many of the factors identified in such studies were present in the lives of Tyrrell, Jacquie, Daniel, Jason and the others.

All except Luke were persistent offenders (if a persistent offender is defined as one who commits frequent offences within a period of about a year) and their crimes were serious. They stole or burgled and some of them robbed or mugged. I interviewed them because of what they had done but it emerged that their circumstances followed a pattern indicated by research about young offenders.

RELATIONS WITH THEIR PARENTS

Parental discord and separation are key indicative factors for juvenile delinquency. Of the eleven young offenders I interviewed, only Jason lived with both his parents. The parents of all the others except for Stephen's were divorced, separated or had never lived together. Some of the young people were too young when their fathers left to be able to remember them now. Josiah, who was brought up by his Dad, was two when his mother left, seven when she faded from his life. Corinne said that her divorce from the twins' father had been acrimonious and Jacquie had witnessed her father's violence against her mother. She got on better with her father than her mother and said that her offending was "nothing to do with them getting divorced . . . It was a couple of years later that I started properly going and stealing." But she also said that it was when her Mum and Dad were arguing and fighting that she took refuge in smoking cannabis. Her mother Pat attributed her older son's truancy to his depression caused by seeing his father beat her.

How does one define a good parent-child relationship? Jason showed his attachment to his parents when he admitted he was worried about upsetting them and they showed their attachment to him by not just telling me how worried they were about his criminal activities and his difficulties with his schools but by praising his achievements. All the parents I saw did their best to tell me about their children's good points. When I saw them, Mark was living edgily with his Mum, Jacquie with her Mum or aunt, Josiah with his Dad and Luke with his step-father, the most stable figure in his life. The others had either left the family home of their own volition, been sent to live with relations or were being looked after by social services. Matthew was with foster parents, Tyrrell was in a children's home, Stephen lived in a bed-and-breakfast hotel, the twins were in a flat. Tyrrell's mother, Matthew's mother, Jacquie's mother, all the parents I spoke to, clearly "loved" their children and were deeply concerned about what had happened to them, questioning and often blaming themselves.

"I just don't understand," said Tyrrell's capable mother who since he was small had earned a good living as a secretary, "what makes a child these days turn to crime, especially a child that was loved." The trouble is that "love" is not always enough to enable a parent to weather the difficulties of rearing a child. It is the start every child must have but in itself it may not be enough to meet his or her needs. Continuity in relationships and consistency are also necessary. It is easy to see why it made sense for Tyrrell to live with his grandparents when he went to primary school and why he was like a son in his uncle's household. He was such an easy, attractive toddler that even the staff at his nursery would take him home for the weekend. He drew considerable strength from happy memories with his extended family and there was nothing unusual in sharing the care of a child in the culture to which he belonged. Yet his grief at the loss of the paternal role his murdered uncle played, his protectiveness towards his drug-addicted father and his longing for a close relationship of his own with a girlfriend and with his child, suggest that what he wanted, as well as love, was stability. It is easy to make such an analysis in retrospect but more complex to show how his mother could have dealt differently with her circumstances.

Another factor in the lives of young people whose parents have separated is that they have to deal with their parents' new partners. They belong to, or feel outside, more than one family. Tyrrell worried about men sponging off his kind-hearted Mum. Mark at seventeen showed how abandoned he felt when he explained, cheerfully at first, that he still sometimes saw his Dad who left home when he was very little, his Dad's girlfriend and their baby. Then he added: "I don't bother ringing him up all the time because he don't bother ringing me so why should I make the effort?" One in four marriages now end in divorce. A fifth of all children under 16 are now brought up by lone parents. They all face similar separations and problems but they do not all run out of control and become persistent offenders—which shows that these are not the only factors in play and suggests there are ways to mitigate the effects as well as to help people avoid creating such situations in future.

None of the parents I interviewed had a criminal record but Jacquie's father had been in prison as a young man and the twins' uncles had been in trouble. Some friends of Jason's older step-brother had used him for their burglaries. Drugs had been a problem for Josiah's Dad as well as Tyrrell's and Josiah had begun offending when living with foster parents whilst his father was sorting out his addiction. I did not get the impression that any of them came from homes which accepted a criminal's life as normal or desirable. On the other hand, many of them testified to a culture in which it was standard to take things that fell off lorries, something I will examine later: "To be quite honest it kind of wears you down," said Pat, Jacquie's mother. And drugs are everywhere available.

As for the way parents bring up their children, the interviews show parents at sea in stormy waters with different guides to navigation. Take Corinne, mother of the twins. She also had an older son who had been in a great deal of trouble and a 20-year-old who she said "listened" to her—individual children may react differently to the same parental style. She had tried everything with her sons: "I talked to them, slapped them, threatened to throw them out, disown them, and at the end of it, I stand by them."

Attitudes to corporal punishment were interesting. There was a lot of hedging and guilt about its use but used it was. Marilyn, Jason's mother said it was no good hitting Jason but a few minutes later told me how she'd given him a bloody good hiding when she caught him stealing her clothes. It often seemed to be a last resort but what was frightening was that it was often used when parents lost control. Corinne again:

> I find a few slaps—I mean I don't batter them in the sense that I hurt them, you know what I mean, but I do punch them on the leg or the arm, scream at them. I don't really know if it helps more because when I get going and I'm hitting them and that, I won't let them leave the room, I push them to sit down and then I say my piece; they're made to listen. Obviously now that they're a lot older it's harder.

Ambivalent attitudes towards corporal punishment but refusal to rule it out were being passed down to the young people. Daniel said he had been beaten when he was little and "If they were really bad I'd beat my children". Of the twins. Cliff—a young man who seemed to have thought a lot about his life—was clear: "If I had children I'd give them freedom but not enough to go off the rails. I'd discipline them not by smacking. I'd talk to them." Young Jason said his sisters as well as his parents hit him to try and stop him thieving and if his children got into trouble he'd hit them. He went further and explained: "People all round here, they have to get hit to learn. You can't tell them . . . *Telling* ain't no use." With due respect to Jason, communication, the way parents talk with their children, is a key factor in improving parent-child relationships and thus preventing delinquency. "We haven't got a good relationship to talk about things," lamented Pat, Jacquie's mother, who knew this.

Joshua, Luke's graduate step-father, identified poor supervision when Luke was staying with his grandmother as the reason why Luke was out late in the evening and got into trouble—and he blamed himself for not realising what was happening. All the parents had rules and sanctions which they tried but sometimes failed to enforce. Jason hated being grounded and his parents said he came in at night at a set time. Tyrrell admitted he had broken his mother's curfews and Daniel said, "I come in at a decent time like ten o'clock at night. I'll tell [my Mum] what time I'm coming in".

Middle-class parents who organize every minute of their children's free time are shocked if children or even teenagers are allowed to roam by themselves at will but it was always a feature of working-class neighbourhoods for children to play in the streets, monitored by the local community. Today most people agree that the risks of such freedom are too great for young children but it is difficult for poor parents, many of whom are single parents, to provide suitable supervision. They are criticised whatever they do. If they do not work, they are spongers on welfare; if they do, they neglect their children. They cannot afford individual day care from their low wages and there is not sufficient day care available in the community or supervision after school. If we take seriously the research findings that poor parental supervision is a factor leading to juvenile crime, we should acknowledge some of the reasons why parents do not supervise their young effectively.

Matthew came from an extremely strict Christian home. His mother said he had consciously rejected her values for those of his peer-group. His history shows that high principles and rules of conduct in the home will not necessarily prevent delinquency. There are no neat correlations. The causes are many and complex but there is a relentless downward escalation in behaviour. Mark explained it well:

> My Mum can't control me. It's a matter over years. It's not just a two-week thing, a three-week or a year thing, it's over the years that I've been bad, you know what I mean.

It emerged that he had a healthy respect for the consistency and authority of the staff at his youth justice centre but the point he made about time is central to any consideration of how to help parents take control of their children. Both parents and children have to learn new ways of responding to each other and they will not learn them overnight, a crucial point politicians should remember when they try to legislate for parental responsibility.

FRIENDS AND SCHOOLS

"Unsuitable peer influence" was clearly a factor with all these young people. They committed most of their offences with others. Daniel had robbed a building society with three older boys. Talking to him I thought it unlikely that he would have thought it all up himself. Most of his friends were in prison now. Jacquie said she usually went shop-lifting with her friends and graphically described how they worked as a team and also their competitive spirit: "It's a thing of 'Who's the best at it, who's got the most guts to go and do this?'" Marilyn and Desmond explained how easily their son Jason was led. His best mate, another Jason, was clever enough not to get caught. With Luke, it was his friend who did the mugging while he watched. "He wasn't a violent person or on drugs," Luke said. Mark and Matthew described outings with their mates that ended in trouble and Tyrrell had been taught how to steal cars by graduates of his children's home.

Matthew specifically blamed his delinquency on getting into a bad crowd. He made an interesting distinction between his good friends and his bad friends, almost as if he himself had two halves. His problem was that he could not say "no" to his bad friends. Mark, too, said, "I think it was being part of the gang really, being part of the crowd, that's how I think you really get into things, one of the lads you know, being in trouble, nicking cars. You don't think about it being dangerous, them sort of things, when you're with the boys."

The boys in question were also usually truanting or excluded from school. For all those I interviewed (except Luke, a special case) the time they switched off school was the time they began offending seriously. For these young people mainstream schooling had been a total failure. "I didn't like school, I didn't like the teachers", said Robert and his mother, Corinne, had suggestions about how his interest might have been retained by a more practical curriculum and more work experience at a younger age. She had done well at school herself but Jason's well-meaning parents had handed on what sounded like a family phobia about school. All of them, female as well as male, had a short fuse to their tempers and a short attention span for conventional lessons. 'Boring' was the word that came up most when the young people were discussing school. I sometimes longed to challenge the pervasive view that everything in life should be entertaining but at the same time wondered if they were not right to resent what may have been poor teaching. Difficult as he must have been to manage, Mark could recognise when he was being taught "brilliantly".

Low achievement at school is another factor which foreshadows juvenile offending. Not all those I interviewed had done badly when they attended school but all had become low achievers because they had not completed the course. Jacquie explained "I could have done my exams" and this would clearly have been possible for Josiah, Matthew, Cliff and Luke (who had been able to continue his studies when in secure accommodation, one of its many advantages over young offenders institutions where some 15-year-old boys are sent).

For others it was difficult to sort out how bright they were because their potential had been dimmed by years of poor attendance and neglect of their difficulties. If they had emotional problems and these had not been spotted, it was hard to know how clever they really were. Tyrrell's mother attributed his first disruptiveness at nursery school to the fact that he already knew what they were teaching him. She said her younger boy was less bright than Tyrrell but more biddable so she did not anticipate the same difficulties with him. Mark was sent to a boarding school for children with emotional difficulties when he was ten years old but his progress was interrupted when the school was closed down.

All of them (except Luke who was atypical in so many ways) were handicapped by their lack of basic skills at whatever stage they were, whether catching up at college like the older ones or in an individual tuition centre like Jason. He told me he hated reading and his parents described his frustration at not being able to read or do the same sums as younger children. He had, however, been assessed and 'statemented' to see if he had special educational needs when he was excluded from primary school. It is shameful but symptomatic of the system that nothing had been done subsequently to meet his needs. Stephen said he got on all right at school when he tried and he now wished he had tried harder but he also told me: "When I was young I was slow. I didn't really want to listen. My Dad spent a lot of time with me reading but not with my sisters. They're fast learners. I was that slow so my Dad had to spend more of time with me, reading books and music and things like that." Who knows now whether professional attention to his slowness would have prevented him running away from home, a teenager who felt different from the rest of his family?

Daniel told me he was in a small school for those with learning difficulties because of his dyslexia. He liked his school and was making good progress. "I always used to be behind. I didn't like primary school. My Mum used to give me help all the time because she used to know about my reading. She used to let me read and that every day." His mum was a teacher and had identified his learning difficulties. He first got into trouble at an earlier school for fighting on the bus. It was clear from talking to him that he was a slow learner on all counts, just the kind of boy to be led by others into trouble, both a victim and a bully. He looked mature for 16 but he talked like a much younger boy. He had little insight into his own position, little understanding of the gravity of his offences and little awareness of where he fitted in this world. His 'moral' development was if anything less advanced than 13-year-old Jason's. Robbing a building society is a crime usually committed by adults—and he was with adults—but I wondered if he was mature enough even for a youth court. The acquisition of a moral sense is a topic I will be treating.

More than half of those I interviewed were in the care of their local authorities, some because they had left home and asked for help themselves, others because their parents had asked for assistance.

Their situations show how difficult it is for the state to assume all the functions of the caring parent, from providing them with somewhere to live to ensuring that they receive a good education. Accommodation in a bed-and-breakfast hotel cannot be right for teenagers and I would like to see its use for young people banned. Several of those over school-leaving age who were being looked after by local authorities were in the vulnerable position of being unemployed or awaiting a college place. Even those in training or on youth justice courses had a lot of free time to fill and not enough knowledge or incentive to fill it constructively.

OTHER ELEMENTS

Only Mark had been drunk when caught for an offence. Stephen was in a drinking set but said he knew when to stop. Josiah stole liquor from an off-licence and Matthew hung around one. Alcohol was mentioned by some of the others but it was drugs that emerged as the universal temptation.

None of those I interviewed admitted to a drugs habit when I saw them, though Jacquie said she used to get through the day by thinking of her cannabis waiting for her at her home and at one stage she stole to feed her habit. The fathers of two young men were or had been addicted to drugs, a painful and possibly salutary example to their sons. However, most of these young people, whilst protesting that they could keep off hard drugs and would not become dependent on cannabis, said they had the odd puff: "only small weed and that", "but I don't do it till I'm out of my head". In their use of drugs they were typical of young offenders and of many other young people. I have no doubt that the ready availability of drugs, inadequate education about drugs and too few treatment centres for young people already hooked on drugs are factors which must be dealt with in preventing youth crime.

The young people I interviewed were selected for their crimes, not their backgrounds, but I have shown that they all have in their backgrounds features that indicate they might be at risk of offending. None of them has all the features which is one reason why identifying potential offenders is difficult and sensitive. They do not all come from families existing on state benefits, though the poverty of their families may be a contributory factor for some. Their lives are complex, often more complex than those of non-offenders, but for every one who offends in their circumstances I am sure others can be cited in similar circumstances who do not.

I interviewed only one young woman which by chance reflects the fact that boys far outnumber girls in the youth justice system. Five of the eleven young offenders interviewed were white, six were black or of mixed parentage. Again this outcome occurred by chance. The proportion of black to white young people in England and Wales as a whole is less than one in eleven, though they form almost half their age-group in certain urban areas. I can only repeat that those I interviewed were suggested to me because of what they had done, not because of who they were. What we know is that there is a higher number of black people in the criminal justice system than is proportionate to their number in the population. In 1995 they formed less than six per cent of the population but 18 per cent of the prison population. About a third of those under supervision to the Inner London Probation Service are from ethnic minorities. By contrast a 1995 Home Office confidential survey of 2,000 young people aged 14 to 25 showed that the rates of offending of African-Caribbean and white youngsters were about the same.

There are many reasons for the high number of black people in prison, especially those of Afro-Caribbean origin. It starts with the fact that more are challenged on the streets by the police. Racial prejudice is hard to prove. If police officers know that in their area certain young people have been convicted for certain offences, they will suspect them in future. Josiah who was black and Mark who was white both protested about being watched and picked on by the police. But fewer black than white young people are cautioned by the police rather than sent to court. This could be because fewer admit their guilt (which is necessary for a caution) or it could be that the authorities do not have confidence in black families once warned to keep their young out of trouble—prejudice. Fewer people of Afro-Caribbean origin are granted bail which may again be because of lack of trust (or should one call it prejudice?). Bail should only be refused on clear indication that the accused may abscond, commit more offences, threaten witnesses or endanger the public. Heavier sentencing of black people may be partly because more plead not-guilty, thus losing a mitigating factor when they are convicted, but it may also be because sentencers do not think they will respond to penalties in the community. There is unconscious as well as conscious discrimination.

Only Matthew of those I talked to raised the possibility of racial prejudice in his account of what happened to him at an off-licence. The man there said, '"We don't like you kind of people being in the shop." I said "What do you mean?" Then it clicked and I thought "Ah! He's talking about different race."' I am white so maybe the other five black young people did not feel comfortable about raising this topic with me.

One final factor runs through most of the stories I was told. When support had been offered to children and families it was often short-term, unco-ordinated and petered out before it was effective. Jacquie's teacher did not follow through her suggestions for homework, Jason's glue ear was never properly treated, the education welfare service told Corinne to carry on taking Robert to school but did nothing to see he stayed there. Tyrrell's mother complained that the schools did not inform her early enough of his truanting and that "If you get to talk to anybody, they'll make a note of it, say they'll get in contact with who they've got to get in contact with, but then it stops: nothing was ever taken forward again." Or, as Jason's mother said, "Your child got excluded from school, got sent to see someone, have them examined, and that was it: end of story."

The next part of this book will look at what alternative ends to the story there could be.

Part Two

Early Years: The Parents' Perspective

"I certainly don't blame parents for how kids turn out," said Corinne, mother of the car entrepreneurs Robert and Cliff, but the majority of the population, most of the media and most politicians do blame parents. In the last few years there has been a two-prong use of punishment as society's means to deter young people from crime. You punish the children and you also close in on their parents.

Common sense tells us as well as numerous research studies that the kind of control parents exercise over their children is one of the key factors determining juvenile delinquency. In particular, low levels of supervision—for example, letting children play outside the home by themselves at primary school age and not having clear rules about where they go—and harsh or erratic discipline have been identified as crucial. But the reasons why so many people blame parents for failing when their children transgress are complex. People may sympathise with the burden of a young single mother. In theory they may understand that she has no mum of her own nearby to give her a hand and she lets her seven-year-old go out to stop his whingeing and give herself some space. What people cannot understand is why some parents manage to control their children's behaviour and others do not.

"I had my difficulties, I had no money, no support but my kids don't cause any trouble," is a frequent reaction. In the search for quick and simple solutions it is hard to recognise that no two families' circumstances are identical and that families which superficially look similar react differently. The analogous problem which many find perplexing is why some children in a family offend and some do not, even when their parents think they raised them identically. Different children react individually to the family's disciplinary methods. "My 20-year-old—I've never had to hit him, I've never had to smack him," said Corinne. *The Sunday Times* reported in wonderment that the boy the media had called Rat Boy came from

> a solid, law-abiding, working-class background and was brought up in an immaculately kept home with his three elder sisters and younger brother. None of the other children has ever been in trouble and there was no sign that [he] would be different.

The importance of the parental role has long been recognised in our courts for children and young people. The old juvenile court, like the youth court today, was able to bind over parents to take responsibility for their children's behaviour. If the child or young person offended again, the parents could lose a sum of money set by the court, and if the money was not paid, the parent could in theory be sent to prison, though such a draconian outcome was rare.

It was hoped that in addition to jolting parents into exercising their authority, this measure would underline to children the importance of obeying their parents (more often than not their mothers) and make them realise that their offending damaged the whole family. As even the most hardened young offender is usually conscious that his mum is the person most likely to stand by him if she can—all the mothers I interviewed *wanted* to help their children whatever happened—there is at first sight some logic in this approach. But it was not a power often invoked. Magistrates from experience of the families they saw in court thought that the threat of such financial penalties might make relations between weak mothers and difficult sons deteriorate further. Fear of losing cash would not empower the mothers to control their sons and in any case, how could people who more often than not lived on state benefits find a fine of £50 by legitimate means?

The threat from the court might be the last straw, confirming parents' fear that they were powerless and bringing nearer the day when they would give up, throw out their troublesome offspring or ask the authorities to accommodate him. The responsibility the law gives to social services departments to take into their care ("accommodate" is the term used by the Children Act 1989) young people who are beyond the control of their parents or homeless is well-intentioned and a necessary safeguard. The outcome, however, is often—usually, one might say—disastrous. And it is easy to understand why in a state that is not Utopia.

The young people may be leaving an unstable, even "chaotic" household—"chaotic" is an overused catch-phrase in the child care world to describe families which cannot manage to conform to the everyday routines of life like getting up in the morning in time for school or work, cleaning the house, oganizing regular meals—but they enter a world where instead of being a member of a small group, however unsatisfactory, with one or two adults in charge, they are one of many in the care of a large organization. There have been numerous attempts to individualise the care given to such young people. They usually now have their own "key" workers (but there is no guarantee the key worker will remain in the same post throughout the period they are away from home); some have 'passports' summarising their health and education records, as important for them with all the moves they are likely to make as for evacuees in a war zone; others make 'life-story books' with their social workers, collecting photographs and memories of their confusing childhoods; most local authorities have complaints systems for young people; and there is always Childline to telephone for help and advice, if they know about it and if they can use a telephone.

Despite such attempts to improve communications and despite greater awareness of the problems, the reality is grim. Placements with trained, specialist foster parents who are ready to suffer the behaviour of damaged adolescents and to give them the parental attention necessary are far too few. Community homes have far too few residential workers trained to the level necessary, or trained at all, in spite of numerous enquiries and recommendations over the years for raising training standards; we learn too late of flagrant abuses. Even the best residential workers have their times on duty and their times off duty, unlike parents, so that individual staff cannot give complete continuity of care.

But the most risky placement for young people who are accommodated is "bed and breakfast": 16 and 17-year-olds (like Stephen when I met him) live in a room in a basic "hotel". There is no warden. Their contact with their social worker is sometimes only weekly. A place at college or on a training scheme may not yet have been arranged and when it is offered may not be full-time. As a result the bored and unoccupied young offenders look to the streets for company and friends—their offending escalates. This was the pattern for Tyrrell, Matthew and the twins once they had left home.

The obvious way to avoid such a downward escalator to an unhappy and possibly criminal life is to make sure that parents carry out their primary roles effectively and that their children conform to the rules of society. But a central question to be answered is "Can the courts *make* parents fulfil their roles satisfactorily?"

PUNISHING THE PARENTS

John Patten, as minister of state at the Home Office, gave his ideas on parental responsibility when he wrote in March 1989 to the UK Federation of Business and Professional Women,

> There are some parents who could cope, but simply choose not to: households where seemingly children are deliberately not taught the difference between right and wrong, where the parents are quite well aware of the child's criminal activity but make no attempt to stop it.

He went on to suggest debate about a new offence of "failure to prevent child crime" which could apply to parents of children up to the age of 16.

Recent criminal justice legislation has not gone as far as to introduce such a separate offence but they have brought parents up to the front line. The Criminal Justice Act 1982 required parents of children under 16 to attend court and made them responsible for their children's fines "unless this would be unreasonable in the circumstances". At first glance these were both sensible requirements. It is right in theory for parents' appearance in court to be compulsory. They are responsible for their children and they should support them, for better or for worse; they should also show that they support the law to maximise the impact of the proceedings; and they should be present in court so that they can communicate and reinforce to their children exactly what is said and why. As for fines, children under 16 can rarely earn money through jobs today so their parents will usually have to find the money, if we leave aside the problem, already mentioned, of fining people who have no money.

It should, however, be remembered that those parents who have jobs may risk losing them for absences caused by repeated attendances at court; and mothers of families such as many young offenders come from, who find it hard to cope with the daily routines of life, often find it difficult to get to court when they have younger or sick children or other dependants at home. The reality of constantly attending police stations and court is grim, as the mothers of Jacquie and the twins explained (see pp.47 and 77).

The Criminal Justice Act 1991 introduced a new requirement. Youth court magistrates when sentencing the child for any offence must also bind over the parent or guardian "to take proper care of him and to exercise proper control over him" if they are satisfied that this is desirable in the interests of preventing the commission of further offences; if the magistrates choose not to do so, they must give their reasons for their decision in open court. The introduction of the provision was widely opposed, not just by social workers and probation officers but by the Magistrates' Association. In its comments on the White Paper which first made the proposal, the association warned that the measure might hasten a breakdown of family relationships.

In practice it seems that few youth courts have been satisfied that a parental bind over will help to prevent the commission of further offences and the provision is not often used. In 1993, magistrates used the power in only seven per cent of cases involving offenders aged under 16, and some areas did not use it at all. The bind over provisions were extended in the Criminal Justice and Public Order Act 1994 to allow courts to include a requirement for the parent or guardian to ensure that the child complies with the requirements of a community sentence. There have been few reports about the reaction of parents to the latest developments but a study in Wales in 1993, described by Mark Drakeford of the University of Wales, Cardiff, in *The Howard Journal of Criminal Justice,* found that parents said the bind over "made no difference whatsoever," was unfair and did not help them to be more effective parents. It may even have made young people think that they could do what they like, since it was their parents who would pay the price.

There is at present a contradiction between what politicians and the public say about young offenders and what they say about their parents. On the one hand it is argued that young people from the age of ten know the difference between right and wrong and are responsible for their own actions. The Crime and Disorder Act 1998 abolished the *doli incapax* rule concerning children. Under this rule, in a case in which children under 14 were defendants the prosecution had to counter the presumption in law that children aged ten to 14 did not understand the difference between right and wrong. In reality the number of children under the age of 14 who appear in court is small and I can count on the fingers of one hand the number of times in 20 years that I heard lawyers argue to uphold the presumption that young defendants were *doli incapax*. Perhaps in the past some children were not prosecuted because it was thought their capacity to understand right from wrong would be challenged but, if this was likely, presumably the decision not to bring them to court was right.

Nothing is asked at the outset about whether older offenders like Daniel, who had special educational needs, have the capacity to understand properly what they are doing. Once they are in court, young people are considered as individuals who are accountable for their choices, subject only to mitigation at the time of sentence about their age, understanding and circumstances. How else to mark the difference between those who get into trouble and those who keep their noses clean?

Thus children are held to be responsible for their actions. On the other hand it is said that parents should exercise proper control over their children, by implication suggesting that children who offend may be the victims of a lax or deficient upbringing. There is confusion at the moment between the two sets of expectation. Do we want children to take responsibility for their own actions or do we hold their parents responsible for what they do? In the present forum of the youth court it may be impossible to achieve a correct balance when attributing responsibility, which is one reason why I shall later argue for a different kind of forum in which to make decisions about punishing and reforming young offenders.

The parents I interviewed all said unequivocally that they wanted their children to keep the law and that they had tried to teach them the difference between right and wrong. It is dangerous to generalise about parents of young offenders—and there have been few systematic studies of such parents—but *pace* Mr Patten I have yet to meet one who did not want his or her child to succeed and to conform in society, whatever their own history. "You've got to develop them and bring them up so obviously you do your best," said Corinne who till her own sons started offending used to agree that the parents of young offenders were to blame for not rearing their children properly. "You don't want your children to make the mistakes you made. You try and teach them right and wrong but what can you do but try?" asked Marilyn, mother of young Jason.

It is argued that the local child curfew schemes, being piloted in 1998-99 under the Crime and Disorder Act, could help parents, for example by establishing a norm for the age when children should play outside unsupervised. It is up to local authorities to introduce such schemes and it will be interesting to see in how many areas the delinquent activities of young children under the age of ten are so widespread as to demand action of this kind.

Applications for the new child safety orders for children under ten, also being piloted, will be made by local authorities in the family proceedings court. An order may require a child to stay at home between certain times or to stay away from certain people or places, as in bail conditions for offenders awaiting trial. The family proceedings court is the right court for any proceedings concerning young children but is it right to restrict a child's liberty and label a young child with such an order without the kind of rigorous proof necessary in a criminal court?

The standard of proof used in the family proceedings court is the civil standard 'on a balance of probabilities'. It does not have to be proved 'beyond reasonable doubt', as required in criminal courts, that seven-year-old Tony or Jim has actually committed what would be an offence in the Youth Court before the court is asked to make a child safety order. Before a supervision or care order is made in family proceedings it has first to be established that the child would suffer "significant harm" if the order were not made. This is a strong test and the magistrates also have to have regard to a welfare check-list. Local authorities, who are empowered by the 1998 Act to request child safety orders from family proceedings courts, may well think there are fairer and more constructive ways of diverting young children from delinquency than applying for a child safety order.

The thrust of recent legislation suggests either that parents know what to do and choose not to do it, or that they choose not to accept help: they are cast as accomplices in their children's crimes. The sense of frustration, embarrassment and helplessness felt by most parents of children in trouble is not recognised in our criminal courts. It is also implied that parents could make the necessary adjustment to their parenting style quickly. To repeat the central question, even if they are well-intentioned but incompetent, can parents be *made* to be competent by order of the court, galvanised if not shamed into exercising their authority? Will they learn if *made* to attend a course by order of the court? And is attendance on a course, no more than once a week for no longer than three months, under the parenting orders being piloted for eighteen months from the autumn of 1998 under the 1998 Act, likely to change ingrained reactions and lifestyles for people who have many problems and may be slow learners?

THE DEPRAVED AND THE DEPRIVED

Since their introduction in 1908, the separate criminal courts for young people have had to balance the regard they are enjoined to have to the welfare of the individual child offender with their duty to protect society. There is now a danger that youth courts will become merely scaled-down versions of the adult court. Recent legislation has emphasised the due process of the law and the nature of the crime. 'Two strikes and you're in prison', the legislation making a custodial sentence compulsory for the third of certain offences committed as an adult, starts counting the offences with those committed as a child.

This tariff flies in the face of all that is known about the pattern of juvenile offending. Many young men go through a spate of adolescent offending and then, most of them, mercifully stop. They may meet a young woman who wants to build a 'normal' home; if they are lucky, they may get a job or start training; or they just mature. The peak age of offending for boys used to be 15. It is worrying that it has now risen to eighteen, suggesting that it takes longer for young men to settle down, but the evidence still suggests that most young men do learn their lesson. They should be allowed a fresh start when they become adults.

It is worth looking at the comparatively new family proceedings courts for a constructive approach to dealing with parents. The old juvenile court dealt with children up till the age of 18, both those who had broken the law ("the depraved") and those who were victims of abuse or neglect or who were at risk ("the deprived"). There were different court sessions for the two types of proceedings but the same juvenile court magistrates dealt with both types of case and everybody knew that the 'bad' children were very often 'sad' children, too. The Children Act 1989 was a watershed. It separated the two types of case, making care proceedings the responsibility of the new family proceedings court, along with private disputes between parents about issues like where their children should live and who should have contact with them.

Children are at the heart of the legislation which brought the family proceedings court into being. Whereas in the youth court magistrates only have to have *regard* to the welfare of the child, in the family proceedings court the welfare of the child is *paramount*. The family court system is still open to criticism on some counts. Children in public care cases, who may be taken from their parents' care only if it can be proved that they have suffered, or are likely to suffer, significant harm, are separately represented by a specialist lawyer and have the benefit of a specialist social worker called a *guardian ad litem* to report on their case to the court. But children whose parents are warring about contact with them in private law cases are not in their own right parties in the case. This means they are not separately represented and a welfare report centred on the child, incorporating the child's views, is not mandatory, despite the importance for children's lives of the decisions being made.

In general, however, the family proceedings court has a conciliatory, non-adversarial approach, with the emphasis on finding solutions, encouraging families to resolve difficulties themselves, take support from the community and manage their own affairs without, if possible, intervention from the state. Before making any order in the family proceedings court, the magistrates have to consider the principle of "no order" and give written reasons if in a given case they think an order *is* necessary. Often the court proceedings give families the stimulus to recognise that they will have to change and take steps to tackle their problems, even serious problems like addiction to alcohol or drugs—and they may agree to attend, voluntarily, parenting courses to learn more about the difficult task of being a parent.

PARENTING ORDERS

The Conservative Government's consultation document, *Preventing Children Offending*, presented to Parliament in March 1997 just before the 1997 General Election, proposed a new parental control order, "to be used where previous attempts to ensure that parents faced up to their responsibilities had failed". It could be imposed in its own right where no offences had yet been committed or instead of the old parental bind over when a child had been convicted. The conditions of the order might include "attending a suitable programme, or ensuring that the child was at home during certain hours or attending school".

And New Labour? The words in the Labour election manifesto were uncannily similar about parents of young offenders. A new parental responsibility order was promised "to make parents face up to their responsibility for their children's misbehaviour". The promise has been fulfilled in the Crime and Disorder Act 1998 as a parenting order which, in the words of the Home Office Consultation Paper introducing the proposal, gives courts "powers to deal effectively with parents who wilfully neglect their responsibilities—or who need help and support in fulfilling them".

The parenting order being piloted from 1998 is available for the parents of a child aged ten to 17 sentenced for a criminal offence or subject to the new community safety order and to a child under ten made subject to a child safety order by a family proceedings court. The order may require the parents to attend training and guidance sessions, no more than once a week for a period not exceeding three months, and to comply with other specified requirements like ensuring the child is at home between certain hours and is escorted to and from school. The penalty for non-compliance is a fine of up to £1,000.

On such specific requirements, we have seen how Corinne in vain tried to track down the twins when she knew they were truanting. Tyrone, Jason's father, described vividly how a parent can deliver a child at one door of the school and the child then runs straight out of another door.

It could be argued, and this is the government case, that it is therefore logical to send parents like Corinne and Tyrone on parenting courses to teach them how to exert their authority over their wayward children. I suspect that as was the case with parental bind overs, courts will be chary about the effectiveness of parenting orders, realising that they are of too short a duration to tackle the deep-seated problems of inadequate parents and that by their complulsory nature they may further antagonise difficult parents.

We have seen that in the family proceedings court the emphasis is on voluntary agreements if possible. Every effort is made to help parents make the changes in their lives that will convince the court that they are "good enough" parents. The decision to attend a course or undergo counselling is ultimately theirs, even though the alternatives if they do not change are bleak: they know they run the risk of their children being taken away from them. In addition, the commitment to learn must be long-term because it takes a long time to acquire new behavioural skills. Learning to be an effective parent is not like learning how to read the instructions on a packet of pasta. It takes cognitive, emotional and communication skills which are easier to imbibe over time than to adopt after a few sessions.

Many therapeutic centres will only enrol parents who agree to treatment and are willing to attend for a sustained period. The reason for their emphasis on voluntary agreement is not sentimental. It is not because of pity for inadequate, impoverished people who may have themselves suffered intolerably in their own childhoods. The reason is that agreements entered into voluntarily, with understanding of the issues and support for their implementation, are more likely to work.

THE DEFEATIST FALLACY

Corinne probably expressed the views of many mothers when she said, ". . . it would be nice to have some help, some support because no one is a robot, you know, to keep on." The parents who feature in this book, including Corinne, all did in fact have some help at some time for some aspects of their children's upbringing but it was not continuing, not co-ordinated and, as Tyrrell's mother said "nothing was ever taken forward." It is easy to blame lack of resources for the gaps in provision, the inability of the health, education and social services to follow cases through and to communicate effectively with each other. Lack of resources certainly accounts in part for the present inadequate, patchwork provision of facilities to help parents. Indeed, the Blair government is at first only bringing parenting orders into force in pilot areas because it recognises that provision for parental training and guidance "may not yet be available in every area". But there is another more deep-seated, malignant cause why so little has been done to tackle the causes of youth crime.

I have come to think that despair and lethargy about the extent and nature of the problem cloud the minds of most people about possible solutions. If "prison works" is a meretricious and false slogan, "nothing works" is a defeatist and false argument applied to both young offenders and their parents. Since the optimistic years of the 1980s, when schemes were set up in the community with government backing to turn round young offenders, there has been a lamentable tendency to let things slide and leave the young people either to grow out of offending or to fulfil their destiny in prison. The problem of young offenders, as presented by the media, seems too big to tackle. Hence the support for measures that shut the worst of them away and contain them for a period, out of sight and out of mind. Similarly, the needs of problem families overwhelm the outsider. It is suspected that child-rearing is something you can learn only through your own experience. Like morality, it is caught, not taught.

The strangest aspect of such defeatism is that for years there have been small schemes, pilot schemes, model projects showing just what can be done. What is more, many of these schemes have been described in the press and on television programmes. Perhaps most surprising, some have been summarised and evaluations of them given in government documents. A Home Office Research Study, *Reducing Criminality Among Young People: A Sample of Relevant Programmes in the United Kingdom* by David Utting, was published in 1996 by the department of the then Home Secretary, Michael Howard, who was at the time busy legislating for increasingly punitive measures against those young people who had already broken the law. The Conservative government's 1997 consultation document, *Preventing Children Offending*, carried as well as the proposal for a parental control order an excellent chapter on 'Early Intervention with Children at Risk of Offending', listing some of the programmes in the Utting Report and research in the US.

It is worth looking more closely at some of the schemes outlined by Utting and others, remembering the point made by the House of Commons Home Affairs Committee in 1993: ". . . investment in identifying and eliminating the causes of crime is clearly preferable to paying for the damage once it has been done." If the mothers I have seen recently had lived within the catchment area of a scheme run by Exploring Parenthood, Home-Start or NEWPIN, just three of the organizations whose work is commended, would they have joined the schemes on offer and would they have learnt more effective ways of handling their children at different stages of their development?

HEALTH VISITORS

In a lecture in 1994 to the RSA (Royal Society for the encouragement of Arts, Manufactures and Commerce, commonly but inaccurately called the Royal Society of Arts) on 'Early Developmental Prevention of Juvenile Delinquency', Professor David Farrington of the Institute of Criminology, University of Cambridge, concluded a powerful endorsement of the evidence for the effectiveness of early intervention with a plea for a greater role to be given to health visitors in identifying and supporting families at risk.

It is at present the duty of health authorities to provide certain health services, including those for health visiting, originally the responsibility of the secretary of state under the National Health

Service Act 1977. When fundholders purchase a service it is the fundholders rather than the health authority who then have to buy a comprehensive health visiting service "within available resources" for their patients. There is no detailed specification describing what a comprehensive health visiting service should provide. Traditionally health visitors have looked at their particular patch of the community and targeted what was most needed. Money has always been tight. They have always had to decide on priorities but now health purchasers want to know the exact value and outcome of what they receive for their money—in numerical terms. It is difficult if not impossible in the day-to-day organization of health practices to quantify the financial savings five years hence of intensive visiting to help, for example, a stressed mother with a hyperactive toddler. It follows that most health visitors today are compelled to offer the minimum input to enable families to cope and leave it at that. Long-term, continuing therapy, mothering a mum who has never been adequately mothered herself, has to be left to others.

The first important point about the health visiting service in the context under discussion is that it is a universal service. Every woman who has a baby, be she a university graduate or a 16-year-old who dropped out of school, a banker with a husband and a nanny or an unemployed divorced woman on her own with several children, they are all on the health visitor's list, initially at least. It is natural for the health visitor to come to your door or for you to go to the clinic. You are not labelled as different, special or deficient in any way.

The next point is that health visitors are perceived as offering practical help and being non-judgemental. Their job is to tell you how to stop the baby crying rather than to blame you for making the baby cry. Social workers, by contrast, are seen by many (but not by all—Tyrrell's mother and Jason's parents were warm in their praise of some social workers) as agents of the authorities who come to check up on you and who may even take away your children.

Lastly, there is no doubt that it is possible to spot at an early age, even in infancy, the child who shows worrying behaviour that his or her particular family cannot cope with. The crying baby may turn into the hyperactive toddler. "He was a terrible baby, he was a horrible child," said Marilyn about Jason. "They were little terrors from the time they were born", said Corinne about her twins (On the other hand, Tyrrell and Stephen were lovely babies). Professor Farrington's view, in the light of American home visiting experiments, was that ". . . it is plausible to suggest that a more intensive health-visiting programme, with small case-loads, might be successful in reducing hyperactivity, school failure, child conduct problems, and ultimately delinquency and crime. Intensive health visiting programmes might be even more effective if they were supplemented by parent management training and pre-school intellectual enrichment programmes."

There is considerable interest at the moment in both parent training and pre-schooling but routine visits to the home and domiciliary services in general are out of fashion. 'They are too expensive', we are told

> and it really will not harm a baby with a high temperature to be taken out on a cold night to a strange duty doctor's surgery or to wait in a hospital casualty department. It is a waste of valuable time for a health visitor to go up and down stairs at a housing estate. Mothers can bring their questions to the clinic. It's only a bus-ride away and there is a play area for any other children they may have to bring. Most of them will come.

Most of them may come in some areas, yes, but the very ones who need advice most, and who perhaps do not know what the questions are that they should ask, will not come or will attend erratically. (In France they have tried to ensure full attendance at mother and child clinics for developmental checks and immunisation by linking attendance with the collection of benefits: if you don't attend, you don't get your money.)

I would like to see the domiciliary role of the health visitor greatly strengthened as part of the new 'Sure Start' proposals. The argument that home visits are an intrusion into the privacy of families is not sustainable if families, the most vulnerable families, find visits by health visitors acceptable because they are "normal". It is often easier for people who find it hard to say what is wrong to talk when they are in familiar, non-threatening surroundings. It is easier for professionals to listen; they can see the conditions in which the family lives and they can also observe the inter-action between family members which may be the key to better relationships.

This is not to suggest that the number of clinics and family centres in the community run by health authorities, sometimes in partnership with the social and educational services or with voluntary organizations, should be reduced. Far from it. Every area, not some as at present, needs a family centre where assessments can be made and families can meet. Such centres can provide specialist groups as required in the particular vicinity. They can also offer neutral ground, acting, for example, as contact centres for separated fathers to meet their children when it is not advisable or cannot be agreed that they should meet elsewhere.

The Askham Family Centre in West London, jointly managed by the London Borough of Hammersmith and Fulham and NCH (National Children's Home) has two main functions. First, it supports and does preventive work with families, running a drop-in group, a group for Asian families, a fathers' group for fathers who do not live with their children, a group for families in bed and breakfast accommodation and a group for children of mixed race. Second, it does assessments for the family proceedings court, works with families under court supervision orders and can be used for supervised contact meetings. Attached to the centre are two flats where families under assessment can stay. The borough child psychology service is based there, too, so the centre is also used by families with children who have difficulties at school.

With the most difficult families, work can only begin once trust has been established. "Sometimes I'd be lucky to get in at the door", one senior administrator at the Health Visitors' Association told me, recalling her days in practice.

> I'd stand there, talking through the letter-box till she opened the door. I'd just go on, talking through the crack in the door and asking just a few quiet questions till in the end she said 'You'd better come in then'.

Her two tenets as a health visitor were "Never make assumptions" and "Be prepared for change": things could always improve as well as deteriorate.

It might be countered that health visitors should be primarily concerned with checking the physical development of babies and young children, spotting physical defects and problems (like Robert's deafness) as early as possible, advising on nutrition, childhood illnesses and the like. Would it not dilute their effectiveness as professionals to extend their role? But health includes mental health: post-natal depression can spread its effects long after the baby years; a hyperactive child can hurt himself physically as well as wear out everyone else; addictions to drugs or alcohol need to be treated before children are damaged. It is perfectly proper for health visitors to be engaged in this field and they have traditionally seen their remit as wide.

And the cost? We will see later the conclusions from American research about the savings over time made by investment in pre-school education programmes. There is every reason to suppose that intensive help at home for vulnerable parents would be cost-effective, although there should be studies to chart the progress of families who have the benefit of such help. It is difficult to quantify events that through early intervention, "anticipatory guidance", never actually happen but it is worth noting that when the health visiting service was completely withdrawn in one London borough in the early 1980s cases of child abuse and cot deaths escalated. What is needed is a new system of accounting for local authorities, health authorities and education authorities which allows the possibility of social auditing, setting off present costs against future savings.

HOME-START

In the meantime health visitors constantly come into contact with families who need special help and they can and do when possible refer such families to others who can take on more intensive work. One organization to which they may turn is Home-Start, started in Leicester by Margaret Harrison in 1973. Nine years later, in 1982, she explained its aims and methods in *Adoption & Fostering*, the journal of British Agencies for Adoption and Fostering of which I was then the editor. *BAAF* is the umbrella organisation for the fostering and adoption agencies run by local authorities and voluntary agencies. As well as training in good practice social workers, doctors and lawyers concerned with children who need substitute families, it has always emphasised the importance of preventive work to stop the need for children to be separated from their first families. Hence the interest in Home-Start which had just widened its remit into a consultancy service funded for an initial two-year period by the London Law Trust.

Margaret Harrison described how a voluntary home-visiting scheme was launched "to offer support, friendship and practical help to families with children under five (their formative years), who for a variety of reasons were experiencing difficulties". After an initial course of preparation, each Home-Start volunteer was introduced to one or two families and undertook to visit them regularly, sometimes twice a week, but sometimes daily if there was a crisis, responding to whatever the family felt was their need.

The guiding principle of the Home-Start approach, as valid today as it was then, is that the volunteers take their lead from the family, they do not walk in and impose an agenda of their own. (Good management consultants would say that this is what they do when they analyse the needs of any business or organization.) They have been likened to older sisters or the mothers we all would have liked. "Only if the parents' needs are met", said Margaret Harrison, "so that they gain self-confidence and a sense of security, can they themselves transmit the love and emotional stability which is so vital to their own children. But it often takes time, and in some cases a Home-Start volunteer may visit for up to two or three years before this can be achieved."

The organization which started with a dozen volunteers, all ordinary parents but trained and supported by a multi-disciplinary group of professionals, by 1998 was a network of 218 home visiting schemes supported by a national consultancy, Home-Start UK. In addition there were 22 schemes operating within the British Forces in Germany and Cyprus. Similar organizations have been set up in Australia, Canada, Hungary, the Irish Republic, Israel, The Netherlands and Norway. It is cited as an example of what can be done, what *ought* to be done, not only in the Home Office documents I have mentioned, but also in the guidance accompanying the Children Act 1989 as an example of services that

> offer parents under stress significant amounts of time from volunteers who are likely to be seen as friends with no power or tradition of interfering in family life and who may themselves have surmounted similar difficulties.

Visiting is still open-ended and the only conditions for beginning are that the family includes at least one child under the age of five and that the family wants to be visited.

Home-Start has been monitored and evaluated more than most other schemes because it has been operating longer, for over 25 years. The results are impressive. In 1995-6 Home-Start schemes in Britain supported more than 11,400 families of which more than a third were headed by a lone parent. The 22,270 children involved included 924 whose names appeared on the child protection registers held by local authority social services departments to monitor children thought to be at risk of abuse or neglect. In March 1996 there were more than 4,600 Home-Start volunteers with another 665 attending training courses. Most Home-Start services are now funded through contracts with local authorities and the surveys suggest satisfaction from families visited, improvements in their lives and beneficial effects for the children, with most of those children who were at risk being kept out of care.

As David Utting comments, preventing delinquency is not among Home-Start's stated objectives but it addresses some of the known risk factors which can lead to delinquency—poor parental supervision, harsh or inconsistent discipline and conflict in the family. It also helps by reducing the risk of children growing up in care and thus being more likely to fall into delinquency. Above all, I would add, it improves their own upbringing so that they do not suffer abuse or neglect and have a better pattern of parenting to pass to their children in due course. It helps to break that cycle of deprivation which the Jeremiahs think is inevitable.

And the cost? The annual cost of visiting a family in 1998 was approximately £500; the cost of establishing a Home-Start scheme including volunteer training, an organizer's salary and part-time secretarial help is put at £37,000 in the first year and £34,000 in the second year. Compare such costs with those of keeping a child in a secure unit for a week (about £2,000). Small wonder that the government Audit Commission in 1994 said it was the type of family support service that should be available in every local authority area.

EXPLORING PARENTHOOD

Exploring Parenthood, The National Parenting Development Centre, was founded in West London 1982 by a group of professionals in mental health who were working at the Tavistock and Parkside Clinics. Carolyn Douglas, its director until 1998, herself a family therapist, says that they felt the formal process at the clinic could demoralise parents further. They wanted to go out into the community and bring their expertise to parents who came on demand, without folders giving their case histories. They wanted a partnership between professionals and parents with the professionals responding to the wishes of the parents.

Exploring Parenthood spread its influence further than might be thought possible for a small organisation with a total income in the year 1995-6 of £316,191, from charitable trusts and foundations, corporate donations and a few government and local authority grants. First, it ran a national telephone advice line. Any parent could ring 0171 221 6681 between 10 a.m. and 4 p.m. and arrange to be called back by an EP professional adviser. Sometimes an extended telephone call may resolve a problem but if not, the parent is offered options for further help and told about local resources which may be available.

Next, Exploring Parenthood offered parenting programmes to meet the needs of a wide range of parents—parents of infants, young children and adolescents; single parents, working parents, black and Asian parents, very young parents, disabled parents and those with disabled children. These programmes were worked out in detail so that those trained to use them could replicate them. The training provided was open to health visitors, speech and language therapists, psychologists, doctors, teachers, nurses, childcare staff, social workers, family workers and also parents who wanted to support other parents. The Moyenda Project worked from 1991 with black and Asian families in London, Luton and the South East and assessed the cultural needs of these families, including the role of fathers.

Two of the programmes offered addressed the connection between good parenting and the prevention of juvenile offending. The Parents N' Kids Programme for parents of under fives "known to be vulnerable and face parenting challenges" aimed to stimulate active listening and communication, and to provide a framework for discipline. How? By teaching skills that would reward effort, considering alternatives to punishment, balancing children's needs with parents' needs and so on. More directly, there was a specific Parents Against Crime Programme for parents of ten to 14 year olds "who already face serious difficulties like school failure, exclusion and brushes with the law". The programme kept the emphasis on enabling parents to find their own way: it facilitated "parents' ability to identify areas for change and undertake new approaches" as well as offering them the opportunity to learn new skills and "providing a forum in which parents can discuss issues with teachers, social workers and the police on neutral territory".

So how did the professionals identify parents of children at risk of trouble and woo them to participate voluntarily in a course that lasted ten weeks? Exploring Parenthood gave guidance on publicity, networking among professional groups, using the local media and selecting a suitable venue, one that is preferably familiar to intended participants and possibly has facilities for a crèche and children's group. The content of the courses was structured but flexible, a series of group sessions which introduced themes like the stages of adolescence, boundaries and discipline, problem solving and assertiveness and negotiation skills, in language that was understandable by all. The exercises suggested were mainly experiential, enabling the parents to draw on their own lives. For instance, when treating adolescence they discussed their own teens, positive as well as negative memories, working in pairs and reporting what each other said.

The organizers recognised that parents with many problems of their own including difficulties with their children, who hated school and were probably unused to joining groups, might come late and not attend regularly. They said that the initial ambivalence was gradually melted by the nature of the course: the atmosphere was nurturing and the facilitator was warm, caring, reliable and consistent (like a good parent). It would be too much to expect a life-time's anxiety and sense of failure to evaporate after a ten-week course and some continuing support was offered after the formal conclusion of the course.

This is the kind of course politicians have in mind for parents of young offenders under the new parenting orders. But if parents were present only by order of the court, the organizers would have two additional hurdles to overcome: their resentment—their feeling that *they* did not commit the crime—and their even deeper sense of failure. With enough skill, no doubt progress could be made but how much better if more parents attended such courses before the crisis. And it is clear that such courses should not be seen as one-off, quick solutions to deep-seated problems.

The results are relevant here of the evaluation by Clem Henricson of the pilot Parents Against Crime project in West London, published by Exploring Parenthood in 1995. Families had been referred during 1993 by the police or social services but took part voluntarily; their children who were offending or on the brink of offending were encouraged to take part in a youth group to confront their behaviour and introduce them to constructive leisure activities. The research found that parents (a maximum of eight in the first group, six in the second) felt they had benefited from the course but could apply what they had learnt better to their younger children than their delinquent sons. The conclusion was that the programme, then lasting only six weeks, was too short. A nine-month course was recommended with the first three months intensive, followed by weekly meetings. It was also found that the young people in the group needed therapeutic work from highly experienced youth workers over a longer period. By contrast the maximum period for a course under a parenting order is three months.

The pilot study was funded in part by the Home Office. The conclusion for legislators would seem to be that yes, such courses are valuable and should be readily accessible in all areas but they are only part of the continuing support which parents of children in trouble need and they are most effective at an early stage. The parenting order smacks of shutting the stable door after the horse has bolted.

Sad to relate, Exploring Parenthood closed in the autumn of 1998 through lack of continuing funding, though it was hoped that individual projects, including the telephone help-line, the training courses and the Mayenda Project, would be carried on by other organizations.

NEWPIN

Among many small, neighbourhood ventures to help families in distress, I was told of a group started by health visitors and run by local childminders. Once a week mothers were given the opportunity to leave their children to play with the childminders whilst they went off to do what they wanted on their own. The only condition was that once a month the mothers had to stay with their children and join in the group's activities. What happened was that most mothers did not take their break. They preferred to stay in the circle of the childminders in the company of other mums; they made friends and helped each other; and they incidentally absorbed from the childminders new methods of relating to, playing with, distracting and disciplining their children. Gradually they took the initiative about the group's activities and asked for information for themselves, about child rearing and about health issues like smoking. The group came to resemble those run in the 1960s by the Pre-School Playgroups Association, used mainly by middle-class parents, in which the mothers played essential roles as play-leaders.

I have often wondered about the logic of the system of day nurseries for mothers who are not at work. Those who work must have full-time, high quality care for their young children but is such care the best solution for depressed, unsupported young mothers who may lead isolated lives and have few friends nearby? Once they have left their children at the nursery they can only return to the four walls of their small flats, usually without the motivation or means to improve their living conditions, find training or work. Nor is their income such that they can buy themselves distraction or a change of scene. The price of a packet of cigarettes is about the only amount they can afford—which is one reason why so many poor young mothers irritate sensible health workers by continuing to smoke. Yet a place at a day nursery is often held up not just as a respite measure but as the bright hope to enable such mothers to improve themselves as parents. What can they learn, however friendly the staff are when they deliver and collect their offspring? May they not be further disheartened by the calm professionalism of the workers who keep the children so happy?

By contrast NEWPIN, a national voluntary agency, demonstrates an approach which nurtures children through their parents. In 1998 NEWPIN had a network of seventeen local centres. Most are in the Greater London area but there are two centres in Northern Ireland and one in Australia. The centres are open to mothers and children five days a week from nine to five, with a 24-hour back up service throughout the year. Women are encouraged to look after each other and each others' children inside and outside the centre, forming a mutually supportive community.

An interesting result of the way NEWPIN works is that three-quarters of the centres are managed by co-ordinators who were themselves initially referred to NEWPIN as mothers wanting help and who over several years have graduated through its ladder of programmes. There are two points to note here: first, mothers who may seem hopeless in every sense mature into competent workers who pass on their skills to others; and second, this process does not happen overnight.

The achievement of NEWPIN is to identify, feed and bring into use the inherent strengths of parents. "I didn't like the problem focus," says

Anne Jenkins Hansen, NEWPIN's director who was a health visitor when she and others started NEWPIN in Walworth, London, in 1982. Her case-load included the highest number of children on the Child Protection Register in the area. She started a small mothers' group in a church hall and brought along her own two-and-a-half-year-old. "The mothers saw me as like themselves," she says, "and were far more open and receptive."

The belief in self-help, and the concentration on building self-confidence and trust, show even in the referral procedures. The form used to refer a mother says, "Please help the mother to fill this in—do not do it yourself". The principle of empowering people to take control of their own lives is there from the beginning and extends throughout the organization, with each local management committee having two user members.

NEWPIN says it can manage 25 to 30 families at a centre. GPs, ante-natal clinics, psychiatrists, psychologists, health visitors and sometimes group members refer mothers (as the main carers for their children). Those mothers referred are socially isolated and often depressed. Many are on anti-depressant drugs. One of NEWPIN's surveys showed that a third had been at some stage in their childhood received into care, 40 per cent had been separated from their parents, a third had experienced harsh discipline or sexual abuse in their own childhoods, half had discordant relationships with their partners, half had suffered significant mental health problems of at least two years' duration and two-thirds were clinically depressed. The same survey showed that of those with significant mental health problems who had been with NEWPIN for over six months 73 per cent improved and 20 per cent remain the same.

When a new mother is referred, the co-ordinator at the centre, goes to see her for a "pre-NEWPIN chat". If the mother likes the idea of trying NEWPIN (and nearly all do), the co-ordinator matches her with an established member who is called her befriender and has taken part in NEWPIN's Personal Development Programme. The befriender helps the newcomer to integrate into the daily routine of the centre and to enlarge her network of support. She gives her the names, addresses and telephone numbers of other mothers in the group so that if she wishes she can call on them as well as herself. "We are facilitators," Anne Jenkins Hansen says. Women monitor their own progress and record the changes in themselves and their children. The co-ordinator will help them with this recording if they have difficulties with reading and writing and there is a programme to improve literacy.

Once the new mother is at ease in the centre ("well attached" would be the NEWPIN phrase since the model used is based on the theory that adults as well as children need secure attachments for good mental health and to grow and mature) and her child is ready to be left with other children and adults in the playroom, she will join a therapeutic support group. She remains a member of that group which meets weekly, facilitated by the co-ordinator or a professional therapist, sharing her doubts and fears, experiences, troubles and progress, for as long as she is at NEWPIN. Then when she is emotionally ready she joins the Personal Development Programme. The pace is structured to further the personal development of the mother without affecting the child's need for emotional security. The mother's progress is never at the cost of her relationship with her child.

At a NEWPIN centre I visited, one mother sat with her two-year-old in the living room, listlessly eating crisps and gently rocking the child. She told me that her little girl did not yet like being with the others. Half a dozen other young children were in the playroom with their mothers and the centre's play facilitator, painting their faces, building Lego or playing with dolls. Every time a mother entered the living room to fetch a cup of coffee or pass on a message she said a cheerful word to the withdrawn figure in the armchair. Eventually another toddler entered, ran round the room and went back to the playroom. The little girl scrambled off her mother's knee and cautiously went to the door. Her mother slowly followed, as wary about entering the playroom as her daughter. It was hard to know which of them would take longer to integrate but it was clear that neither would be rushed: the other mothers understood and respected their feelings.

The Personal Development Programme has four modules: Parent Skills Training which looks at the needs of both children and parents; the Family Play Programme which helps mothers to play with their children as well as showing the point of play in children's development; the SEERS (Support Empathy Equality Respect and Self-determination) course, concerned with attachment and befriending, communication, listening and support skills; and during the second year of participation at NEWPIN, Learning for Life which consists of preparation for work and further training and is sometimes linked to NVQ training. Some mothers choose to remain with NEWPIN to develop their skills in family support and become co-ordinators or play facilitators, an internal career ladder.

Alice, one of the co-ordinators, and Shirley, the administrator at the same centre (not their real names), now shoulder great responsibility. Alice is in charge of the well-being of all at the centre, its financial as well as its therapeutic development. She reports back to her own management committee and has a weekly supervision session at National NEWPIN. When she was referred to NEWPIN in 1982 she had post-natal depression and she says she soon saw she had been suffering from depression for years. She had done well enough at her secondary modern school, leaving with some O levels, to work in a bank and had fulfilled the expectations of her family by marrying at 18 the boyfriend she had met at school. She says she felt nothing for her first child when he was born and had no insight into her own problem, why she could not get dressed in the morning, why she cared nothing about anyone. At NEWPIN she started to feel she was being looked after herself and thus became interested in and able to meet the needs of her own children and of others.

The group is the key to NEWPIN's success. Shirley went from job to job before she met her husband, fell pregnant and married him. "Motherhood wasn't as exciting as I thought," she says. There were constant rows and she grew more and more depressed. Then she heard of NEWPIN locally and "I was human again," she says. She reckons there has been an improvement in her marriage, it has made her a better mum and above all "I really feel somebody now." Her latest achievement is to have raised the funds to buy a computer for the centre which she hopes to use not only for the administration but also to teach other women computer skills.

Following good results from a pilot project, NEWPIN now has a fathers' group which it is hoped to replicate. The fathers who have been through the NEWPIN programme at the centre concerned will befriend other fathers who are referred. NEWPIN would like to build up a similar service for fathers in prison or on probation.

National NEWPIN is supported through the Department of Health and the usual, sought-after trust funds. The local centres are mainly funded by local authority health and social services which realise the value of NEWPIN as a preventive service. The cost for an individual family in NEWPIN, a mother and her children, averaged in 1997 £3,300 for a year, not much more than the cost for a week of secure accommodation for a child or prison for a young person. Bargain rates, it would seem, but local authorities have many claims on their funds and they have to make choices, between the young and the old, preventive care and support for those already in trouble. As a result, despite the plaudits (from citation in the guidance to the Children Act given in 1991 by the Department of Health to winning the Henry Kempe Award for Significant Contributions in the field of Child Abuse and Neglect) NEWPIN is available in only a fraction of the number of areas where it would be welcomed. In 1996 the Bristol branch was forced to close because local authority support was withdrawn when the county of Avon ceased to exist.

WHAT WORKS

It is clear that there are ways to help parents who are in difficulties to take charge of their own lives and thus become responsive and effective care-givers to their children, protecting them from harm and controlling them properly. There is no single blueprint for success in this field which may be one reason for the sparse and almost serendipitous scattering of provision. David Utting and his colleagues classified the different kinds of schemes for families into universal services offered to any parent or family who might find them helpful, neighbourhood services available to families under stress, and 'intensive care' family preservative interventions aimed at families under severe stress whose children might otherwise be accommodated. They all could be said to help reduce criminality among young people.

The new approach to break the present posture of punitive despair about problem families, the underlying feeling that it's all too late and 'nothing works', must be based firstly on a universal, non-stigmatising, domiciliary service to identify and support families at risk. Next a variety of schemes are necessary, ranging from pioneering clinical work (such as the programme for severely aggressive and disruptive children and their families at the Child and Adolescent Psychiatry Unit at the Maudsley Hospital in London) to small neighbourhood schemes in every area which meet the particular needs of a neighbourhood and are sensitive to the culture of local families. The neighbourhood schemes must have a guarantee of continuing funding, subject to their meeting agreed standards, because of the time-scale necessary for their work.

Voluntary participation in any remedial scheme is the key to enabling parents to change. Parents' needs have to be met before they can care properly for their children and when parents with sole charge of children return to work, they must have flexible working hours and conditions so that they in their turn can meet their children's needs. It must be accepted that changes will take time. The real answers are long-term but they do exist, they do save money and, combined with other measures, to be discussed in the chapters which follow, like preparation in schools for parenthood and citizenship, they could break the cycle in which so many families of young offenders are sadly locked.

Education: Staying and Learning

Of the young people I interviewed, only Luke had coped with mainstream schooling. Daniel at 16 was in a small special school where the teachers could address his dyslexia and other problems. Significantly, he liked this school and thought it helped him. Jason, the youngest, was attending an Individual Tuition Centre which he, too, liked but he could go there only ten hours a week and there seemed to be little hope of returning him to an ordinary school. He was only 13 years old.

All the others, with the exception of Luke, a special case in many respects, had been excluded from their schools or, like Jacquie, had gradually faded out through not attending. Low attainment at school and disruptive behaviour in school are normal for children who break the law. It is easy to see from their own accounts how difficult it would be to cope with these young people: hyperactive Tyrrell, playing the class clown and urinating into the waste-bin, or high-spirited Mark, tussling with the teachers at his boarding school. And it is not just aggressive physical behaviour that teachers have to manage. Verbal abuse is the reason why a significant number of primary school children are excluded—all that effing nonsense.

Bored students (like Robert, the car-fixated twin) become disruptive. A number of questions follow from that fact. Is it always exclusively the fault of the children that they are bored and disruptive? Tyrrell's mother was convinced that he became hyperactive at nursery school because he already knew what the staff were teaching the children and they were unable to engage his interest. Could schools of all kinds do more to fire the imaginations of their students and to change their attitudes? Would some of the young people who fall foul of the system have fared better in schools which had more effective strategies to manage difficult pupils?

Michael Rutter showed as long ago as 1970 in his landmark study *Twenty Thousand Hours* that two schools in the same area could have completely different results. The style of the head teacher and the ethos of the community spirit in one school enabled it to overcome the difficulties of the environment in which it operated. When inspectors reported on the Ridings School in Calderdale, where the breakdown of order caused a press furore in 1996, they found that more than two-fifths of the lessons offered were unsatisfactory. Ofsted also said that there was too little information about pupils' achievements—lack of praise for success, low expectations of pupils and negative attitudes help to cause a downward spiral of failure.

We do in truth know a great deal about what makes schools successful. In the first place, success should not be defined and measured only by academic achievement. The academic league tables are welcome. They chart one aspect of a school's work and they give a baseline from which to note progress on that front for that particular school with its specific catchment area and traditions. However, it is unhelpful to compare the GCSE results of a school based in a middle-class suburb, where the majority of parents have benefited from further or higher education, with those of an inner city school where most of the parents left school without qualifications and themselves had difficulties at school. This is not to say that children from poor backgrounds cannot achieve well academically but to acknowledge that in order to achieve their potential they may need more support and to have their expectations raised.

But the emphasis on measuring only one aspect of the work of schools has led us to forget that people have different capacities and manifest their intelligence in different ways. It puts at risk the intention of the Education Reform Act 1988 that schools should prepare pupils for all the "opportunities, responsibilities and experiences of adult life". It is unfortunate that the league tables are seen as indicating the main points of difference in schools, the only way that parents can evaluate schools or that schools can sell their merits to their communities. Of course it makes sense for parents with high academic hopes for their children to seek schools with good examination results but good schools encourage other achievements, too. It was welcome news at the end of 1997 that consultations were taking place about introducing aspects of 'value added' into league tables.

The other questions parents should ask about schools range wide. Do students have opportunities to take part in music, drama and sport? Do they learn how to be active, responsible citizens by participating appropriately in the governance of the school as well as by learning civics? Are they equipped with the skills to look after themselves and others as they grow older? Do boys as well as girls learn about child development for when they may become parents, about cookery, the point and the fun of family meals, about budgeting? Is there sensitive education about sex and relationships, about health and drugs? Are they encouraged to develop enterprise and compassion by taking part in voluntary activities in the community as they grow older?

The system of funding schools introduced by the last government put them in competition with each other. If schools are funded in proportion to the number of pupils who actually attend school daily, they will be tempted to erase from their rolls as soon as possible troublesome students who make their performance look poor in the league tables, are taught under special arrangements off-site or do not attend regularly. The number of final exclusions from schools in England and Wales increased from 3,000 in 1991 to over 13,000 in 1995. Such an increase cannot be attributed wholly to sudden, escalating problems in behaviour. It may also have been caused by the reaction of governing bodies (who make the decisions about exclusions) to the system of calculating their funds which was introduced in the early 1990s. Schools would have more incentives to meet the needs of difficult children if they were not penalised for keeping them on their rolls.

But at the root of the problem of poor schools is the position of teachers in our society, underpaid, undervalued and undertrained. In other cultures, teachers and learning *per se* are better respected. The projected General Teaching Council should improve morale and by setting out the standards for training and conduct may help to give teachers the professional status and respect doctors and lawyers safeguard through their professional bodies. However, if wealth is most people's main criterion of success, teachers will not be role-models for their students and teaching will not attract the brightest graduates. There was rightly a warm welcome to the increased sums given to education by the Chancellor of the Exchequer in July 1998 but there should have been stronger protests at his short-sightedness in ruling out any substantial increases across the board for teachers' pay. It is not only 'superteachers' who ought to be appropriately rewarded.

These are long-term strategic considerations. Meanwhile, David Blunkett, secretary of state for Education and Employment, can take heart from the stories of schools which are thriving. Even without funds to make the size of primary school classes smaller, to pay and train teachers better, to provide adequate text-books and computers, to repair buildings—all of which are needed—some schools have already found ways to become model communities with lively teachers who can engender delight in learning in children from difficult backgrounds. In the last decade some schools have pioneered ways of making parents their partners, a vital ingredient for ensuring the progress of the most vulnerable children. Others have effectively tackled bullying and truancy. Some have employed special tactics to reintegrate excluded or truanting pupils. The approaches they have initiated should now be built on and the benefits they bring extended to all areas according to local needs. They are particularly relevant to preventing difficult children from becoming young criminals.

PARENTS AND SCHOOLS

If a mother has herself liked school at least some of the time, she can pass on a positive view of school and the satisfaction of learning to her children. On the other hand, if she could not cope with school, even i f she acknowledges the value of education and wants her children to take part in normal schooling, she may find it difficult to give her children the support they need. It emerged when I was talking to Marilyn, the mother of Jason, that she had herself been excluded from school. So had her older son, who had a record of juvenile offending, so had her older daughters and now so had 13-year-old Jason who was already in serious trouble with his offending. She and her partner Tyrone were always ready to go up to the schools and talk with the teachers when there were complaints. She wanted her children to succeed at school but somehow her pattern of poor attendance and failure at school had been passed on. What can be done to help such families break the cycle of educational deprivation which often results in offending?

The first solution is through well structured early pre-school provision for young children who are at risk. The achievements of the Perry Pre-School Programme in a disadvantaged, black neighbourhood of Michigan in the US have been demonstrated by long-term research and, most important, well publicised. By the age of 27 those who had attended the programme were more likely than a control group to have completed their schooling, to be in jobs earning adequately and to own their own homes. They were less likely to have been arrested for drug-related offences or any offences at all and less likely to have needed social services. The girls were less likely to have become pregnant as teenagers.

These and other American findings established a clear link between the right kind of quality early education and the prevention of subsequent offending by children. So what has been done in Britain to adapt the Perry Programme for vulnerable young children here? In 1996 about 42,000 children a year attended pre-school groups in Britain which used the same approach as the Perry Pre-School Programme, following a pattern of 'child initiated learning'. The children for most of the time choose and 'review' their own activities so that they have to think about what they want to do and learn how to do it.

The relevance of inculcating from the earliest years the habit of thinking before acting is obvious when the histories of young offenders are considered. If Jason's nursery had used this structured approach with him, would his mother now be saying "My Jason doesn't stop to think"? And would a nursery school which was fully aware that hyperactivity such as Jason showed was a warning sign for later delinquency have intervened more actively to shape his behaviour? Marilyn complained that there was no plan at nursery. "It was actually *left* until it was beyond repair", she said, a common criticism voiced by parents. "Think before you move", was what Mark's youth justice worker was trying to teach him at the age of 17.

The statistic most quoted about the Perry Pre-School Programme is that for every one dollar invested there has been a return to the taxpayer of over seven dollars in savings from reduced crime and lower expenditure on welfare services. Less often mentioned but crucial to the success of the Perry Programme was the involvement of parents. Each family was visited at home every week for one and a half hours. They were helped to understand and reinforce at home what their children had learnt at school.

I argued in the last chapter that enabling parents to fulfil their role effectively was a fundamental factor in preventing later delinquency for their children. For those children most at risk of failing at school and falling into delinquency I suggest that a partnership between home and school is also essential. Parents and teachers must share overarching aims and agree a clear strategy for the benefit of the children.

The inclusion of parents in the school scenario and their support for the school, from nursery days onwards, is vital to a school's success with its students. We have progressed a long way from the days when notices on school doors said, "No Parents Beyond this Point". Parents are now members of school governing bodies which have awesome powers to determine the futures of schools. All the same, only a minority of schools have what might be called an inclusive approach to parents. Not all schools set out clearly the relationship between the school and the parents. Few see it as a need, let alone a priority, to help the parents as well as the children to learn and to enhance their capacities. Perhaps the best example of official failure to see the significance of including parents in special provision is the fact that the key feature of home visiting was omitted when the Home Office Programme Development Unit supported the introduction in North Tyneside, Lewisham, Manchester and Liverpool of nurseries based on the Perry approach.

HOME-SCHOOL PROJECTS

In 1993 the RSA (Royal Society for the encouragement of Arts, Manufactures and Commerce) set up a two-year project 'Parents in a

Learning Society'. The RSA is a difficult organization to define but i t has been an important engine for change in our society. Since its foundation in the eighteenth century it is has been responsible for many initiatives to promote British enterprise in manufacturing, good design, a sustainable environment and continuing learning for the whole population. For the last decade its membership of 20,000 Fellows has sponsored projects to encourage 'A Learning Society', including the development in schools of practical partnerships with parents.

This kind of partnership casts parents as partners rather than consumers. They have responsibilities as well as rights. In its basic form the partnership can be symbolised for parents when their child joins the school by a simple contract. At Kate's Hill Community Primary School in Dudley a document is signed by a teacher, the parents and the child. It states that the school will describe the day's routine, explain the method of reading used, arrange regular meetings to discuss progress and "encourage the child to do the best he or she can". The family will make sure the child gets to school on time and attends regularly, themselves attend a workshop about the work in school, agree to share information and attend progress meetings. All three 'parties' sign the agreement. The last Education Bill of the Conservative government gave official blessing to such agreements being a condition of a child's admission to a particular school, stating "admission arrangements may provide for homeschool partnership documents".

Such pieces of paper, however, are only a start, a statement of intent. Participating schools in the RSA project went on to involve the parents in identifying the educational goals for their particular child and then to plan with them how they could support the child to attain those goals. When Pat, the mother of Jacquie, the young woman I interviewed, went to her school to see if she could do anything to help her daughter to catch up on the schooling she had missed, a friendly teacher promised some course-work for her to do in the holidays but never produced it. In a school operating a systematic partnership scheme with parents such a situation would be unlikely to arise. Jacquie's absences from school would have been taken up with her mother earlier and considered in the light of the plans they had made together for her future. Pat would have known the type of course-work Jacquie was doing, her request for assistance would have been acted upon and the outcome monitored.

Selwood Middle School in Somerset, one of the schools in the 'Parents in a Learning Society' project, developed with parents a 'school link book'. It contained factual information about the school, lists of the student's teachers and timetable, a weekly diary to record details of homework and a message box. In one book I saw the note "Nicola has an orthodentist (*sic*) appointment on Wed 15 and so will be away until the afternoon"; this was initialled and acknowledged the next day. There is less scope for truancy when all absences are noted as a matter of course. Nicola's homework for each day was also listed. There could be no arguments about what she was meant to be doing each evening and her mother must have had a clear idea about what she was learning that term in each subject.

But what about parents who have missed so much education themselves that they can barely help their children to practise reading? What about those for whom English is a second language which they may speak badly and cannot write well enough to fill in a school link book? The ten schools in the RSA *Parents in a Learning Society* project helped parents to gain confidence in their own skills. Monson Primary School in a run-down area of the London Borough of Lewisham held Saturday reading sessions to share ideas about the teaching and learning of literacy and language—and they encouraged parents to improve their own skills. Parents joined their children at computers to learn how to use them and were given certificates of accreditation for what they learnt.

A parent from one of the project schools said: "I have gained more knowledge and understanding of helping my child with reading and maths. I have learned a little bit about how the unemployed centre works. I have also learned that I am not 'just a mum', that I have still got a brain and am still capable of learning and developing." Like the Mums in the NEWPIN centres described previously she had been 'empowered', with consequent gains for her child.

New Labour's plans to boost family literacy in 500 centres in the summer of 1998 were welcome. Courses help parents to improve their own skills and to learn how to encourage their children's. Four pilot schemes set up by the previous government showed good results for both parents and children which were sustained after the course ended. Such courses should be available nation-wide. But they would be even more effective (and less likely to make parents feel conspicuous and embarrassed because they attend) if they were part of a school's integrated approach to including parents as partners in their children's education.

The times when a child transfers from one stage of schooling to the next, particularly from primary to secondary school, can be difficult for children and their parents. Most primary schools are smaller than secondary schools and many seem friendlier. Most parents understand what their children learn in the early stages but many are overawed by the fuller, more advanced secondary curriculum which will have changed from their schooldays. Transfer time is risky for potential truants. Although much truanting starts towards the end of the primary school years, it becomes worse at the age of 14 or 15 and the hope of reintegrating students with poor attendance recedes as they grow older. To ease the transition, Rush Common County Primary School and Fitzharrys Secondary School in Oxfordshire, also in the RSA project, linked pupils and parents in the final year of the primary school with those in the first year of the secondary school.

All the schools in the RSA project designated a member of staff, sometimes the head, to co-ordinate their home-school initiatives. Saturday workshops and parents' meetings are yet another claim on the time of busy teachers but the benefits of changing the culture were clear to the teachers in these schools. In the short term parents could take over some tasks assisting teachers. However, the main rewards of home-school partnerships were agreed to be long-term and fundamental. They stemmed from the increased commitment of the family to the school and hence improved progress of the students, with subsequent savings of time spent on dealing with difficult students.

BULLYING

A boy of 14 is waiting by the bus-stop after school. No one else happens to be there. Two or three boys, maybe slightly older and slightly bigger, maybe from the same school, maybe from a rival one, approach him. "Give us your money," they say. He says he has only his bus pass and 50 pence. They jostle him into a side turning and one of them searches his pockets while the other pinions his arms. They take his change and the chain round his neck. He falls to the ground and grazes his chin. They are school bullies and in the eyes of the law they have committed the criminal offence of robbery.

Bullying in schools, as in many institutions, can take a variety of forms. It may start with teasing and name-calling in the playground. This kind of bullying can be undermining enough to affect the victim's progress at school. It may even cause the victim to truant from school, or worse. In 1997 a 16-year-old in Stornaway, the Western Isles, committed suicide because of bullying by her schoolmates. The psychological wounds often go deep and what is called teasing should not too readily be dismissed as part of the rough and tumble of growing up. Physical bullying, applying brute force to take a football or to exclude someone from a group, is sometimes minimised by adults who would be shocked if it were officially—and correctly—termed assault or robbery.

In general, only about ten per cent of crimes committed by young people involve violence. It is adults who commit most crimes of violence. By contrast, young people are more likely than adults to be the victims of personal crime. (It is significant that three-quarters of young people convicted of the most violent and serious offences have themselves been physically, sexually or emotionally abused.)

Although some offences by young people which are classified as robberies are for crimes against strangers—mugging people in the street, snatching handbags (a crime which Jason thought was sick) or seizing Rolex watches from drivers waiting at traffic lights in stationary cars—many robbery cases before the youth courts are examples of schoolboy and schoolgirl bullying. There are schemes in some schools to stop bullying at an early stage and to help to prevent it escalating into more serious offending.

Archbishop Thurstan School, also one of the RSA's 'Parents in a Learning Society' project schools, is situated on a large housing estate on the eastern fringes of Hull. Long-term unemployment is endemic and there is considerable family poverty. The school, with about 760 students, boys and girls aged eleven to 16, had always prided itself on its open, caring ethos. Its then deputy head, Barrie Wyse, was therefore shocked to find that a boy who had been bullied regularly for six months had not spoken to anyone about what was happening to him. The discovery of this case led to the development of a systematic procedure to involve the whole school—pupils, teachers and parents—in an anti-bullying strategy.

Writing about the scheme in the *RSA Journal* of June 1995, Lesley James, then head of education at the RSA, and John Bastiani, project director of 'Parents in a Learning Society', explained that the first step was to open up the problem. Pupils were given a questionnaire asking if they had ever been bullied, how, where and who, if anyone, they had told about it. A letter was sent to parents explaining what the school meant by bullying and pointing out that their help was essential if the issue was to be tackled effectively. The school's Parents in Partnership group, which had previously developed initiatives for parents whose children had learning difficulties, then drew up with other involved groups of parents, teachers and education welfare staff a structured approach to deal with and prevent bullying.

The system was based on the use of 'Help Cards'. It was agreed that students would find it easier in the first instance to write down sensitive, often highly personal information than to approach a member of staff and talk about it. The cards have proved an effective means to get students to report bullying whether of themselves or of others. Careful (and confidential) records are kept of the nature of the bullying, which staff were informed, and how parents were included in discussions about what action should be taken.

The high-profile scheme is reinforced by a long-term programme of Personal and Social Education classes to which parents are invited. "Although not many actually come to the lessons," James and Bastiani reported, "all know they are taking place and what issues are being considered." Through role play and similar methods pupils are encouraged to think about other students' feelings. They are also asked, "What should the school do", so that they see how responsibility is shared. Students, parents, teachers all "own" the policy because it was developed with them and is constantly reviewed with their help. The key point is that everyone in the school, from the chair of the governors to the dinner ladies, to the parents, from the oldest child to the youngest, knows about the policy and the system.

Bullying will not disappear just because there is a strategy to deal with it, however excellent and well understood that strategy is. A nurturing atmosphere in a school may not outweigh the influence of a home where arguments are won by force. It is not always easy to see why some children are bullied, others are not, why some bully and others do not, why some seem to have the self-esteem to protect themselves and others do not. But the Archbishop Thurstan model and others like it have shown that every school should develop a strategy in partnership with parents and pupils, first to acknowledge and then to tackle the problem of bullying, with clear procedures for dealing with it and long-term social education to prevent it.

TRUANCY AND EXCLUSION FROM SCHOOL

Truants come in various shapes and sizes. Not all are noisy class clowns like Tyrrell, disrupting lessons to win popularity until they get excluded. Not all go shop-lifting as he did when he first absented himself, using his travel-card to visit the Aladdin's cave of a toy emporium. There are also shy, introverted children who cannot bear the hurly-burly of school and are not supported at home. Some fear bullying or extortion and some may want to stay at home to protect or look after their mother or the rest of the family. But all are at risk, not just of missing out on their education. Truancy is an early predictor of juvenile delinquency, adult criminality, frequent job changes, unemployment, poverty and even marital discord.

The fact that all truants do not commit offences has to be set against the fact that most young offenders have been permanently excluded from school—nearly 80 per cent of them. They hang round shopping centres or housing estates with little to divert them from boredom except stealing from shops, breaking into cars or vandalising property. So what can be done?

Research studies confirm the obvious that early detection is essential. One in four persistent truants start skipping school towards the end of their primary years. Schools with good attendance figures make a point of stressing with parents from the outset the need for regular attendance and punctuality. They keep proper records—it is no good pupils getting their mark at morning or afternoon registration and then slipping out of the gates—and have clear procedures to follow up absences immediately and to monitor the effect of the remedies they set in train. Ensuring parents are in the picture and engaging their commitment to the school from the start is crucial—we have seen how this was done in schools participating in the RSA 'Parents in a Learning Society' project. Links between primary and secondary schools, as described in the project's Oxfordshire schools, can ease that difficult transition period. And there must be support to re-integrate those who have been absent for whatever reason and therefore missed class-work and lost touch with their classmates.

But nipping truancy in the bud is not just a question of checking the register to see who is absent. The real detection should be into the reasons why children vote with their feet. It may be a minor incident or it may be constant, low-level failure that triggers the first absence. Extra help with basic skills is the obvious answer for children who are falling behind. The charity Volunteer Reading Help reckons it costs just £70 to help to change the attitude of a child lacking the motivation to learn to read. VRH links volunteers from the local community with children aged from six to eleven whom teachers think would benefit from individual attention. In 1997 it had 22 branches and over 1,000 volunteers helping 3,828 children in 671 schools. This is a small contribution to a major problem but it strikes at the root of the problem: all children must learn to read before it is too late.

A feature of schools with good attendance records is that they reward good attendance and good behaviour. Most truants have low self-esteem and like most of the boys I interviewed are defensive and really rather ashamed of their lack of accomplishment. They should be praised for what they do well and encouraged to do better. (It has been suggested that to give less homework to the less able students carries the message that they are not worth bothering with—they count for less.) Truancy should not be seen in isolation: tackling its causes should be part of a school's total strategy. Corinne took Robert to school every day but he did not stay there. A parenting order requiring her to escort him to school would not have helped matters in their case.

Taking children to the family proceedings court for non-attendance or making attendance at school a condition of a supervision order in the youth court is to use a blunt instrument too late.

Co-operation and good communication with specialist agencies—the education psychology service, the education welfare service, social and health services—will help schools sort out the problems of individual pupils but the school by its own structures and attitudes can itself do most to prevent truancy and exclusion. I greatly admire the work in local authority pupil referral units where excluded pupils are sent as a last resort. These centres are sometimes disparagingly called "sin bins" but their pupils benefit from individual attention and a curriculum tailored to their needs. Like Jason they learn to respect their teachers. The pertinent question is this: if all schools could at the first signs of disruptive behaviour call in trained specialists to give difficult pupils individual attention for a period would there be a need for pupil referral units?

The financial costs of leaving intervention until it is too late are high. At a conference on "Truancy, Exclusion and Youth Crime" in November 1996 Dr Carl Parsons of Christ Church College, Canterbury said it took on average approximately £2,000 a year to educate a pupil in a secondary school, approximately £3,000 to give a child only five hours a week home tuition and £4,500 to £8,000 a year for a child in a full-time special school. Then there are all the peripheral costs of letters, telephone calls, assessments and meetings triggered by the exclusion process, followed by the long-term costs of allowing young people to leave school without skills and job prospects—possibly a life on state benefits. Training teachers to deal with issues of non-attendance, enabling them to support weak pupils, enlisting specialist therapeutic help also costs money but less money with more positive results.

The community, too, can help to stop a culture in which truancy is condoned. At Hanley, Stoke-on-Trent, a "Truancy Free Area" was launched in September 1993 by a partnership between the local chamber of trade, the education welfare service and the police. They first of all tried to raise public awareness of the problem through an information campaign. *A Parents' Guide to Truancy* was sent to all parents of high school children in Staffordshire. Posters in public places and on public transport asked parents whether they were sure their child was at school. The vulnerability of children to criminals and paedophiles was stressed as well as the mischief the truants might do. Participating shops displayed a "Truancy Free Area" logo and staff were trained to ask suspected truants "Shouldn't you be at school?" Police officers in uniform, in company with education welfare officers, walked round shopping areas at irregular intervals, approaching suspected truants, "enquiring into their welfare and advising them where appropriate, to return to school". Details of suspected truants were sent to the education welfare service to give to schools and parents.

One can see potential pitfalls in such an approach. There are legitimate reasons why young people may have a day off school and they could rightly resent too much intrusion into their lives. Shops do not want to deter the lucrative trade they enjoy from schoolchildren out of school hours. They do not want to risk kindling the kind of bad feeling that exists in some inner city areas between the police and young people, especially black young people, who feel they are stopped and questioned unnecessarily on the streets. It is also much easier to see such an operation being effective in a small town than in a city whose shopping precincts are a magnet for young people from a wide area and from schools with different half-terms and attendance requirements.

Nevertheless, the raising of public awareness about truancy must in itself be helpful. The evaluation of the Staffordshire initiative was summarised by Inspector Edwin James Lewis in 1995. Police statistics showed that there was a 30 per cent drop in crime related to vehicles in the town centre over a four month period; a 16 per cent drop in juvenile shoplifting; and a 48 per cent reduction of juvenile arrests during school hours. The schools reported the same level of unauthorised absences— the local education authority stressed that truancy in the area was below the national average—but that a number of persistent truants had returned to school because it was more difficult for them to go undetected. The traders all supported the initiative and thought it was a success, with their shops more "comfortable" for other customers. One chamber of commerce member wrote: "It was also very encouraging to be part of something we all believed in . . . "

The Staffordshire Truancy Watch initiative continues, as do other similar schemes, many of which have been supported by government Grants for Education Support and Training (GESTs) funding. As is often the case with evaluations, research on the GEST schemes has shown that what many people had been saying for a long time was true. According to David Utting's 1996 Home Office Research Study, "The most efficient and effective interventions in terms of value for money are those which work preventively before hard-core absenteeism develops". The new powers of the police under the Crime and Disorder Act 1998 to pick up truants in public places and take them back to school or another place designated by the local authority, must be operated as part of a strategy developed with the co-operation of local communities.

FURTHER EDUCATION COLLEGES AND CITIES IN SCHOOLS

"I'm going to try to go to college", said Daniel who at the time I met him could barely read or write. College to most of the young people I saw was a ray of hope, something normal, something for people who were going to be successful, a means to their aspirations. Tyrrell was beginning to accept that he would have to get proper qualifications i f he was to achieve his dream of owning a garage. Josiah, a bright lad, went to college regularly four days a week. Matthew put it like this: "My 'good' friends don't get into trouble. They go to college, they have a job, they work". Even Robert, who seems to have assaulted a tutor h e argued with when he was at college, said that if he could travel back in time, he'd stay at college.

It is indeed a cause for hope (and a tribute to their youth justice workers and often their parents) when these young people see the point of qualifications and the connection between skills and jobs. What is less certain is whether they will have the staying-power to stick to their intentions, given their histories of non-attendance at school and the way they are easily distracted by those whom Matthew called his 'bad' friends. Cities in Schools is one organization which has developed "bridge courses" to help young people who have truanted or been excluded from their schools to settle into colleges or sometimes back into their schools.

The Beethoven Centre of City of Westminster College when I saw it in 1997 was situated at the heart of one of the most deprived areas of London, next door to a housing estate notorious for crime and trouble. Unemployment was far above the national average, especially among the higher than average proportion of young people. Many single parent families had been rehoused in the estate. Many of the young people had been excluded from school. The centre's handsome but antiquated buildings went back to 1893 when they were built for a school which was a pioneer of technical education, subsequently Paddington Technical College.

The centre has long had a tradition of taking in school leavers with no qualifications and a history of poor school attendance. It is used to teaching basic skills and preparing young people for vocational programmes. Pat Squires, head of faculties, explained that as a further education college they were not constrained by the national curriculum when they took in children of school age and so could devise programmes with a practical bias that suited the interests and attention span of entrants.

The day is made as easy as possible for students to manage. A nine o'clock start is difficult for young people from households where no one has to get up in time to go to work so the classes usually begin at 10 a.m. Coddling them? Giving in to them? Call it rather facing facts. Lateness was often one of their problems when they were enrolled for school. Once they grow into the routine of attending college regularly and enjoy it, then the start to the day can be made earlier. To meet their problem of poor concentration, they have short spells in the classroom interspersed with periods in the workshops—painting and decorating, motor mechanics, art, computing—where they learn to apply basic literacy and mathematics. They don't have long breaks during the day which might result in them hanging round the estate and getting into trouble.

The programme such students follow is broken down into small units with clear goals and rewards so that there is always a next step before them which they can achieve. Their records of achievement note not only academic progress but what they do during work experience and other activities. As well as working for City and Guilds qualifications in English, numeracy and IT, they do science, art and design including printing and photography, and sport. They also follow a personal and social development course—including consideration of drugs, crime and parenthood—and take part in the ASDAN Youth Award.

Since 1995 the centre has had a contract with the organization Cities in Schools to integrate into the college 14 to 16-year-olds who have been permanently excluded from school or have not attended school for a substantial period. At any one time there are six groups of students; each group has a maximum number of ten. CIS has a project manager for every group who accompanies the students throughout the day, into classes and at break times. The students attend college for half the week and their manager arranges work experience or other activities for them for the rest of the week. Some go on to full-time GNVQ Foundation programmes and to GCSE programmes, still supported by their project managers. The small groups enable personal learning plans to be made and implemented.

Such a scenario—a suitable curriculum, personal attention, a minder in class—looks fine on paper but what happens if a student does not arrive for class? Or two students? The project manager who knows each student's parents, carers and situation, will immediately go to the student's home to fetch him or her. The managers see themselves very much as intermediaries, working as a team with teachers, carers and other supporting services.

At the Beethoven Centre the system works well. The Cities in Schools students often have brothers, sisters or friends in the mainstream of the centre which has a local catchment area. A high proportion of the students are African-Caribbean, reflecting the composition of the local population. The students are easier to manage than they were at school because they are taught in small groups by dedicated teachers (in both skills and commitment). As the site is comparatively small it is easy to monitor everyone's movements and most of the teachers know most of the students. It is not an anonymous place. The atmosphere is relaxed and friendly, with less emphasis on security than in some schools where every classroom is locked when empty.

In 1996 16 of 20 students from year ten and 26 of 30 students from year eleven finished their year's course. Three of those in year ten moved away from the area (though they also had behaviour problems at the centre) and one was excluded for sexual misconduct. In a community containing many vulnerable young people from different cultures there has to be a clear code of conduct safeguarding everyone's rights and stating everyone's responsibilities. The rules about bullying and harassment are made plain from the outset.

Funding is the stumbling block to further expansion of the scheme for younger students. The college can only take school-age students if the local authority will agree to pay for them. The inclusive cost of a bridge course for ten students in 1996 was between £45,000 and £50,000 a year. This compares favourably enough with the annual costs of off-site pupil referral units or home tuition provided by local authorities but local authorities have to consider numerous factors when deciding how to put their money to best effect. The success of such bridging courses also requires good co-ordination between many agencies, something which it is not simple to achieve. Everyone in the institution, from the schoolkeepers to the technicians to the other students, has to accept and back the project. The concurrent counselling has to be constant, surveillance close and much depends on the ability of the project manager, who is not a teacher, to work well with the teaching staff.

Cities in Schools originated in the US in 1977 and has been working in the UK since the early 1990s. "To reduce the number of incidents of crime" is one of its objectives. In 1996 it had 75 projects and claimed that 75 per cent of 16-year-olds who attended its bridge courses went on to further education and training. It also organizes re-integration courses to slot younger children back into school with support in class after an intensive programme to tackle their behaviour and to enrol them in constructive leisure activities. On the preventive side, Cities in Schools has worked with schools to help with aggressive behaviour and truancy, to encourage links with parents and to set up strategies against bullying. Their work shows yet again that we know what is effective in reconnecting young people to education but we fail to universalise the methods.

Lambeth College in London has between 8,000 and 9,000 students from many ethnic groups including 38 per cent of African origin, 35 per cent African-Caribbean and eleven per cent Caucasian. Most of them are over 18 years of age and well motivated, returning to education because they see it as a key to future success, but over 1,000 are 16 to 18-year-olds who have missed much of their basic education. Beulah Coombs, head of student welfare, explains that most have financial problems. Their fees will be paid but not their living expenses. The college's hardship fund had in 1997 £14,000 a year to give one-off grants but there was no possibility of paying students' fares—and the most common reason students gave for dropping out of the college is that they could not pay the fares to get there.

The college has developed a welfare system to help the younger students cope with their various difficulties and to reduce the drop-out rate. Two youth workers try to help them not only with practical problems but with their motivation. Some have enrolled reluctantly to comply with the wishes of parents, teachers or social workers and have little interest in their courses. Others have ended up at the college out of boredom, to fill their time. The college's code of conduct is strict on violence, drugs and disruptive behaviour with clear disciplinary procedures. Class sizes are comparatively small—15 to 20 students—and everyone has a personal tutor. They meet their tutor each week, one-to-one or in a small tutorial group. The tutorial groups follow a programme of life-skills.

The college has recently started a mentoring scheme linking volunteers from the community with young people who want support. In 1995, the first year of the scheme, the mentors were all former students of the college who had graduated to university. The emphasis is still on finding role models with whom the students can identify but other mentors now come from local businesses and organizations. The mentor meets the student regularly, every four weeks for the academic year, and helps the student to plan for the future, encouraging attendance and punctuality to begin with, building the student's self-confidence and ambition, giving information about further courses and higher education. Mentors are linked with members of the college staff who know the students.

The College of North West London also serves a diverse community in a deprived area. It has a College Learning Support Service which includes language support for students whose first language is not English, basic mathematics and support for students with dyslexia, hearing or visual impairment. The Foundation Programme helps students with literacy and numeracy and "to develop personal skills necessary for work". They choose from a range of vocational options, from catering to motor mechanics, and work for basic qualifications. Cities in Schools have a similar bridging course in the college to the one in City of Westminster College. Once students who were excluded from schools have completed their initial Cities in Schools course they can join the mainstream with special weekly support from the college.

Anita Dell who runs the special needs department is realistic about the "totally dysfunctional" backgrounds of many of the students. In many of their homes no-one has ever worked and no-one gets up in the morning. Some parents are addicted to drugs—tranquillisers as well as hard drugs—and there are many poor single parents. The college does its best to engage their support, starting with a parents' evening for everyone on the Foundation Programme. If parents don't attend, she tries to contact them afterwards because she thinks it so important to involve them.

To meet some of the financial problems of students, the college has won funds from the European Social Fund to pay £16 a week to younger students for their fares. If they do not attend, they do not receive the money. Some of the students have part-time jobs (stacking shelves in supermarkets, delivering pizzas) encouraged by the college as complementary to its own work experience programme. The placements the college can offer are unpaid but in addition to acquiring skills the students learn to work in a team, take orders, get on with the rest of the staff and even to arrive on time. The college also has a Young Enterprise project to make money through schemes suggested by students—they were selling framed pastiches of Van Gogh's 'Sunflowers' when I was there.

All these colleges say that to be successful with their students they have to combine support with firmness. The rules are clear. Anyone found with drugs, for example, is sent home and the parents or carers informed. Permanent exclusion is reserved for serious offences like attacking staff. The root of their success is that students know the college will "bend over backwards" to keep them and help them if they conform.

A SPECIALIST COLLEGE

In spite of the ways these mainstream colleges have adapted their courses to acclimatise difficult young people to normal education, there are some students who fall out or have to be excluded. The students at Lennox Lewis College in the London Borough of Hackney had all failed to fit in anywhere else. The black boxer Lennox Lewis, who established the College in 1995 with a gift of over £1 million and funded it, with his business manager Panos Eliades, set the tone for the college when he said on television:

> I got expelled from school and I still survived. In a sense that made me a better person . . . Given the opportunity some could go one way, some another. I've given the opportunity so that they can choose.

He was both a benefactor and a role model.

The students aged 15 to 19 had a history of truancy, exclusion and usually criminal offences. Not many lived at home. Most were accommodated by local authorities and most came from one-parent families. When parents were available they were welcomed to the college and they as well as their children had to make a commitment to conform to the college's aims and rules. But the emphasis at the college from the outset was on success: "We provide a positive learning environment where young people are given the opportunity to achieve and succeed."

The curriculum as elsewhere for this kind of student was vocationally biased with intensive work to catch up on basic skills— social skills as well as literacy and numeracy. Classes had a maximum of seven students to one member of staff. Every topic studied and each task set had a clear objective and took at most 20 minutes. This timescale was the maximum the students could sustain. But the difference from other colleges that struck me was the lavish equipment, from the gym to the music studio where I saw two young men totally absorbed in reggae composition. The rhythms they were making on the keyboard and hearing through their headphones were zigzagging across their computer screens. Their tutor was a mathematics graduate who had turned professional musician.

In the media room Leroy was writing a story on his word processor. It was about two policeman in their patrol car waiting for something to happen. Although the situation in his story was hardly original—such is the start of many a television drama—he caught with precision the boredom and frustrations of routine patrol duty and it was interesting that he, a persistent young offender, chose to begin a story from the point of view of the police. Over in the building section some of the youngest students were measuring pipes ready to plumb in a bath and basin according to a plan. Others were stripping out wiring in a model house before beginning to renew it.

You could see scenes like this in many colleges (and indeed in some young offenders institutions) but few have as small classes or more potentially troublesome pupils. Someone pushed the door against us when we tried to enter the plumbing class, pretending to shut us out. It was all good fun but the teachers had to know where to draw the line—and they did. "We do not tolerate bad behaviour, we confront it," is the rule. Liz Jones, the principal in 1997, explained that the overarching aim was to make the students responsible for their own actions including their own learning. If they broke the rules, they were immediately challenged and not allowed to go on denying something which it could be proved they had done. Staff had to be up-front and have the wit and vocabulary to stand up to the students.

Yet behind their tough façade the staff had also had to believe that these students who had failed everywhere else could succeed there. The message the College gave was, "Don't come here if you don't want to achieve." Liz Jones told the young people she interviewed: "This is not a place for fag-end students." She told me:

> They think no-one is on their side, that no-one is prepared to listen to them or to help them—and they can't see what's going to happen as a consequence of their actions.

All the time the system both encouraged success and inculcated a sense of responsibility. Every day began for each student with a short session with his or her tutor at which an action plan for the day was agreed. At the end of the day the student saw the tutor again and if all had gone well was rewarded by a blue dot on the record sheet.

Extra blue dots could be won for any helpful behaviour, from opening a door for the caretaker to resolving a fight—and blue dots could be awarded by the domestic staff as well as the teachers. On the other hand, if you were ten minutes late in the morning or if you screwed your friend's finger into the vice during a plumbing class, that would be noted, too, and recorded by a yellow dot. At the end of a week when you had received only blue dots for work and behaviour you won a certificate, signed by the principal, saying:

> Congratulations! For a whole week you have
>
> - Been on time
> - Been prepared
> - Worked productively
> - Respected yourself and others.
>
> Well done, keep on meeting the challenge.

The student also received a £1 token for records or cosmetics and there were other prizes—£10 for the best student of the term in each curriculum area. The system of dots for good behaviour was like that in many nursery schools and it was equally successful, being well fitted to the emotional and social maturity of most of these damaged young people.

Although the college was a last chance for many rejected and alienated young people, it was in a sense selective since it admitted only those young people it thought wanted to change their lives. It took about 56 students a year, mainly young men. About ten had dropped out in the first four months of the 1996-97 academic year, not a surprising number considering their histories. The fact that even this dedicated college could not open its doors to all and had some failures is yet more proof of the need for earlier intervention to prevent the downward spiral into self-destruction and crime.

Why do I write this account of Lennox Lewis College in the past tense? Sad to report, the college closed in July 1998, the year after my visit. Lennox Lewis' generous purse had limits, the fees charged local authorities did not cover the costs and there was no long-term development plan in place to obtain sufficient outside funding to keep the college going. The building was owned by Panos Eliades and there was some hope that the college would be relaunched when suitable long-term funding had been secured but the failure of such a constructive venture for the most difficult young people in society underlines the shortcomings of much government policy about funding. It is comparatively easy to find seed money to begin a venture but often impossible to obtain funds for it to continue. Communities need not so much funds to start ventures as funds to continue them subject to stringent monitoring.

All the courses and colleges which compensate for past educational failures have certain features in common. They see the difficulties of the young people in the round; they offer small classes, individual attention, tuition attuned to the interests and attention span of the students, practical and social skills; they have clear rules but rewards as well as sanctions. My final question is this: "Could not their approach be replicated earlier in the lives of young people who are at risk, with the concentrated resources they require deployed earlier in mainstream schools?"

Teaching Morality

At the trial of the two ten-year-old boys who murdered two-year-old James Bulger in 1993, both their head teacher and their former class teacher testified that the boys knew the difference between right and wrong. Robert Thompson and Jon Venables (who were truanting the day they abducted the toddler) received moral education at their primary school. Only recently, the head said, they had learnt about the Good Shepherd, and from the moment they entered school children knew, for instance, that it is wrong to strike another child.

In *As If*, his searing reconstruction of the Bulger trial, Blake Morrison tells how their class teacher explained that in the last year the class had discussed "cruelty to animals—pulling the wings off insects, etc.—and this led on to talk of human cruelty: bullying, teasing, fighting in the playground". So the experts answered "Yes, yes, yes and yes" to the questions about whether these ten-year-olds knew right from wrong. The law was satisfied that they were not *doli incapax* (were not, literally, incapable of having the evil intention necessary for the commission of a crime). Morrison goes on to ask his own questions: "Do they have a sense of the awful irreversibility of battering a child to death with bricks? Can death have the same meaning for them as it has for an adult?" His answer to them is "No, no, no and no". The *doli incapax* rule in the law relating to children aged between ten and 14 was abolished by the Crime and Disorder Act 1998 but the questions it raised about the comprehension by children of the seriousness of their crimes remain.

How then is an active moral sense acquired, a conscience, a super-ego which stops us doing wrong? All the mums I saw, like no doubt Robert's and Jon's, thought that they had taught their children the difference between right and wrong. It was not a question I put to them directly but most of them raised it spontaneously in the course of our conversations. Marilyn and Corinne both used the words "You teach them right from wrong" and Matthew's mother vehemently protested, "This is a Christian home. I teach them values."

Discussions about teaching morality are often side-tracked by confusion between religion and morality or ethics. It is obvious that for some people (like Matthew's mother) their practical morality is fiercely grounded in their faith. For many more their adherence, whether nominally C of E, Catholic, Jewish, or Muslim, is mainly to a cultural tradition from which they have imbibed principles of conduct. Although only 8.3 million people were calculated in 1995 to be active members of religious organizations in Britain, a poll in 1996 found that two-thirds of the population considered themselves to be Christians.

There are no figures available for the number of people appearing in court as witnesses or defendants who take an oath to God that they will tell the truth compared with the number who affirm that they will do so without swearing on any holy book. My impression over the past 20 years is that most people, including children, still take the oath, whether or not they attend church, temple or mosque. But most of us would agree that those who affirm are just as likely—or unlikely—to tell the truth. Faith, religion and its sanctions may strengthen the will to avoid wrong-doing and to tell the truth but that is another point. The basis of our society today is an implicit agreement on fundamental principles whatever way they have been reached.

Of the Old Testament ten commandments murder is still a universal taboo but among many people there is a disturbing degree of relativity about some of the others, from adultery to stealing and lying. The excuses I heard about stealing were especially revealing. There was the distorted Robin Hood principle: Jacquie said that the big stores were not going to miss what she took and she had often stolen clothes specifically for the children of a neighbour on social security. Then there was the get-out clause that the crime had no victim: Josiah said that the insurance would pay and thought that the government, that great anonymous provider, paid insurance claims. Finally, there was the ostrich attitude: "I can't think about the people," said Daniel, adding: "I won't do it if I think about them".

When children learn to read, they usually take a long time, several years until they have an adult reading-age. No one expects a toddler, having learnt the ABC and begun to connect sounds to the individual letters, next day to read the leading article in *The Times*. The Campaign for Plain English in official forms and notices is important not just to save time and to avoid misunderstanding for everyone but because many people in this advanced democracy never reach adult standards of literacy. One in seven of the homeless young people who find their way to the Centrepoint charity in London cannot read or write properly. Although most people would agree that it also takes time for a toddler to learn good behaviour, there is little understanding about the complexities of understanding the difference between right and wrong—and then applying that understanding to your own situation.

There are of course fundamental reasons why people should not steal or break other laws, just as they should not kill. Some people will accept absolute rules of conduct because they respect and automatically obey those who transmit them. But we no longer have a society in which everybody accepts authority without question and children are no longer dominated by their parents. They are bombarded by other influences from infancy and they are used to asking why and being told the answer. You don't cross the road without looking *because* you might be run over; you don't take sweets from strangers *because* they might harm you.

KNOWLEDGE IN MORAL DECISIONS

Since Eve gave Adam the apple, a basic component of making a moral decision has been knowledge. It is essential to know the relevant facts if you are to understand the consequences of your actions. The knock-on effect to consumers of shop-lifting, the millions stolen every day (by employees as well as by shop-lifters, by white-collar workers who use the photocopier as well as by labourers who take the slates off buildings) should be explained; so should the sad fact that lower profits hit the lower paid more than the fat cats at the top.

Most young men when they are first caught driving a car without insurance are totally unaware of how the insurance system works. Yes, they may have heard their Dad grumbling about paying the insurance on his car but they think it is one of many onerous, amorphous taxes adults pay if they cannot avoid them. Its relation to compensating victims of accidents (including drivers and their passengers) is not usually discussed in the home or taught at school. "I didn't realise before about insurance, running someone over," Mark said. Jacquie raised this point when she said that at primary school they taught about not going with strangers, about road safety, about what do in a fire but "They don't really teach you don't steal". No doubt "Thou shall not steal" came up sometimes in morning assembly or RE classes but she is right about the need to be specific: the facts about the economic and social consequences of theft and the purpose of motor insurance should be taught to young children, just as they are taught the physical consequences of playing with fire.

The importance of teaching the facts in sex education is clear. To persuade young people not to have unprotected sex, you have to explain the elements of reproduction and the way a fatal disease like AIDs is transmitted. Otherwise young men are not going to see the point of using condoms or young women the need to ensure that their partners do so. It never occurs to many parents to explain the purpose of car or motor bike insurance but embarrassment is the reason why many do not go into the reasons for or mechanics of contraception. They leave a dangerous vacuum for young people who have grown up with the belief that the sexual act is primarily for recreation rather than reproduction.

Knowledge about the needs and development of babies and children is also essential if young people are to become responsible parents. It is still sometimes argued that you cannot be taught how to be a good parent. Parenting skills are learnt from one's own experiences as a child, caught rather than taught. From this perspective there is little hope for the young man who had little attention, little consistency and a lot of harsh discipline as a child. Small wonder that he cannot sustain a commitment to his girlfriend or his baby. Small wonder, too, that girls from harsh backgrounds fall pregnant in their teens because they want a baby of their own who will 'love' them. It is not surprising that they are not mature enough to put their responsibilities to their baby first in their lives and often do not see the dangers of holding on to an unsupportive, even violent partner.

As long ago as 1977, during 'the great education debate' initiated by the last Labour government, I argued in *The Times* that "There are few conditions more glamorised than motherhood, and few more ignored than fatherhood". In addition to improving basic standards of literacy and numeracy, education should stretch to meet the wider needs of young people as they grew up. The need for education for parenthood was central to the work of the late Dr Mia Kelmer Pringle, Director of The National Children's Bureau from its foundation, but it is still not accepted. Why not?

The argument that 'good enough parenting' (to use the child psychiatrist Donald Winnicott's realistic standard for our aspirations) cannot be taught is another example of the defeatist fallacy which I have mentioned before. It is known from research about adoption that many children who have suffered appalling treatment recover and grow up as well-balanced people once they have experienced a nurturing environment. I have shown how organizations like NEWPIN (see p.119) offer young mothers the compensating support they need to develop their confidence as individuals. An integral part of the successful parenting programmes I have described is to help people to become aware of the needs of children and then to teach them how to handle them.

Many cases of cruelty to children are caused at least in part by the unrealistic expectations of young men about how babies and toddlers should behave. Crying is naughty. Two-year-olds should not wet their pants. So when you are tired and infuriated, you lose control. You hit the baby who cries, stub out your cigarette on the toddler to teach him a lesson and tie him to the leg of the table. If all boys as well as girls learnt about child development at school, there would be less risk of abuse as well as a greater understanding of the seriousness of bringing a child into the world in the first place.

AWARENESS OF OTHER PEOPLE

If someone had explained about insurance to Josiah, an intelligent young man, before I did, would the factual knowledge alone have altered his attitude? Not necessarily. Knowledge is an essential component of being able to make a moral decision and knowledge empowers its owner ("Knowledge enormous makes a God of me", said Keats's Hyperion). However, the possessor of the facts has to decide whether or not and *how* to apply his or her knowledge. It is possible to conclude, as Daniel did at his stage of development, "I don't care about that. It's their business. People do what they want to do."

The second component in making a moral decision, and perhaps the most important, is awareness of other people and the ability to imagine what they may feel. Awareness of others was not a quality much shown by the young people I interviewed. On the contrary, they could all be described as self-absorbed. Many adolescents are introspective and preoccupied by their own concerns—and selfish about sublimating their own to other people's wishes—but these young people had so many troubles that they often seemed completely isolated by them. Those who had received a measure of counselling, even therapy, like Tyrrell, still had more problems to unravel and work through. Robert saw his girlfriends as satellites to his life. Jacquie liked analysing and talking about her life but it was as if she saw herself as a heroine in a novel. Daniel gave the clue about the relevance of thinking about other people when he said, "I won't do it if I think about them". The younger and more immature young people concentrated wholly on their prospects for today rather than tomorrow.

The third step, when you have knowledge of the facts and appreciate the consequences of the your actions, is to apply what you know and feel about others to specific situations. Mark, like many teenagers, knew that he maddened his mum by slamming doors and playing loud music but he went on behaving badly: "There is rules at home but I break them. Sounds silly," he said. The idea of compensating the victims of crime who were strangers had caught his imagination as fair and constructive but he had not advanced equally far in handling his own personal relationships. I did not meet his mother so it was impossible to tell whether their situation after so many years could improve if both could learn to listen to each other more and to negotiate agreed rules.

The point is that it takes a combination of cognitive and emotional understanding to make an informed moral decision. In addition, it takes social skills to act in a morally correct way, especially the ability to say "no" when your mates ask you to join in a dodgy enterprise. It was his inability to react quickly and according to his own principles that made Luke party to a serious act of robbery through which a woman in her late fifties was crippled for life. It takes considerable confidence to be able to say, as Mark says he can now, "On your bike, pal, see you later". Several of the young people I interviewed repeated like a mantra that they must think before they act. Their youth justice workers who are teaching them to analyse their 'offending behaviour' and their parents hope that they will be able to apply the theory to real life when the occasion arises.

Moreover, understanding deepens and is strengthened with increasing maturity. The facts have to be presented repeatedly and differently according to the age of the child. It is now generally accepted that adopted children should be told that they were adopted at an early age. But "telling" about adoption is not a matter of a statement of fact which a very young child may accept without question. The topic is returned to over the years, as and when the child raises it, as and when the occasion for telling more arises, so that there are no secrets. The child's security with his or her adoptive parents is strengthened by shared knowledge about the child's roots. Telling about adoption is a long, cumulative process and so is teaching children and young people to make and implement decisions about right and wrong.

TEACHING RESOURCES

When I was 12 years old I was given a little, leather-bound Bible, published in 1790 in its eighth edition. Its frontispiece explained that it was:

> A curious hieroglyphick Bible or select passages in the Old and New Testaments represented with emblematic figures for the Amusement of Youth: designed chiefly To familiarise tender Age, in a pleasing and diverting Manner, with early Ideas of the Holy Scriptures.

I loved the clarity and literalism of its simple wood-cuts. In the passage "The *Lord* hateth proud *Eyes*, a lying *Tongue*, and *Hands* that shed innocent Blood; an *Heart* that deviseth wicked Imaginations, and *Feet* that be swift in running to do Mischief" (Proverbs VI, 17, 18), *Lord* was illustrated by the Hebrew lettering for Yahweh in a sunburst star surround, *Eyes* by a pair of gimlet eyes under beetling brows, *Tongue* by a sinister, swollen organ complete with tonsils, *Hands* spread out sideways with a cuff on each wrist, *Heart* in conventional, valentine shape but as large as one of the hands and densely cross-hatched, and

Feet suitably bare and attached to muscular calves. "Wicked Imaginations" were left to your imagination. Pictures linked by words filled the page within a garlanded border and at the bottom ran the full text. It was great fun working out the meaning of the pictures and then checking your answers with the translations at the bottom of the page.

People since earliest times have used pictures and words to instruct as well as to entertain. There is a didactic element in epics handed down through the oral tradition from the *Iliad* to the *Maharabata,* and in classical drama; the parables had their clear purpose; and Bruno Bettleheim spelt out what everyone suspected about fairy-tales. Closer to our times the Victorians favoured romances to inculcate moral principles. The redoubtable Harriet Martineau, political journalist and social commentator, wrote novels to interpret economic theory—Smith, Mill and Malthus—for the working man. She embodied the principles she wanted to explain in her characters and their situations.

The combination of story and picture as in the strip cartoons of teenage magazines was a format I developed with Gillian Crampton Smith in the 1970s to reach disaffected young people who did not want to listen to warnings about their health or behaviour. Between 1972 and 1983 we produced the *Thinkstrip* and *It's Your Life* series of cartoon-stories, aimed at 14 to 16-year-olds.[1] The subjects were sex and birth control, babies and parents, smoking, drinking, race prejudice, advertising, gender roles in society and why there are laws. Gillian wrote gripping stories in the current teenage idiom and a professional illustrator who worked on IPC comics drew the pictures. They looked exactly like the magazines that teenagers could buy and were often mistaken for them. Young people could identify with the characters in the stories, see the relevance of the problems raised to their own lives and were able to discuss the choices the characters had to make without feeling personally embarrassed or threatened.

Our first comic was for the South West London branch of the Family Planning Association in 1973. I was working there as part-time education and information officer at a time when free contraception on the National Health Service was about to be introduced. The problem then, still not solved, was to reach the most vulnerable in the community, young girls and young men, to ensure that "Every child is a wanted child". The FPA had many admirable leaflets about the various methods of contraception but you almost needed a university degree to understand some of them. I had read the work of John Wilson and his philosopher colleagues at Oxford on making moral decisions

---

[1] The pictures on the cover of this book are from this series

and as a journalist was convinced that the way to capture the attention of young people was through their own interests. Stories were the best way to give them information and to help them understand the issues: the facts included in the plot, plus the concern for the characters, and an awareness of their own feelings might enable them to make informed, responsible choices. All the stories could tackle the perennial, underlying problem of how to say "no" to your peers.

It is hard 25 years later to believe the furore our first comic *Too Great A Risk* provoked. The FPA itself was nervous about the venture and the first copies were published by the South West London branch using a £500 donation. Headquarters was right that it would interest the press. Newspapers carried frames from the comic, the hero Harry saying "I never thought it could happen to me" or lovely Eve, who looked like an Andy Warhol model, crying "It was only once". In a couple of months some 70,000 copies had been sold, mainly for use in schools and youth clubs, accompanied by the information file I wrote with the factual background and ideas for using the comics as "triggers" for discussion and further projects. "The girls liked it because it was true to life and the boys liked it because it was about sex", we were told in one reply to the questionnaire we sent to schools which had used it. The FPA took it over as a national publication and it remained a popular resource until it was withdrawn after legislation following Victoria Gillick's campaign made illegal the frame which said "Will they tell Mum?", "No, it's a secret between you and the doctor".

It was the launch of our second comic *Don't Rush Me!* in 1975 that confirmed we were reaching our audience. *Don't Rush Me!* was published by Wandsworth Council for Community Relations. It, too, gave information about birth control but of the three main characters two were black and one white. At a time when teenage magazines and educational material ignored the existence of black British children we wanted to produce pictures with which all young people in our multi-racial community could identify. On publication day there were 180 column inches in newspapers from *The Times* to *The Sun*. Radio and television programmes followed. *Nationwide* on BBC television showed the comic with actors voicing the parts and Giles used it for a cartoon in the *Daily Express*: "Grandma says she could have written a better strip when she was eight".

As I explained in the publication about the project which I wrote for the Community Relations Commission (precursor of the Commission for Racial Equality), the outstanding point about this coverage was that it reached a popular audience. In homes all over the country sex education was discussed. The heading in the *Sun* was "The comic with lessons in love" but the feature that followed was accurate: "A three penny comic aimed at cutting Britain's alarming pregnancy rate . . . It is a situation hundreds of young girls face every day". The headline to the leader in *The People* was, "The Right Way To Teach Sex To Teenagers" and the *News of the World* commented: "Congratulations to Wandsworth Council for Community Relations for having produced a novel way of contraceptive education . . . the idea must surely get home to kids".

The News of the World was correct. Through the Community Relations Commission I was able to conduct a research study on the use and effectiveness of *Don't Rush Me!* as a teaching resource. The respondents to the questionnaire about the comics were mainly co-educational comprehensive schools. They found total enthusiasm for the format and story. Copies "vanished" from display racks. The period under review was short but many offered evidence that young people had retained the information given in the comic and had shown increased understanding of the issues. They were also able to empathise with all the characters, black or white.

We went on to write a series of "Thinkstrips", complete with teachers' notes and exercises for classes, later combined in a series of books on each of our chosen topics called *It's Your Life*. The story *It'll Never Be the Same* was about life for a young couple with a new-born baby—not as glamorous or as initially rewarding as Joanne thought it would be. "I always wanted to have a baby," she sobs while Alan storms, "You might at least make my tea when I come home". Teenaged boys are often not interested in thinking about the days ahead when they may have a family. ("I don't know about getting married," said Daniel, doubtful about the serious involvement it entailed.) Through stories about people who look like them and who enjoy the same music and fun as they do, they may begin to see themselves in a future situation.

In *Losers, Weepers*, Dave steals a purse to get money to buy an amplifier for his pop group. ("We need that amplifier" says one of the group.) Charlie, another member of the group, discovers that the purse by chance belonged to his girlfriend Sally—she put it down while trying on a coat in a shop ("All my holiday job money and a present from Dad"). He sells the amplifier to the consternation of his mates and asks Sally to tell the police she's found the purse, creating a series of new dilemmas.

I have discussed this comic with groups of young offenders who argue vehemently about the rights and wrongs, the loyalties they feel to different groups, whether lifting things from shops is different from stealing from people, who in the story broke laws and who broke agreements, whether Sally should lie to the police or her parents and say she had found the purse again. At one point, before he discovers that it was Sally's purse, Charlie says, "Anyone walking round with that much can't need it like we do", a view I have often heard voiced by young men who mug people for their Rolex watches. The contradictions in young people's thinking abound. "I'd never nick a handbag," Jason told me. "It's not good to do that, to run and just take it off her." Yet he was a boy who was apparently willing to be used to gain entry to someone's flat to burgle it while they were asleep. Teaching that stealing is wrong *per se* is not a simple matter. The strip-cartoon stories we developed were one way to help young people to see the implications of their actions and to anticipate future problems.

Our comics were greatly praised. Wandsworth Council for Community Relations won an award from Fleet Street Industrial Editors as "Communicator of the Year" for its housing and employment campaigns and for *Don't Rush Me!* (The dynamic Campaigns Organizer for WCCR at that time was Greg Dyke, now Chairman of Pearson Television and a candidate in 1999 for director generalship of the BBC). The Open University used the *It's Your Life* series for a teacher-training module. The Inner London Education Authority, the Health Education Council and the Department of Health and Social Security all showed interest in developing further series but in the end it was a commercial publisher, Longmans, which took the risk. Over half a million copies of the *Thinkstrip* and *It's Your Life* series were sold until they went out of print in 1991, when their illustrations and some of the situations—there are few holiday jobs today—but not the topics had become out-of-date.

DRUGS, DRINK AND VIDEOS

Two youths aged 16 and 17 appear in the youth court on a charge of robbery, a joint enterprise. It is said that the 17-year-old sat in a car while the 16-year-old snatched the handbag of a woman in her fifties. Police officers on surveillance saw what happened and the youths were immediately arrested. The 17-year-old had been in trouble but the 16-year-old had never been in court before, his mother was educated and supportive, and he had passed (not just taken) several GCSEs at a high grade.

Why did he get involved? Was he just weak, doing what his mate asked him to win esteem or out of fear? He could give no excuse. "I don't know why I did it," he maintained, but a clue to his behaviour lay in the single police caution on his record: he had been cautioned for possessing a small amount of cannabis. Moreover, it would emerge after the case was proved that the 17-year-old was in custody awaiting trial for supplying drugs. In all likelihood the robbery was attempted to get money to buy drugs or to pay off money owed. His supplier said: "Go on: get it".

The Metropolitan Police have established that over half of burglaries, thefts and robberies in London are perpetrated by young, unemployed men, low-achievers under the age of 25 who are involved in the drug scene. The connection between crime and drugs has reached the youth courts for those under 18, hardly surprising as drugs of one kind or another are readily available to young people and soft drugs are cheap. In 1997 a small amount of cannabis, enough for a smoke, cost only a few pounds; a tablet of LSD only about £4.50; an Ecstasy tablet about £15. Cocaine was a different matter, £100 a gram; you needed about £400 a week to feed a moderate habit.

None of the young people I interviewed admitted to using drugs regularly although several said they smoked cannabis from time to time. I suspect that when I first interviewed one young man he was slightly withdrawn and hazy having had a smoke of cannabis *pour courage* before meeting me. On the other hand, all of them testified to the dominance of the drugs culture. Jacquie put the difference between her and my cultures graphically when she explained to me:

> Maybe when you come here you'll bring this grapes and strawberries for us to eat, for refreshing because we're sitting here talking [it was a hot day and I'd brought some fruit along]. My friend comes out to my house and what we'll have there is a drawer, Rizla [papers for making cigarettes], cigarettes, a lighter and we sit down and smoke. Do you understand what I mean?

The case for legalising the use of soft drugs has influential supporters. The headlines sensationalise their arguments. One in the *Daily Telegraph* shouted in June 1997, "Cannabis Does No Harm Says Stoppard" and in *The Independent* in the same month Polly Toynbee's column was billed, "It's a Waste of Money Being Hard on Soft-Drug Users". In fact, Dr Miriam Stoppard was saying that drug-taking had become so much the norm among the young that it was fruitless for adults to take an authoritarian line against it. Smoking the occasional joint did little harm and people smoked to make themselves feel happy. Polly Toynbee quoted the recent Home Office British Crime Survey which found that nearly half of all young people used drugs at some time and pointed to the devastating effects of harsh punishment for involvement in drugs on young people whose prospects were otherwise promising. Her solution was for the police to concentrate on catching hard-drug users who should then receive intensive treatment for their addiction.

Another pragmatic argument came from Charles Glass in a pre-election series during 1997 in the *New Statesman* of "unorthodox prescriptions for improvements to the state of the nation". He suggested that the only way to put the drugs barons out of business was to license and tax their trade. And in the autumn of 1997 *The Independent on Sunday* launched a campaign to decriminalise the use of cannabis. But is acceptance and tolerance of the *status quo* at any level really a solution? Taking Ecstasy may be endemic now in the current dance/rave scene but fashions about how young people spend their leisure change. Everyone agrees about the appalling effects of hard drugs. My experience of seeing young people who take drugs suggests that the use of soft drugs, too, is detrimental to the development of young people and that the usage of all drugs has to be seen as connected. Some disciplined young people may be able to control their use of drugs but many more, often the most vulnerable, cannot. Education is the key, as Polly Toynbee indicated, but it is no good just concentrating on hard-drug users—in addition to receiving education young people must be diverted to alternative ways to spend their time.

I call to my support in deploring the effects of smoking cannabis Jason, Jaquie and Mark. Jason, at 13 years old, analysed the physical effects thus:

> What's the point of doing cracking? Say the police come and there's a time for you to run: you've been smoking—you'll collapse, especially if you're smoking cannabis. It makes you just high, when you don't know what you're doing . . .

Jaquie confirmed that cannabis prevented her from undertaking purposeful activity. She would not smoke cannabis and then go shop-lifting. It messed up your head, she said. She also revealed her disturbing dependence on its comforts—what kept her going for the day was the thought of it waiting in a drawer at home. Mark said: "I've had loads of friends die from drugs. It's digging a grave."

There is plenty of medical evidence to support the long-term damage the recreational use of cannabis can have, both physical and psychological, but another argument put forward for legalising its use is that alcohol is just as damaging to the human body and mind, if used excessively, and so is tobacco, if used at all. We don't ban them. We let people assess the risks and make their choices as mature adults. So why not let young people smoke pot at 18, just as we let them drink in public houses and smoke?

If the tobacco weed were introduced into this country today rather than in the seventeenth century by Sir Walter Raleigh, no doubt we would prohibit its use as an insidious, deadly poison. But we are not starting from scratch and legislation to ban smoking totally is not yet acceptable, though it is remarkable how easy it has been to ban it on public transport and even in restaurants. Some day soon public opinion may force a government to have the courage to balance the revenue from tobacco taxes with the costs to the National Health Service of tobacco-related disease and ban the sale of tobacco (to the Third World, too). Today the effort has to be educate young people from an early age not to use tobacco by weaning them from the illusion that it is smart, "cool", to smoke.

There is also an argument that alcohol can be seen differently from tobacco and other soft drugs because it is not damaging when taken in moderation and even can be helpful for some medical conditions. But education about the detrimental effects of alcohol is essential so that young people do drink only moderately and in appropriate circumstances.

Where soft drugs are concerned the libertarian arguments for legalisation fall short. I would apply John Stuart Mill:

> The sole end for which mankind are warranted, individually or collectively, in interfering with the liberty of action of any of their number is self-protection.

Too many people's lives are destroyed by drugs for their minority use to be tolerated by the majority. It is another example of the defeatist fallacy to give in and say drugs should be legalised because they are part of the present youth culture and give many young people short-term pleasure.

So what is to be done about drugs? An independent inquiry into Britain's drugs laws has been launched under the auspices of the Police Foundation. The 'Drugs Tsar' appointed by the government may be able to co-ordinate action but he will not be effective without funding. Money is needed firstly to wean from drugs those already addicted and secondly to train teachers of Personal and Social Education. The aim must be to deflect young people from experimenting with them in the first place. There are not enough centres easily accessible in the community to treat those on drugs and there is a dire shortage of centres which will tackle the problem at all for young people under 18, let alone tuned to their special needs. "Druglink" in the London Borough of Hammersmith and Fulham is one agency which tries to contact vulnerable young people who appear in the youth court. A drugs worker in the waiting area gives information about local services and arranges, if appropriate, for confidential advice.

One point about drugs education in schools is that those who take drugs are also likely to smoke and (if they do not belong to a culture like Rastafarianism which forbids alcohol) to drink. Young smokers and drinkers have similar problems about not wanting to stand out from their peers by saying "no". It follows that children and young people should learn about all drugs (from cannabis, amphetamines and Ecstasy to heroin and crack-cocaine), alcohol, tobacco and solvents, together.

A second point is that teaching should be from an early age, structured according to the stage of the children's cognitive and emotional development. Some children start experimenting with solvents at primary school and pushers of cannabis are now known outside primary school gates. Middle-class young people tend to postpone drug-taking till they reach college—maybe they would not have passed their examinations if they had started earlier or maybe parental supervision is stronger for them while they are at home—but the poorest are at risk at a very young age.

Thirdly, as far as drugs, alcohol, solvent abuse and smoking are concerned, it is useless just to give the facts about the dangers. As we have seen, decisions about such choices demand emotional insight and sophisticated social skills. "Emotional Intelligence" is the term recently coined by Daniel Goleman in his best-selling book with that title. He cites among other studies one from Harvard Medical School which pinpoints the emotional difficulties of drug addicts and he argues that the idea of emotional literacy has scientific foundation in the structure of the brain. Goleman believes in the effectiveness of projects which develop emotional understanding and which teach young people how to control their anger and to develop their social skills.

The current trend in drugs education is to concentrate on making sure young people, if they are going to use drugs, know how to use them safely. First, they must make sure they touch only pure products. (Quite how they do this in a necessarily unregulated market I have never understood.) Then they must take only small amounts, in the company of responsible friends who will look after them if they react badly and they must be in a safe place—no sharp edges to fall onto or windows to fall out of. This may be common sense but it gives a double message. By teaching young people how to manage drugs it suggests that drug-taking cannot be stopped—the defeatist fallacy again. It is possible to empower people to make responsible choices against the prevalent trend but only if it is clear that it is not all right to take drugs in any circumstances.

How then does one avoid the authoritarian, thou-shalt-not method which is destined to make teenagers do the opposite to what they are told? Once again, imaginative methods are needed, engaging the emotions and tackling the social pressures. Young people almost need a script to help them react in the situations to which they are exposed. Gloom and doom, threats of death, are unlikely to convince them, as pilot campaigns against teenage drinking by the then Health Education Authority in the 1970s showed. Youth seems eternal and invulnerable when you are 15. Young people are concerned with the here and now. Their hopes and fears are about their relationships, their day-to-day activities—what will happen at college tomorrow or clubbing on Saturday night. The heroine of the comic Gillian Crampton Smith and I published about smoking wouldn't take a cigarette not because she was afraid of cancer but because it would make her breath smell.

The most recent research on the effects of video violence on young offenders already convicted of violent crimes showed that these offenders liked violent films and were more likely to identify with violent characters than non-violent offenders of the same age. Offenders spent significantly more time than non-offenders watching video films but their actions and values were influenced more by the actual violence they had themsleves experienced or witnessed in their homes. The researchers left open the extent to which violent films reinforced their predisposition to violence caused by other factors but noted that, in general, offenders had reached a lower level of moral development. Increasing their ability to empathise with victims as well as aggressors through suitable methods of education might help to counter the pervasive influence of violence throughout our society.

LIFESKILLS IN THE CURRICULUM

The importance of developing emotional understanding alongside giving factual information is now well established. Stories, writing them as well as reading them, are an obvious way to open discussion on sensitive matters. So is drama. Specialist groups like the Geese Theatre Company perform at young offender institutions, as well as in schools and at conferences, to make real the dilemmas of growing up, the temptations of crime and drugs, the need for children and parents to see each others' point of view. Their audiences are directly engaged and participate in the action. Ten years ago, when I was doing research for my first book on juvenile offending, youth justice teams like the one at the Juvenile Offender Resource Centre, Surrey, were already incorporating such methods in their work with both groups and individuals. One book, *Offending Behaviour, Skills and Stratagems for Going Straight,* by James McGuire and Philip Priestley, sometimes described as 'the Bible of Intermediate Treatment', was particularly influential in suggesting imaginative approaches to confronting young people with their offending behaviour.

There have always been two difficulties in introducing this kind of approach in schools. Firstly, where do lifeskills fit in the curriculum— whether you are talking about sex education, education for parenthood, the practicalities of daily life from budgeting to cooking, education about drinking, smoking and drugs or education for citizenship? Where do media studies fit and when do you teach young children to analyse what they see on television, to deconstruct advertisements and to be aware of how they can be manipulated? Secondly, how do you give teachers the confidence and sensitivity to use imaginative approaches in a purposeful way?

Personal and Social Education (PSE) is now a requirement of the National Curriculum for all pupils but for only one teaching period a week. It covers most of the agenda I have sketched, including health education, and so is an essential plank in the programme for preventing young people from falling into offending. To have a foothold in the National Curriculum is a good start but the limited time available underlines the importance of structuring the syllabus well. The syllabus for PSE is proposed by the individual school working under broad headings with its OFSTED inspectors who have a proactive as well as supervisory role. "Spiritual and moral" development, citizenship, cultural and environmental awareness, health issues, sex education, preparation for careers, all these have to be covered. The plan for sex education has to be agreed by the school's governing body after consultation with parents and then approved by the local education authority.

Most of the older boys I met were "into girls", as Josiah put it, and some of them, the twins for example, had steady relationships. A steady relationship usually includes a sexual relationship. It is obviously vital for these boys to understand and use contraception but among the many lessons they will have missed through their erratic schooling are probably those on sex education at a time when it was most relevant to their lives. As I have said, the majority of parents are too embarrassed to discuss sex with their children so what knowledge these boys have about methods of birth control and protection from disease will come from their mates. It will be partial and without the context needed to motivate them to use it. Boys are less likely to pick up informed, sensitive views from other sources because much information is still targeted mainly at girls. Girls are better informed than boys, partly because their mothers may warn them about the risks of pregnancy but mainly because they read more magazines. Teenage magazines have a good record of giving information about contraception and discussing the emotional aspects and responsibilities of relationships.

Tyrrell fathered a child when he was only 16. The mother was a girl he met at the children's home where he was living. He said they had told him about safe sex in the home and condoms were readily available there. However, he did not like using them because "I don't enjoy myself with them". He did not know whether his girlfriend was on the pill or not—that is to say, the possibility of her conceiving a child was probably never discussed. "Children don't worry me," he blithely told me. He claimed he had got two girls pregnant "for an abortion" in two different homes. The relationship with his girlfriend meant a lot to him. She was a good influence on him, wanting him "to get some education" and he wanted to be able "to give my daughter a job some day so she won't steal". He told me, "I've never stolen a car since I've been away from my girlfriend and since she had a baby" and she would never risk stealing again lest the baby would be taken from her. He thought they were close but his girlfriend was ambivalent about her feelings towards him and he was only allowed to visit the baby under supervision of social workers. There seemed to be little hope that the baby would grow up under the roof of both her parents.

A sad and shocking tale. This young man, who had a loving mother but a disturbed upbringing and an unstable father who never took responsibility for him, was "happy" he had a child of his own. What about the child? Tyrrell had no understanding of the needs of that child or any children, except perhaps for their material care. His story shows the necessity for proper sex education (which is about relationships as well as methods of birth control) and for education for parenthood which is about the welfare of children. Pages and pages of newspapers and magazines, hours of time on radio and television, are devoted to discussing the demise of the old-fashioned family with two parents married to each other and 2.2 children. The increase in the number of single parent families, especially of mothers who have never married, is pruriently examined. Many single parents do an excellent job of rearing their children and the problems of others often go back to their poverty rather than their marital status but the basic question at the heart of the matter is usually avoided. Becoming a parent is not a right to be entered on casually: parenthood entails responsibilities from both of those who create life and children need consistent care and familiar people throughout their childhood. It is still argued sometimes that sex education merely encourages children to be sexually active but it is a fact that those areas which have well-publicised birth control clinics which specialise in helping young people also have lower pregnancy rates for teenage girls and fewer girls having under-age sex.

One good local set of OFSTED guidelines I have seen defines Personal and Social Education as being concerned with "qualities and attitudes; knowledge and understanding; abilities and skills in relation to oneself and others; social responsibility and morality". Moral development is to be judged by the extent pupils display "an understanding of the difference between right and wrong; respect for persons, truth and property; a concern for how their actions may affect others; the ability to make responsible judgements on moral issues; moral behaviour". Briefing notes for a training day for teachers who were going to deliver the curriculum listed, alongside the topics to be tackled for each year-group, the strategies and resources to be used. The topic for Year Eight "Decision Making—Who influences you?" had a worksheet series as its resource; the topic "Teenage and Parent Conflict" had "Parents' Sayings"; drama was used in Year Nine in the consideration of prejudice and discrimination and the police were to be called in to talk about 'Goodies and Baddies and Drugs'.

But the notable omission at present from the general guidelines to PSE in the National Curriculum is education for parenthood, particularly serious because education for parenthood at school age is one way to prevent the need for compulsory parenting orders in future. Some schools offer child development courses as an option but it is not a compulsory module. For the reasons I have given, the needs of babies and children (emotional as well as physical) should be a compulsory subject, for boys as well as girls. Until education for parenthood is compulsory, OFSTED inspectors should press for its inclusion in the syllabus as a concomitant of sex education. And Inspectors should also make sure that schools involve parents as much as possible in the PSE programme. As I have shown, schools which treat parents as partners in the education of children do more than just inform parents of the topics that are studied. The need for a combined, complementary approach by school and home is especially important for personal and social education.

Another essential topic for the curriculum which is particularly relevant to the prevention of offending is citizenship—the balance of duties and rights, the workings of the political, economic, social and legal systems and the point of the democratic process. One in four adults failed to vote in the last general election. Of the parents I interviewed, Pat expressed her disillusion with the political climate after 18 years of Conservative government and attributed the lawlessness of young people to a general disregard of community values. The cult of individual success was at the expense of the community, she thought, and individual greed rather than the fruits of prosperity had trickled through from the rich to the poor. It was she who gave me the idea for the sub-title of this book, *Everybody Does It,* when she said "You think everybody does it".

Voluntary organizations like the Citizenship Foundation have led the way in this field. The best methods for teaching young people how to grow up to be active citizens are often in themselves participatory, giving children a voice as well as information. In Richmond-upon-Thames there is a primary pupil parliament consisting of two representatives from each of the participating schools. Twenty-four schools took part in 1996. In 1997 they were joined by a school for children with special needs and two local independent schools. Propositions are put to the members of the parliament to be debated and decided. The parliament has exerted its pressure for more initiatives against bullying and racial harassment, the introduction of first-aid classes and the publication of a booklet about pet care produced with help from the RSPCA.

But whatever the curriculum, the style and ability of the teacher in this field is crucial. I have seen splendid projects developed from the "Thinkstrip" stories which I had not anticipated. I have also seen the comics given to students to read in class and a feeble discussion follow because the teacher was not receptive to the reactions of the young people and could not take further the points that were raised. Sometimes failure is because teachers are not comfortable with or have not thought through their own feelings on the topic. Alternatively, they go too far. They are set in their own opinions and want to tell the students exactly what they should think and do, without letting them come to conclusions themselves. They may be good at conveying factual information but poor at ensuring its relevance is understood and that young people have the social skills to apply it to their own situations. And sometimes they are nervous about using unconventional material. Comics in the classroom?

To be effective, teaching in this field must have clear goals and those who teach must be specially trained. High quality training, both initially and in specialist refresher courses, is the obvious answer but such training is expensive and has had to fight for its share in a school's budget since LMS (Local Management of Schools). A crucial question is who should do the teaching. In the past, especially for sensitive subjects like sex education, it was usual to invite specialists into schools on a sessional basis. There is still a place for visitors in their professional capacities, whether community nurses, police officers—the Metropolitan Police in 1997 had 200 officers whose main job was talking about drugs in secondary schools—politicians or trades and business people, but there are limitations to the role of outsiders. I have argued that making decisions in these areas is a complex operation. Understanding comes slowly and according to the maturity of the students. The FPA in its years of patient work on sex education has always said that sex education was not just a question of demonstrating once how contraceptive equipment works (the plumbing on its own). There must be both continuity and development in the mode and content of teaching and learning.

A welcome trend, therefore, is for training in personal and social education to be delivered by the teachers who have the responsibility for the pastoral care of their students each year. It makes sense for the teachers who have continuing contact with the young people and their families to have this responsibility but it underlines the need for OFSTED inspectors to ensure that they are properly trained and have access to good teaching material. I would go so far as to say it should be compulsory within a given period (say five years) for teachers with such pastoral responsibilities to have obtained a specialist qualification for teaching PSE along the range of topics I have outlined. If they were all properly equipped for their work and the complexity of teaching PSE were fully recognised, much juvenile offending would be prevented and much human misery averted.

Community Matters

One of the central planks of the theory of communitarianism as proposed by Amitai Etzioni is that law and order can be strengthened by increasing a sense of mutual responsibility between citizens. He suggests that a positive approach is likely to be more effective than restricting individual rights or creating a fortress society in which property is preserved by elaborate protection. Although I argue against specific proposals he supports which stigmatise offenders, I believe Etzioni's basic premise, that people must unite to show their commitment to the law, to be right. The social contract is founded on voluntary agreement about what is best for the majority.

Did the concentration on individual success in the Thatcher years erode people's sense of responsibility about others? Pat, Jacquie's mother, said: "There's not like the sharing and caring attitude there was maybe 20 years ago." As reported, she thought it was the new individualistic values rather than prosperity which had trickled down from the rich to the poor. On the other hand right-wing commentators often argue that it is the existence of the welfare state which enables people to shrug off their sense of collective responsibility, in spite of the widespread participation in voluntary work which is a heartening characteristic of life in this country.

During the 1997 election campaign New Labour adopted most of the rhetoric of the Conservatives against crime, especially youth crime, in order to win the confidence of a frightened majority. I believe it is another defeatist fallacy to think that people will always be so frightened of being mugged, raped, robbed or cheated that they will prefer spending money on short-term retribution and defensive measures rather than on plans to attack the underlying causes. The public is psychologically stuck with short-term retribution because the alternatives have not been sufficiently explained or demonstrated. The only solutions people can see are firstly to shut away those criminals who can be caught and secondly to protect themselves in their homes, cars and shopping centres with all possible security measures. But if there really is a universal wish, a 'general will', for a law-abiding, peaceful society, surely then change can be brought about by effective education, publicity and community action against the causes of crime.

SAFER CITIES

Etzioni has set out the plans of the Communitarian Network in the USA showing that "it takes a village to prevent a crime." The Truancy

Free Area in Hanley, Stoke-on-Trent, which I have described in the previous chapter, is only one example of many ventures initiated by communities in this country to tackle social problems which are relevant to offending by young people.

The trouble is that such ventures until now have been piecemeal and often not co-ordinated with similar projects in neighbouring areas. They have been essentially short-term, introduced on a wave of enthusiasm but not embedded in the local systems and with no guarantee of continuing funding. The Blair government has legislated in the Crime and Disorder Act 1998 for local authorities and the police to work in partnership to formulate strategies to reduce crime. Some lessons can be learnt from previous government initiatives.

The Safer Cities programme was set up in 1988 to give a national boost to crime prevention schemes. It ran for seven years in 20 cities or boroughs as part of 'Action for Cities'. In 1996 the Home Office Research and Statistics Department published studies on its impact in reducing the risk of crime and the implications for future partnerships to increase community safety. As every city or town is different and every scheme was different, each with its own co-ordinator, funding and steering committee, results were bound to vary. But some elements emerged as crucial: first, the importance of creating a genuine partnership between all sectors of the population, second, the need for clear goals and stringent evaluation for projects, and third, the need to understand the nature of crime in the particular area.

There was a strong bias in these early schemes for using "situational" rather than "offender-orientated" schemes. It makes sense to improve the lighting on estates and encourage home owners to have proper locks on their doors but such 'situational' measures do not tackle the root problem. Most burglaries are not committed at dead of night; they happen at tea-time when school is out or before midnight. It is foolhardy to leave the front door on the latch or the kitchen window open, but it is just as foolhardy for communities not to ensure that young people have somewhere to go after school where they can do their homework or play sport. In the holidays and evenings they need somewhere safe and attractive where they can enjoy themselves with their friends rather than hang round the streets. But the ultimate shame for a comparatively rich nation like ours is not to be able to guarantee that all young people of school age, however difficult, are in a supervised establishment and learning during school hours. Would Jason have got into trouble again if he had been able to attend full-time the Individual Tuition Centre which he enjoyed and where he was making progress? The pragmatic approach, reducing opportunities for crime, must be combined with a longer-term approach, addressing the reasons why some young people turn to crime, for an effective youth crime prevention strategy.

In the Children Act 1989 there was a provision which put a duty on all local authorities to keep children and young people from offending. The potential of this section was tremendous but its effectiveness was sadly limited by the all-embracing vagueness of its provisions which left it to local authorities to define and finance the work. In 1991 a Juvenile Crime Prevention Strategy Group was formed in the Royal Borough of Kensington and Chelsea to achieve what it could under the aegis of the Children Act. It had no specific funding. The Royal Borough includes not just the leafy residences of Kensington Gardens and Campden Hill but the terraced streets north of fashionable Notting Hill Gate where many languages are spoken and jobs are few.

The impetus to form the group came from the Kensington and Chelsea youth court users' meeting. The court users met quarterly with representatives from all involved in the administration of the courts (magistrates, justices' clerks, the Crown Prosecution Service, defence lawyers, security, the police, youth justice, probation, and education). They found they had no time to discuss long-term strategy like the prevention of youth crime. The new Strategy Group was led by the social services department, with the assistant director in charge of families' and children's services in the chair. The strength of the new group was that it crossed traditional boundaries. It spanned all the relevant local authority agencies (housing as well as social services and education), the police and the magistracy as well as probation and the local youth justice team, and voluntary bodies working in the borough (including Exploring Parenthood) as well as the local youth service. Its first move—and here I must declare an interest as I was the representative of the local youth court magistrates—was exemplary. In 1993 we commissioned Crime Concern, the national independent crime prevention organization, to assess the level of crime committed by and against young people; to assess the effectiveness of existing preventive policies and practice; and to recommend how an approach to prevention might be developed, taking account of financial constraints.

The survey collated previously disparate pieces of information: the type of crimes committed by young people in the borough (mostly theft, burglary and vehicle theft, not much violence); the fact that half of those who committed offences in Kensington lived outside the borough; the cost of their crime (nearly £17 million a year); the incidence of such crime compared with that in neighbouring boroughs; the times when crimes by the young were committed (in the afternoon or evening); the number of persistent young offenders known to the police (by the police definition there were nine) and the measures taken by all the various agencies to reduce the risk of crime. It then identified gaps in different parts of the borough, assessed priorities and suggested which agencies might undertake which tasks. The decision-makers were presented with a number of choices. Should they target resources on a single area or on a single type of offender? Should they tackle immediate or underlying problems?

Of particular interest were the interviews Crime Concern conducted with nearly 1,000 young people aged between nine and 25 who lived in the borough. Of 60 young people who admitted being involved in crime, Crime Concern said 27 saw crime as a way to supplement their incomes, 20 committed crime for recreation or to increase their status with their peers, eleven saw crime as a business or way of life, and two used it for 'self-destructive' motives. On the other hand 90 per cent of the young people thought breaking into homes was a very serious offence.

The group, with council approval, decided to concentrate on a single area identified in the report, the Lancaster West Estate, and developed a two-year action plan in consultation with the residents. The estate was purpose-built in the mid-1970s, with one tower block and 900 properties. It was split into two areas separated by North Kensington Sports Centre, round which a lot of vehicle crime took place. The residents set as priorities the involvement of the young people themselves in tackling community safety and crime prevention and in suggesting what activities should be available to them; the provision of activities for young people and the promotion of play centres based on schools; and attention to the needs of parents, ethnic groups and the pervasive fear of crime. Residents were particularly anxious about the way young people gathered at night in the communal doorways and walkways.

Crime Concern identified gaps in local provision. For example, there was little provision for young people who were out of school, little intensive support for families in crisis and the nursery schools did not follow the kind of curriculum known to prevent later delinquency in children who started life in difficult circumstances. Detailed suggestions were set out for action by various agencies, voluntary as well as statutory, on early years provision, play facilities, the contribution of local schools, facilities for older teenagers, safety devices like improving the CCTV scheme of monitoring buildings by cameras and better facilities in the community for those young people who had offended.

The specific aims agreed for the action plan were to reduce crime on the Lancaster West Estate by 30 per cent, to reduce anti-social behaviour by young people and to reduce the fear of crime among the residents. A co-ordinator was funded for six months to take forward some of the suggestions of people on the estate and to make contact with young people at risk and their parents. Holiday activities were offered to vulnerable children through SCAM, a vocational training project run in the summer by the Metropolitan Police, the Royal Borough's youth and education section and the local social services team, in conjunction with Raleigh International. The social services team also started a 'homeworking' club and the Estate Management Board tackled problems caused by the design of the estate, improving the lighting on walkways and in the garage area. A second post was funded jointly for two years from 1996 by the Estate Management Board and the youth service for a 'detached' youth worker to work with young people aged 14 to 25 and to try to involve them in local groups and activities.

At the mid-point review in 1997 the residents asked for the focus to be changed to younger children, from the age of eleven, and their families. The residents believed that many of the hard core of youths who had caused trouble when the scheme started had moved away from the estate. Their fears were now about young children who were exposed to drugs and who had begun to steal to pay for drugs.

A useful development on the estate was the work of Family Friends, a small organization which trains volunteers to befriend and support families with children at risk. It was started by Sheila Paget in 1994. She says that her work for Barnardo's with boys in care made her see the need for work with families at an early stage to prevent the breakdown of family relationships. In 1998, the charity had a paid co-ordinator and a part-time administrator who supported up to 25 volunteers. The style of the work was reminiscent of Home-Start's but on a smaller scale. The aim was to find and boost a family's strengths, especially mum's; to put the family in touch with community resources; and to enable them to find their own solutions to their problems. The volunteers, nearly all women and over half from ethnic minorities, visited the families with which they were linked once a week for three hours. The children in the family might be of any age.

Sheila Paget says that what gets results is the time devoted by a mature, experienced person who is not judgemental. The volunteers, some recruited by word of mouth, others from *The Guardian* newspaper's page in which voluntary organizations can advertise at low rates, are subject to police checks and given training. They have been particularly successful with refugee families who are bereft of their roots as well as being desperately poor. Funding is from charities and City Challenge grants. Family Friends works closely with the social services team on the Lancaster West Estate but has not sought funding from the borough because of the need for continuity in its work, a guarantee local authorities cannot give.

The Juvenile Crime Prevention Strategy Group had always seen work at the Lancaster West Estate as part of a rolling programme to meet the needs of all the borough. Attempts to get funding from the Millennium Fund failed but in 1997 the Group hoped for more support from the borough after the Audit Commission showed the relevance of such collaborative local ventures in its report *Misspent Youth*. The report recommended that "To provide a local focus, local authority chief executives should consider initiating forums in which all relevant local authority departments and other agencies participate." Kensington and Chelsea was one of 63 per cent of local authorities which already had such a forum with a multi-agency membership and had started work in a high-risk area but its achievements were limited by uncertainty about funding and continuity.

The Crime and Disorder Act 1998 now puts a statutory duty on local authorities and police to develop similar partnerships to prevent crime. Splendid news—but unfortunately the key question remains: will there be the funds to underpin action? The Home Office consultation paper introducing the new framework in September 1997 had three paragraphs on funding. The new strategy, it said, promised to produce substantial savings for local authorities, for example by reducing vandalism. The strategy did not require them to introduce new services but to plan and co-ordinate existing ones with crime prevention in mind. "For these reasons," it concluded, "there will be no additional money from central government to accompany these proposed new duties."

The government's argument is specious. Teachers or teacher aides who staff centres for children after school hours have to be paid. Even where 'situational' measures are prescribed, better street lighting to deter crime means more street lights as well as choosing the best model for this purpose. How can local authorities budget future savings from a current account already strained to its limits? It is excellent in theory that all areas will now have partnerships between the relevant agencies aiming to reduce crime but there is little hope for real change unless a new form of social auditing is introduced and the strict Thatcherite rules on balancing books annually are modified.

A SENSE OF COMMUNITY

The Kingsmead Estate in Hackney, the most deprived borough in London, ranks high on any indicator of urban deprivation. In 1996 a third of the 2,300 residents of the estate were unemployed, double the average rate for Inner London. Nearly half of the residents were from ethnic minorities, children and young people formed a higher than usual proportion of the residents and one in eight households was headed by a lone parent. Until recently the estate had the worst crime rate of police beats in the borough. As a result people did not linger for a chat on the way back from the shops or the doctor's and did not go out in the evenings because they were anxious about leaving their homes unattended. The reputation of the estate was so bad that in 1993 three-quarters of people offered flats there refused them. As a consequence a quarter of the flats were empty and there were many squats.

The turning point for Kingsmead came in 1993. Hackney council's housing department co-operated with the police to take action against a small group of young people who were responsible for a large amount of burglary, robbery, vandalism and intimidation. It also took steps to fill the empty flats by offering them to people regardless of their placing on the waiting list. And it provided advice to a group of residents on setting up a Community Trust for Kingsmead to attract funding for specific projects to improve facilities on the estate "for the youth, single parents and women returners, the elderly citizens and persons with disability." About 25 community development trusts of a similar kind nation-wide belong to the Development Trusts Association.

From its offices in the community hall the Kingsmead Community Trust acts as a link between the residents and local agencies and also develops its own initiatives. A third of the trust's management committee are tenants, the rest high-ranking council officers and representatives of the police, the local drugs prevention team and voluntary organizations. The trust employs a part-time administrator and fund-raiser. In the report on its achievements published in 1996 by NACRO (National Association for the Care and Resettlement of Offenders) the role of the trust in reducing crime is spelt out. Activities for young people not only give them something to engage in other than crime but also enhance their sense of belonging to the community so that they are less likely to want to harm other members of that community. (When Jason said, " I won't shit on my own doorstep," he was afraid of getting caught. He wanted it to be "nice and normal" where he lived.)

The estate in 1997 had a general advice centre with a full-time worker and two part-time workers as well as volunteers; a junior youth club for eight to 13-year-olds in the refurbished community hall; and a senior youth club for 14 to 25-year-olds which had sessions two nights a week at a nearby youth club. The senior club has been successful in attracting many of the most disaffected young people who live on the estate, with about 40 attending each session. There was a part-time worker concentrating on drugs prevention education with younger children and the local primary school had a play centre staffed by the council which was open four nights a week until 6.30 p.m.

The Kingsmead Estate still faced daunting problems of poverty. The community trust had provided the impetus for local advice and advocacy, and for improved leisure facilities for young people. Its focus changed to increasing opportunities for employment. It was creating links with local employers, starting a garage project for young mechanics—it was a pity the twins I interviewed did not live there—and setting up workshops for small businesses to recycle furniture and make jewellery. These were long-term projects but the trust's results in preventing crime were already impressive. One measure of them was the better reputation the estate enjoyed. The police felt confident to patrol all corners of the estate and residents to walk without fear. There were 139 domestic burglaries on the estate in 1992 and 24 offences of robbery. From August 1995 to January 1996 there were 20 burglaries and only one case of robbery.

Co-ordinated, concerted interventions can make a difference. The Kingsmead model could obviously be replicated in many other urban areas according to local needs. There has until now been too little central encouragement for such initiatives in local community safety and crime prevention plans. As a result the wheel, or in this case the project, is constantly being reinvented. With the Crime and Disorder Act 1998 all local councils will set and monitor targets for the reduction of crime in their areas. There will be big savings of public funds in the long run but, as I have said, new money will be needed to initiate the crime prevention plans now.

How does "zero-tolerance" policing fit into the government's new framework for local action about youth crime? Progress at Kingsmead could only begin when police had taken action against a delinquent group on the estate. Operation Bumblebee against burglars by the Metropolitan Police in London has reduced the number of domestic burglaries. However, that kind of action is against known offenders. Zero-tolerance as practised in New York by William Bratton when he was police commissioner and now advocated in parts of Britain is different. It entails not just stopping criminals in the act of committing a new offence but stopping, searching and questioning citizens who may be going about their lawful business: only eleven to 12 per cent of those stopped are arrested. Certain groups, black people and young people, feel they are unfairly targeted: one in five people stopped are from ethnic minorities who form only one in 20 of the population. If Mark, Josiah and other young offenders I interviewed felt harassed by the police, how much more resentful are others with no criminal record?

The Tottenham experiment in London during 1995-96 showed that there was disquiet locally about stopping and searching procedures even when those stopped were given a leaflet explaining police powers and their rights as individuals. Stopping and searching people unless there are grounds to suspect them is a crude and wasteful way to use police resources to prevent crime, less effective than the admirable work the police undertake as partners in community projects. As Amitai Etzioni says, "to mobilise communities to censure crime strongly, they must be treated as true partners with the police."

HOLIDAY CAMPS AND BEFRIENDING

"I am always surprised," says Mary Aldred, co-ordinator of Tower Hamlets Safeline Befriending Scheme in East London,

> after seeing a 'young offender' on paper and knowing not much more about them than the offences they've committed, how young and vulnerable they are when you meet them face to face. There is no 'mad, bad, threatening and evil tearaway' in front of you but an ordinary teenager, with the same hopes, dreams and fears as any other schoolboy. What is different is their experience of life so far . . .

Her words could apply to any of the young people I interviewed. Take Tyrrell who stole and drove cars in a way that endangered the lives of others and had committed many crimes along the line. His dream, to own a garage, is that of many teenage boys and he, too, wanted his dream girl and his own family. As for his life so far, have many teenagers had their favourite uncle murdered, lived in as many homes as he or fathered and lost a child at 16?

Tower Hamlets Safeline Befriending Scheme is one of the projects initiated by Toynbee Hall to divert children from crime. Volunteers are trained and matched for six months to vulnerable young people. They have to be both enthusiastic and available. They have to devote their time, their energies and their knowledge. They have to arrange frequent meetings, to tolerate being stood up by those they have arranged to meet, to report back and always to be reliable, consistent and accountable. They befriend young people who are in trouble with the police, often when they are cautioned, sometimes before that. When a befriended young person successfully completes the scheme the benefits go directly back into the community as well as to the young person. Family, friends, teachers and local residents all will gain.

All of the Toynbee projects are examples of community projects, employing a small core of professional, co-ordinating staff but depending on volunteers, over 300 every year, and working closely with other voluntary agencies, the statutory services and the police. Stepney Children's Fund is another Toynbee Hall project for children in East London. As well as offering support and guidance to children and families in the borough of Tower Hamlets, it runs summer camps for children with emotional, behavioural, learning and other difficulties. These are the kind of holidays which for years have been condemned in the tabloids as rewards for wrong-doers. Why should Darren, who smashed the windows of the corner-shop, go rafting in Wales, when Leroy in the same class, who keeps his head down and studies for his exams, does not have a summer holiday? Pat, Jacquie's perceptive mother, reflected this view when she said about her daughter's driving lessons, "I'm pleased for her getting an opportunity but it doesn't seem fair really . . . "

The justification lies in the results. "Burglar jailed despite safari trip therapy," protests the headline in a reputable newspaper but the overall evidence shows that young people who are disruptive at home and whose potential for trouble is growing learn practical and social skills on such trips. They receive individual attention, they are challenged to change and on the whole they enjoy it. Their awareness of the needs of others grows with their increasing self-esteem.

The organizers of the Stepney summer camps do an annual survey of the views of the young people who attend. Some of their opinions make dismal reading. Asked what do you think of the police, they show almost universal distrust. In one group of 30, seven described the police *tout court* as "wankers", six as "bastards", five as "cunts", five as "racist", three as "bullies", two as "shits"—a good spread of the vocabulary of opprobrium. It was left to a girl of 14 to venture, "They are OK and can help you in a crash or accident" and one other person commented, "Do their job". Magistrates were perceived as "rich geezers", "gits" or "posh"; significantly one reply said "My Mum hates them"; sadly two said, "They don't understand" and one, "They work for the police." Seven said, "Don't know any" but four said, "Have to do the job to protect people".

Asked what crimes they would not commit there was a general taboo on arson, murder, rape, sexual assault and hard drugs. There was a disturbing lack of sympathy shown by this group towards the victims of crime. "Tough", said one, "it's every man for himself. Lock it up if you don't want it nicked." "Sorry for some but not shop people and factories people. They're rich," was another view. Only one older girl said she felt "guilty about them" and the general consensus was, "Never really think about it". But most revealing were the comments on why they thought young people committed crime. Boredom came out top, followed by "Need dosh for drugs, tapes and trainers. Sometimes food", and "To get money and to have a laugh".

There was no survey at the end of the camp to see if their views had shifted but signs of hope showed in their reactions to the camp itself.

All of the young people in the survey I saw said they would like to come back another year. They complained a little about the chores they had to share but thought the activities were "good fun" and were proud of the certificates for the skills they mastered which were added to their school National Record of Achievement. The organizers aim to enable them to qualify for awards at the camp and back in London through the Duke of Edinburgh's Award, Guide and Scout Association awards and the Stepney Children's Fund's own Young Leader and Skills Instructor qualifications, which range from qualifications as a first-aider to those for an assistant chef. Whatever they do is intended to develop co-operation between children and between children and adults, and to improve day-to-day behaviour, including the foul language and verbal abuse which is almost a natural part of some children's social intercourse.

If the work of Toynbee Hall and other similar organizations is so successful, even with the kind of children who are generally seen as too difficult to handle, is there any cause for concern? Why can't they continue their good works in partnership with the statutory authorities who can identify children to take part? The first cause for concern is the one I have already indicated about pre-school education and provision for families: it is patchy, a matter of luck if you live in an area where there is such voluntary support. Secondly, there is the question of whether voluntary organizations should be providing well-tested facilities like adventure camps rather than trying new ideas which they are well placed to pilot. Thirdly, the need is far greater than the voluntary sector can manage. To quote the 1997 fund-raising appeal by Bob Le Vaillant, down-to-earth director of Stepney Children's Fund,

We see a growing number of families falling beneath the various safety nets. We see diminishing statutory and other cushioning resources, mounting debts and hopeless relationships each inflicting impossible burdens on struggling parents some of whom are little more than 'children' themselves. We see increasing violence within and outside the family and we see too many bright but disillusioned young men and women being attracted by what is worst rather than best in today's society.

INCLUDING BUSINESS

The old stereotype of the aims of business was simple: the aim of a company was to make money. Who for? The owners and shareholders were the obvious answer but there have always been pioneers and idealists who have added other candidates or stakeholders—the employees, the suppliers and the community as a whole. The arguments for including workers in profits and planning are hard-headed as well as idealistic: participation can improve productivity and enhance loyalty. In an age when the nature of work is changing fast, when trade is global rather than local, when more and more people are becoming self-employed and the barriers between employers and employed have shifted, the mission of companies increasingly includes the creation of wealth for the whole community of which they are part—and not just by paying taxes.

The Centre for Tomorrow's Company, which was set up in 1996 after an RSA inquiry into the role and responsibilities of business, has suggested that companies in their annual reports, alongside the detailed description of what they have achieved for shareholders, employees, associates in the supply chain and customers, should explain the value they have created for the community. For example, they could show the costs and benefits of improvements to their work experience schemes for young people. They could measure the costs and benefits of helping to tackle local traffic problems or reducing pollution of the environment. It is also possible to show how many employees have gained strength and experience by working in the community. Social auditing of this kind would add a welcome new dimension to the bottom line.

Most voluntary organizations now look to local businesses and the charitable trusts of companies for funding. Partnerships between statutory services and local business are becoming more frequent— Raleigh International helped the youth and education section of Kensington and Chelsea in London with its summer holiday activities scheme, the Kingsmead Community Trust in Hackney is involving local business, the public as well as private sector, in its plans. But business involvement can go further than providing money. It can mean businesses seconding people for a fixed period to do a specific job or encouraging employees to take part in local initiatives as volunteers.

The London borough of Hammersmith and Fulham has cultivated links with local businesses for over 30 years. Anyone who drives from central London to Heathrow airport across the Hammersmith fly-over and then along the raised section of the M4 motorway will realise that in Hammersmith resident local businesses often have international names. Businesses which have provided partnership support to education include Seagram, General Electric, United International Pictures and Coca-Cola as well as the Midland Bank, Habitat, Marks & Spencer and other chain stores. Their Education and Business Partnership aims "to help young people prepare for the world of work, realise their full potential and help ensure the economic well being of the community".

All secondary schools and most special schools for those with learning difficulties offer work experience through the partnership, visits to firms and careers fairs. Teachers have placements for three to five days to learn about opportunities available to their students. Half the schools in the borough used to participate in Compact, a national initiative through which local employers set goals with students for their attendance at school, their punctuality, and completion of course work and work experience. A number of primary schools have taken part in science, technology and art curriculum projects. In addition some firms encourage their staff to become "mentors" to individual students, meeting them regularly to support their progress and help them achieve agreed goals.

Marks & Spencer is well known for its interest in participating in community affairs. In 1996 a link was forged between the local branch and two Hammersmith secondary schools. The M & S representative spent time in the school to see what it was like and in what ways there might be scope for M & S personnel to contribute. Similarly the school's representative spent time with the store. The schools had a named link person who could quickly set up a project, whether to send a speaker to the school to give advice on careers or to organize end-of-term work experience for senior girls to shadow senior managers at M & S head office.

Another Hammersmith school has a small mentoring scheme through which students who—for whatever reason—are thought not to be achieving their potential are paired with volunteers, primarily from the BBC (whose White City studios are in the borough) but also from other local companies. They meet the students regularly for a year, help them to find constructive activities, offer them a listening ear and generally widen their horizons and raise their aspirations. These are the kind of young people who are at risk of being drawn into offending so in the wider sense this scheme contributes to youth crime prevention. There were plans for three more such schemes for 1998-99.

In 1997 Lorraine Lawson, the borough's education and industry officer who administered the partnership, had 1,850 employers on her books, small ones as well as the giants. Her aim since she took up her post in 1990 has been to embed into the systems of the companies with which she works a tradition of practical partnership with local schools. At the beginning there was much goodwill but it was often dependent on the motivation of individuals. A senior executive might have a personal commitment to community service or in the case of American companies have experienced community action by businesses at home. The problem was that if he or she were posted elsewhere, the scheme might not be renewed. The experience of the Hammersmith Business and Education Partnership demonstrates how important it is for the commitment of business to be long-term and not dependent on the interest of individuals.

The dilemma for volunteers in increasingly competitive organizations is how to ensure that the time they spend on outside commitments is valued by the company and by colleagues. Even companies which give formal permission for approved public service may prefer to promote a member of staff who does not take days off for worthy activities. (Any JP will tell of the frustration felt when colleagues infer that the minimum 26 days a year spent in court are some kind of holiday. Benches should be balanced with magistrates coming from all walks of life but the Lord Chancellor's Advisory Committees find it easier to recruit the self-employed than those with careers to nurture in organizations.)

The commitment by the volunteer for schemes like mentoring has to be for a regular slot for a fixed period. An executive who may have to fly to Dubai at a moment's notice, however well motivated, will not be able to sustain regular meetings on set days with the young person he or she is befriending. The most vulnerable young people need regularity in their meetings to sustain the momentum of the relationship and they should never be let down because they have been let down too often previously in their lives. Consistency is one of the qualities mentors offer.

Approval for volunteering and joining projects in the community has to be part of the culture of the company, its benefits listed in the company report. And partnership has to be based on knowledge by each side of each other's needs and working conditions. Thus Seagram has a social investment programme with the goal of providing opportunities and expanding horizons for young people in all of Greater London but primarily in Hammersmith and Fulham. Projects it has developed include a Summer Challenge programme for eleven to 18-year-olds, a Youth Information Programme which gives counselling, advice and confidential support to young people aged 16 to 25 and Adopt a Primary through which Seagram volunteers run an IT club for pupils in a local primary school.

Hammersmith must be almost unique in the number of big companies i t can work with but Lorraine Lawson thinks that small companies can also offer much to schools. They may not be able to second staff in working hours on a regular basis but they can offer work experience and contribute to group meetings about careers. Businesses of all kinds can help to foster the sense of mutual responsibility that can prevent crime.

At the moment it is left to organizations like Training and Enterprise Councils (TECs) or the Centre for Tomorrow's Company to raise awareness in business and industry of their responsibilities to the community in which they operate. It would make sense for the government to encourage and reward good corporate citizenship by giving tax incentives for good governance and attention to social as well as environmental issues. It goes without saying that business should be a partner in local authority strategies for crime prevention of the kind planned by the Blair Government and suggested in the Audit Commission's *Misspent Youth*.

MENTORING FOR YOUNG OFFENDERS

When the *Daily Telegraph* in August 1997 first reported that the Prime Minister's policy unit was planning to set up a network of adult mentors to advise teenagers on careers, relationships, and problems such as drugs, it quoted Francis Maude, the shadow Culture Secretary, as saying, "Teenagers already have mentors—called parents. Young people are better off getting guidance from their mothers than from one of Mandleson's mentors." Maude's response was a sound-byte, typical of opposition for opposition's sake. To suggest that parents are the only guiding influence on young people in any society is nonsense. They should be the main influence, yes, but what about the much vaunted extended family and what about teachers? And what about those young people whose parents, for whatever reason, do not give adequate guidance?

The value of having an outside "reference figure" is surely not a matter for controversy. It is useful for teenagers to be able to call on someone not enmeshed in the family relationships, with different skills and with a different perspective. Every family has limitations and most welcome support from sympathetic outsiders with a clear brief. Women and men are equally effective as mentors but single parents may appreciate the opportunity for their children to have a suitable mentor of the opposite sex.

What evidence is there that mentoring is effective? The United States has about 15 million young people who are thought to be at risk, "children from families that are poor and often dysfunctional". It is calculated that about half overcome the odds stacked against them and lead productive lives but a young person who falls by the wayside can cost society a million dollars over a lifetime of jail and welfare. A three-year study about the prestigious Big Brothers/Big Sisters mentoring program for ten to 16-year-olds in eight cities found on drugs education alone that those in the program were 46 per cent less likely to start using drugs. The efforts of the mentors were especially successful with African-American youths who were 70 per cent less likely to start using drugs.

An umbrella group launched in the USA in 1997, "America's Promise: the Alliance for Youth", has a target for the US of a million mentors by the year 2000, using business in partnership with voluntary organizations. Poor co-ordination was blamed for the fact that there were then only 100,000 mentors in Big Brothers/Big Sisters. The basic idea of putting vulnerable young people in touch with individual mentors may be extended to creating links with friendly families, in the way some local authority social services departments in the UK find "foster uncles and aunts" and "foster grandparents" for children they look after.

The impetus for mentoring schemes for youth at risk in the UK accelerated rapidly in the 1990s, with the voluntary sector at the fore, anticipating government approval which came with the Crime and Disorder Act 1998. The Act gave the Youth Justice Board it created responsibility for encouraging and monitoring preventive schemes. One of the schemes which had impressed government was the Dalston Youth Project in East London, an independent branch of Crime Concern, set up in 1993. This mentoring project is designed not just for offenders but for any young people aged 15 and over who have been excluded from school and children aged eleven to 14 who are failing at school.

Participation is voluntary. Indeed, there is no experience to indicate what will be the effect of ordering young offenders to participate in mentoring schemes, as has been suggested as a possibility under the pilot schemes for the Crime and Disorder Act's final warning schemes (to be administered by the police) and the action plan orders (to be made by youth courts). I would argue against compelling attendance, on the same grounds that I believe short-term compulsory parenting orders will have less effect than the voluntary engagement of parents in schemes to help them over a longer period.

Of the 30 young people who had mentors in the Dalston scheme in 1996, 73 per cent found full-time jobs or returned to full-time education and there was a 61 per cent fall in the number of arrests of group members. Seventy per cent of the young people were of African-

Caribbean origin and so were 85 per cent of the mentors—which confounds Jeremiahs who say it is impossible to find sufficient volunteers in the black community to act as role models to black young people. The mentors ranged from professional people, to women at home, to students and included some former offenders.

A central feature of the Dalston scheme is a residential week at the beginning for mentors and their charges to get to know each other and to 'bond', and for the goals of the year to be explained and individually set. It is a pity that the expense of a residential start is prohibitive to many who are trying to introduce mentoring schemes. In truth, none of the other excellent features of the Dalston scheme—the 'taster' courses provided at the local community college or the opportunities for pre-employment training—comes cheap. Effective mentoring like most other interventions is only cheap when compared with the alternative of doing nothing and allowing youth crime to escalate. It costs about £3,000 for each person on the scheme for a year, less than it costs to keep a young person in a secure unit for a week.

Before the 1998 Act there had been a spontaneous increase in the number of mentoring schemes concentrating specifically on the prevention of offending by young people. DIVERT—the national charity for the prevention of youth crime which succeeded the National Fund for Intermediate Treatment (the IT Fund)—created a post of London Mentoring Development Officer in 1997 to promote and support mentoring initiatives in Greater London. In a West London area which already had mentoring schemes in schools, Hammersmith and Fulham Partnership against Crime (HAFPAC), a forum for crime prevention representing local businesses, the council and police, provided 'start-up' funding for a pilot mentoring scheme for young offenders aged 14 to 18.

This new scheme had clear aims. It was designed to reach the most vulnerable young offenders as soon as they began offending, at a stage when they had been cautioned by the police or had appeared in court for the first time. Priority was given to young people looked after by the local authority or leaving its care, those who were temporarily or permanently excluded from school and those who were habitual truants. Thus the scheme hoped to intervene early in the delinquent careers of the kind of teenagers who were known to be most at risk of continuing offending, who had been caught by the criminal justice system but who had not received any compulsory measures of supervision or any formal help to change their behaviour. The project aimed to match them with mentors who in the course of a year would divert them from offending by offering them advice and company, and by helping them gain access to alternative activities, from education, training and employment opportunities to sport, leisure and social events. In addition to meeting their mentors each week, the young people could attend workshops for developing skills in IT (computer training), photography and sport (training sessions at Queen's Park Rangers Football Club, an obviously popular option). Other workshops, for cookery and drama, for example, were being planned.

The scheme offered regular training, support and expenses to volunteers who could commit themselves to meet a young person at least once a week for a year. The co-ordinator of the scheme was based with the local youth justice team. The youth justice workers, with probation, the police and others working with young people, identified possible participants or young people could refer themselves (as nearly a third of the first year's intake did). Joining the scheme was voluntary. The young people chose to belong. Mentoring was seen an opportunity, not a punishment, but it was recognised from the beginning that the voluntary nature of the scheme did not remove the difficulty of retaining the interest and involvement of the young people. Skill and patience would be needed to build a trusting relationship and gradually help the young people to change their lives.

The weakness of the scheme's structure, and that of other similar ventures, lay not in the proposals for the scheme itself, the recruitment and training of the mentors or the identification of activities for the young people, but in the short-term nature of its initial funding, £35,000 for its first 18 months. Its future was dependent on hand-to-mouth fund-raising. Its budget was not sufficient to buy an external evaluation which would attract outside funding most easily. However, as rigorous an internal evaluation as possible was planned. Eighteen months was a short duration for measuring the key outcome of whether the young people continued offending or modified their anti-social activities, returning to mainstream education and pursuits. It is a tribute to the hard work of all involved in this scheme that by June 1998, when the scheme had been running 16 months, it had attracted further funding and was set to continue.

What kind of people decide to become mentors of alienated young offenders? They make a considerable commitment of their time and are not paid for their contribution so what is there in it for them? The first 23 mentors to be approved on the Hammersmith and Fulham scheme were aged between 21 and 49; nine were men, 14 women; nine classified themselves as white, ten black, and one mixed race; one as Portuguese, one Mauritian. Some worked full-time, others part-time, others were unemployed or students.

Two of the three initial mentors I talked to just before they were matched with young people had been drawn to the scheme because they had known young people who had been in trouble with the law and felt they had helped them. Both had done voluntary work before. The third had himself offended as a teenager and thought he had the empathy to be an effective influence on a young person. "There's always a way you can achieve something," he said. "I'll tell them knowledge is empowerment. Pursue something to give yourself skills." This was a formula that had worked for him. His parents were both nurses, born overseas. After his delinquent spell he had returned to education, taken a degree in anthropology and then worked as a care assistant in mental health. He wanted to train for youth justice work and saw mentoring as experience which would help to qualify him.

In the first months of the scheme, from August 1997 when the matching process began to June 1998, 26 young people had taken part in the project and a further nine had been referred but decided not to join. Eleven classified themselves as white British, one Irish, five black, five mixed race and one Chinese. The majority were aged 15 or 14 on referral. Of those in the scheme in June 1998, four were accommodated by the local authority. Two of the 26 were attending college; the rest did not go to school, eight being temporarily excluded, eight permanently excluded and eight being habitual truants.

What effect has the mentoring scheme had so far on the lives of these young people who through their law-breaking, missed education and family circumstances met the project's criteria as being particularly at risk? By June 1998 it had been possible to find full-time work for two young people and part-time work for four. Another four were attending a mechanics course one day a week, a good start for them which had sometimes been difficult to negotiate with the schools they were meant to be attending. Permission to attend courses in school hours has to be obtained for young people who are still on school rolls. The attitude of schools towards pupils who are suspended or truanting is that they should start attending their own schools normally before the question of their attending outside courses can be addressed. This view of priorities is not helpful for young people who are habitual truants or have been excluded from school because of long-standing problems.

Of the 26 young people who had enrolled on the scheme from the beginning, seven had drifted away. They may have been initially attracted to the activities the scheme offered but then found it difficult to make a regular commitment to meet their mentor and to agree goals. Some of them had not reoffended. But was the Hammersmith and Fulham scheme diverting from crime those who met their mentors regularly and took part in the activities offered? Nine had been in contact with the police while on the scheme but for most the frequency of their offending had been greatly reduced and the type of offence had not become more serious. One boy's offending had escalated because of his dependence on crack cocaine which there had not been time to address and another began reoffending when there was trouble in his family. It is easier to analyse factors determining or precipitating offending than to eliminate them over a short period.

It would be misleading to see mentoring as a panacea. A supportive relationship for a year with an older person is not a substitute for stable, life-long family relationships through which more fortunate children learn how to live with others as adults. Re-integrating young people into education in their teens is not a substitute for ensuring that they benefit from learning throughout their early years. But mentors can extend young people's horizons and ease them into new opportunities; and mentoring can help when children have to live away from their families or when family relationships are poor. In many areas members of the community and people in business are beginning to see the part they can play.

The perennial question of securing long-term funding for proven community ventures cannot be evaded. Even the Dalston Youth Project was in 1997 funded mainly by private trusts (59 per cent), with contributions from City Challenge (15 per cent), Hackney Social Services and Education Departments (23 per cent), and the Inner London Probation Service (2 per cent). Its programme for eleven to 14-year-olds was initially funded for only three years by the Home Office. This pioneering project's future, like that of so many others, depends on a precarious combination of resources. Successful projects of all kinds, as long as they are rigorously evaluated, deserve the guarantee of a tomorrow in order to thrive today.

Part Three

Dealing With Young Offenders

Politicians agree in theory that the only way to prevent juvenile offending for the future is to tackle the causes of crime but they are convinced that the public will not support money being spent on preventive measures unless satisfied that "something is being done" about young offenders who threaten the peace now. It is also clear that children who have broken the law need to master alternative ways of living and behaving, for their own sakes as well as for the sake of others.

So what happens to children who break the law? On an average day there may be 50 cases on the morning list of an inner city youth court. I have seen lists of over 70 in Inner London. In such populous areas youth courts usually sit for a full day each week and may take trials in contested cases on a second day. Some of the young people will feature in more than one case, some of them may not arrive, some cases may be listed in error but if there are 50 cases to be heard between 10 a.m., when the court session begins, and 1 p.m., when the court staff need to take a break before the separate afternoon list, that leaves less than five minutes for each case.

What is the experience like for young people of appearing in court? When they enter for the first time they must feel like actors with a walk-on role in a vaguely familiar drama. They will recognise the setting from television. The magistrates in youth courts do not sit on a platform or wear wigs and robes like judges, there are often no police present and the young people are not in the dock. In West London, for example, they now sit behind a table in front of the magistrates, next to a parent or social worker and their lawyer if they have one. Yet the place is clearly a court of law. The young people usually see, sitting behind another big desk beneath a coat of arms on the wall, three middle-aged, middle-class representatives of middle England— despite the efforts of the Lord Chancellor's Advisory Committees up and down the country to recruit magistrates from a wide spectrum of society, including more people from ethnic minorities.

Some of the dialogue in court—"Do you plead guilty or not guilty?"—is part of a script they know but much of the rest that happens in their short appearance on stage will not be clear unless it is carefully explained by the court chairman or the court clerk. The whole episode is so fleeting that it hardly gives young people time to take in their surroundings let alone what is said. But the most blatant deficiency of the present system is that they hardly contribute themselves to the proceedings. Their roles are usually non-speaking except to give their name, address, age and eventually to plead guilty or not-guilty.

This passive role is partly caused by the presence in most cases of lawyers who speak for them and effectively prevent most direct communication between them and the bench. There are good reasons why young people should have legal representation when they appear in court. The law is complex so they may not understand whether or not they have broken it. "I was only the look-out," "It wasn't me that hit her," is not a defence against joint enterprise, as Luke (p.84) learnt to his cost. Youth court defendants are by definition immature. They may not be able to identify, let alone marshall, all the points for their defence or see the difference between accepting facts and explaining any mitigating circumstances. For as many young people who are street-wise about the system, using every trick to put off the evil day of a decision on their case, there are as many who even with their parents' support have no real understanding of how the system works.

There are also those of limited intelligence whose *mens rea,* intention or sense of responsibility, is questionable. The Crime and Disorder Act 1998 removed the requirement for it to be proved that children aged ten to 14 know that their actions are seriously wrong, the *doli incapax* provision. Younger children now need even more than they did before the help of a skilled professional, who is both well-informed on the current state of the law and good at communicating complex matters simply, to explain to them what is happening and to mitigate for them.

On balance I believe that lawyers have a place in youth courts as the courts are now constituted but they should be specialists who appreciate the demands of this work. There are some excellent firms of solicitors who regularly take these unremunerative briefs but all too often youth court cases, especially when a barrister is brought in, are given to the most junior member of the chambers who is longing to be off to higher places and uses forensic cross-examination, as if in the Crown Court with a jury to sway and an audience in the gallery. Lawyers are in court to do their best for their clients but where young people are concerned it is not helpful to encourage them to persist innocence in cases where the evidence is stacked against them, to prolong the agony with an unnecessary trial or to use technical loop-holes to abort proceedings.

Joshua, Luke's father, was sure that his son's lawyer should have advised him to plead guilty. The Audit Commission in *Misspent Youth* commented on the increase in the number of "not-guilty" pleas in youth courts entailing expensive trials. "The legal aid fee structure," it said, "introduced in 1993, which pays lawyers more if their clients plead not guilty, may contribute to the problem." (On the other hand, lawyers may have previously avoided trials in cases which required them because they were not paid enough.) It is customary for lawyers who appear in the family proceedings court to be members of the Law Society's Child Care Panel. They are trained and examined in child care law and communication skills. There should be a similar panel for those who appear in the youth courts.

A degree of formality is helpful in a youth court, not least in lowering the emotional temperature, but the proceedings must be understood by those who are, after all, at the centre of the drama. We are told a lot about young offenders cocking a snook at the courts, laughing with scorn rather than relief as they leave. Sometimes bravado is a symptom of nervousness; so is fidgeting and yawning. Middle-class children are taught to look adults in the eye when they are addressed. In some cultures it is rude for children to do this and it is a sign of shame to look away. The evidence from the little research there is shows that what young people feel in court is not scorn or fear but boredom and incomprehension. Even under the Scottish system, where young offenders appear with their parents before a panel which discusses future action with them and their parents, young people often emerge as confused about what is said and why, though less bewildered than young people in youth courts in England and Wales.

Everyone in court, from the magistrate in the chair to the clerk, to the Crown prosecutor, to the lawyers, should speak plainly enough for the defendant and the parents to grasp what is happening. And the magistrate in the chair should ask if everything is clear to them and, as appropriate, for their response to what has been decided. Sometimes parents of those under 17 must wonder why the law insists that they attend since their presence is virtually ignored. It does not delay matters unduly to interpret anything complicated and to ensure there is a dialogue at suitable points. Too often young people and their parents are talked over as if they were invisible and dumb.

DELAYS

Another failing of the youth courts at present is the long time most defendants have to wait before their case is called. The day's list in some areas is organized so that those making a first appearance are seen early and those coming for sentencing after reports from social services, probation or the new youth offending teams are seen later in the morning or in the afternoon, with trials of contested cases in the afternoons or on a separate day. However, the administrators in most areas are reluctant to try a full appointments system partly because it is impossible to forecast how long individual cases will take and partly because of the poor time-keeping of most defendants.

They may all be bailed to be at court by 9.45 a.m. but they find it difficult to get up in the morning, let alone catch a bus in time. Their lawyers may have more than one brief on the same day and so may be dodging in and out of court. If they have no lawyer but want to see the duty solicitor, he or she may have a queue of clients. But if they do happen to be punctual, waiting around all morning does nothing to enhance for them the authority of the courts. It should be possible to cut the waiting by assigning cases to hourly bands, as is done already in some court areas and in many outpatients' departments at hospitals. This would also help parents who should be present but who have difficulty taking time off work or finding minders for younger children.

The Audit Commission in *Misspent Youth* made a damning indictment of the length of time it took for a case to be completed in the youth court. The whole process from arrest to sentence took on average 70 days in some areas to 170 in others. Jack Straw, as Home Secretary, was right to see such delays as unacceptable and to introduce stricter time limits between arrest and first appearance in court and between conviction and sentence.

It obviously takes time to collect all the information necessary for a pre-sentence report (PSR) which youth court magistrates need to make decisions in cases serious enough for a penalty which limits a young person's freedom by a punishment in the community or by custody. The youth justice or youth offending teams who prepare PSRs must see parents or carers as well as the young person and verify the young person's position as regards education, training or employment. They must collect enough information to give a view about how much risk there is of that young person reoffending. They must then put forward possible programmes for the young offender, according to his or her needs and the availability of local services. The younger and less mature the offenders, the more important it is for their circumstances to be reviewed and for action to be taken quickly.

The Audit Commission analysed 200 youth court appearances and found that 79 per cent were adjourned. On average a young person appeared four times in the course of one case. Some of the reasons for these adjournments were unavoidable. Pleas of not-guilty (entailing a trial when witnesses can be present) or calls for reports about the defendants made up 12 per cent of the cases. But the administrative failures which cause so many other adjournments must be ended. It is absurd for cases to have to be adjourned because the Crown Prosecution

Service has not got the file from the police or from its own office; it is wrong for the defence lawyer not to be present or not to have been briefed (as in 15 per cent of the cases) and for papers giving the details about the case not to have been sent immediately to the defence (eleven per cent); legal aid should be sorted out in time and young offender institutions should not be so understaffed that they cannot produce in court any young people they are holding.

The Audit Commission helpfully suggested that youth court user groups should set targets for speeding the process to an average of 80 days from arrest to sentence and that there should be reviews before trials to check that all the participants will be ready on the day set so that the trial is not adjourned at great expense and inconvenience to all. In areas where systems to decrease delay are being tried out, the problem remains of inadequate resources. There are often too few people to do the work and too few modern machines to help them, from the police stations to the offices of the Crown Prosecution Service to the court buildings.

Some caution is advisable on the proposals for a fast-track system for persistent young offenders, defined as those who have been sentenced on three or more separate occasions and arrested again within three years of the third conviction. Young offenders often go on a spree of almost simultaneous offences which are tried as separate cases. Sometimes an offender who is beginning to change his or her behaviour will nevertheless get involved in trouble, perhaps of a less serious nature than previously. I am hesitant about the principle of labelling some young people as "persistent offenders" and possibly confirming for them as well as others the idea that they are criminals. It is the system as a whole that should and could be quicker.

Under the Crime and Disorder Act 1998 for the first time stipendiary magistrates are allowed to sit alone in youth courts. Stipendiary magistrates are experienced barristers or solicitors appointed to preside in magistrates' courts. They are often perceived by the public to be judges, a fair enough conclusion as they are paid professionals exercising the functions of a judge in conducting cases (and of a jury, too, in deciding the facts). For historical reasons they are appointed mainly in metropolitan areas. In some parts of the country there have never been regular stipendiary magistrates but in London the Metropolitan stipendiary magistrates were responsible for all criminal matters involving adults until 1964 when they were joined on the bench by lay colleagues. There were 49 stipendiaries in the London metropolitan area in 1998.

As far as youth courts are concerned, until 1998 designated stipendiary magistrates were able to take the chair accompanied by lay colleagues but most youth court benches consisted of three lay magistrates, one at least of whom had to be a woman. The principal argument for allowing stipendiaries to sit alone presumably was that their professional skills would enable them to reduce delays. They would save public funds by dispatching business more quickly, without having to stop to consult lay colleagues about decisions.

There are, however, no figures to show that a stipendiary manages a list in a youth court significantly more quickly than a trained lay chairman with his or her colleagues. The delays, as we have seen, may be through unnecessary adjournments but they are more often caused further down the line in the marshalling and exchange of information. And the stipendiary will have to move fast to create savings when his or her salary is taken into account. Like the unpaid lay magistrates stipendiaries have the services of a legally qualified court clerk. The comparative costs are £9.5 million for some 30,000 lay magistrates in all the courts and £6.1 million for the 90 or so stipendiary magistrates nation-wide.

But the main objection to this change is that the youth court is about more than list management. Good communication is essential in the youth court and though it is dangerous to generalise, lay magistrates are not on the whole burdened by legal jargon and so may speak more directly to people in court. Moreover, their day-to-day lives are not confined to the criminal justice system so they are less likely to become entrenched in their perceptions of offending. As active members of the outside community in their working as well as personal lives, they may be more familiar with the resources in the community to tackle offending by young people. Consistency in sentencing and interpretation of the law can be improved for all magistrates by better compulsory training.

I shall be describing the changes in the youth court I would like to see but they do not include a greater role for stipendiaries, certainly not sitting alone. The use of lay magistrates is unique to this country. Its overarching virtue is similar to the jury system's. Justice is seen to be handed down by more than one person and not just by professionals. Magistrates in youth courts have the responsibility of both a jury deciding guilt and a judge presiding over the case and sentencing. Three minds offer more safeguards to defendants against the prejudices a single individual may have and it is important for young people to have people of both genders with as much outside experience as possible looking at their circumstances when sentencing.

Even initial proceedings contain important decisions affecting civil liberties. Should a young person have bail? What about jurisdiction. Although youth courts can deal with all offences other than those involving homicides,[1] if the case involves some other "grave crime" is it so serious that the young person should be sent for trial at the Crown Court? To put such decisions in the hands of single professional who spends all his or her time in the courts is against the spirit of the legal system as it affects young people. The questionnaires from the Stepney Children's Fund camps show how young people have confused perceptions about the "posh" people who decide their fate in court but the fact is that lay magistrates are ordinary citizens, albeit specially chosen and trained, there are three of them and they include members of each sex. In addition, there are at the moment proportionally even fewer stipendiary magistrates than magistrates who come from ethnic minorities.

EFFECTIVE PENALTIES

It is easy when discussing the youth court to be bogged down by its procedures. To an extent that has already happened to the Blair government which has put as a priority reforming the court process. What matters most are the court's powers and the effect of its sentences on the young people who appear before it.

There is one heartening statistic about juvenile crime which is too often overlooked. Seventy per cent of young people cautioned by the police under the system being replaced under the Crime and Disorder Act 1998 did not reoffend within two years. The shock of the formal caution (now called a "reprimand", to be followed by a single "final warning") by a uniformed senior officer at the police station was enough to galvanise the majority of children and families to change or they may have taken up informal offers of support and opportunities for structured activities.

The new final warning[2] after a single reprimand automatically triggers referral of the child to the local youth offending team for assessment so that, if appropriate, he or she may be enrolled in preventive programmes. Such early, preventive intervention is

---

[1] For an outline of the jurisdiction and powers of the youth court including an explanation of the "grave crimes" provisions under which youth court magistrates can commit to the Crown Court for trial, see *Introduction to Youth Justice*, Winston Gordon, Philip Cuddy and Jonathan Black, Waterside Press, 1999. There are no mode of trial proceedings in the sense that these exist in the adult court, just these special provisions relating to homicides and other grave crimes. The point is that the decision whether to send their case to the Crown Court is a quite momentous one in the life of any child or young person.

[2] See *Introduction to Youth Justice*, Footnote 1, above

welcome. It is only odd that it is not seen as a natural development from the old cautioning schemes which, in defiance of the facts about the success of cautioning, are too often disparaged as having let young offenders off the hook.

Nor are we operating in the dark about the comparative effectiveness of different sentences. We do not have to rely on gut beliefs like 'prison works' or the equally dangerous belief that 'nothing works'. Research about what works to reduce re-offending is readily available and the government of course knows about it since much of it was conducted by its own Home Office Research Department and it was clearly outlined in the Audit Commission Report *Misspent Youth*.

To summarise briefly, effective programmes are based on improving the understanding of young people about the consequences of their behaviour (very much as discussed in my chapter on teaching morality) and on giving them practical skills. The young offenders must be fitted back into education or into training or employment. To achieve these ends, short interventions are not sufficient. Programmes must last six months or more and the young person must attend at least twice a week for 100 hours or more. The best programmes are community-based because it is in the community that the young people will live and practise what they have learnt. The programmes themselves must have consistent aims and methods, be delivered by well-trained and skilled practitioners, and be carefully matched to the needs of each individual.

We also know what is *not* effective with the most persistent offenders. General counselling, family counselling and psycho-dynamic therapy may be helpful to the individual but they do not directly address the issue of anti-social behaviour. Putting young offenders into groups which have no clear purpose to address offending behaviour may reinforce their bad behaviour by throwing them together with other delinquents. (This is an argument against attendance centres which young offenders may be ordered to attend on Saturday afternoons. They usually do physical exercise there and learn some practical skill like first-aid. The discipline is strict—the centres are usually run by police officers—but the emphasis is more on accustoming young people to accept authority than enabling them to understand why they get into trouble.) Finally, programmes which only give punishment tend to harden attitudes. Effective punishment has to be immediate and comprehensible to the individual and also show alternative ways of behaving.

As far as custody is concerned, the tabloids ask the public to believe that locking serious young offenders up for a period, away from the area to which they will have to return, will deter them and others from further crime. Certainly Robert, just back from a young offender institution did not want to return and Stephen had hated his month in custody when on remand. Others like Daniel and Jason had a macho, *che sera, sera* (whatever will be, will be) attitude to the prospect. Both Jacquie and her mother Pat thought a spell in Holloway would cure Jacquie of shop-lifting. Pat seemed to think that prison had made her former husband see sense. It is true that after imprisonment he stopped offending but he was violent to his wife and had a serious drinking problem which had grievous effects on his family. I do not like to think of the consequences for Jacquie if she were exposed to the temptation of drugs which are readily available in women's as well as men's prisons.

Desmond, a 17-year-old I did not interview but was told about, had been sentenced to supervision with 30 days "Intermediate Treatment" (activities decided, in this instance, by the youth justice team) for several burglaries and theft, with eleven other matters he admitted to be taken into consideration. He had two previous convictions. It emerged that he was addicted to crack cocaine and committing crimes to feed his habit. He was required to attend drug counselling sessions. He responded well to supervision and counselling, stopped using drugs, his offending was curtailed, he obtained employment and his relations with his family greatly improved. He then appeared at the Crown Court, having just turned 18, for a burglary which pre-dated the imposition of the supervision order. He was sentenced to 18 months custody. He successfully appealed against this sentence but had served three months in a young offenders institution before he was released. On his release he was back on crack cocaine.

The statistics about imprisoning young people in Britain tell a terrible tale. Fifty-four boys and six girls tried to kill themselves when in custody during 1997. Two succeeded. In the first eight months of 1998 two 17-year-olds on remand and one 16-year-old convicted of robbery had committed suicide. A further two 16-year-olds killed themselves in police cells. Nine young people in custody under 18 had committed suicide by the end of the year.

The government wants to end remands in custody for 15 and 16-year-olds and since 1 June 1999 courts have been able to remand the 'most vulnerable' 15 and 16-year-olds into secure accommodation rather than to young offenders institutions, provided a place for them had been identified. But there are two reasons why this concession is inadequate. First, there is not sufficient secure accommodation available and second, how are the most vulnerable to be defined?

The Howard League Troubleshooter Project at Feltham Young Offender Institution in 1997 found that over a three year period about a third of the young people were in public care, either removed compulsorily from their parents because of abuse or neglect, or with parental consent. Eight out of ten had been excluded from school or been long-term truants. One quarter had no previous convictions but a majority had been in custody previously. Fewer than half had committed or were accused of crimes of violence. The project assessed three out of ten as being particularly vulnerable to bullying, self-harm or suicide and three 15-year-olds in the period reviewed had committed suicide. Indeed, there is a plaque on the wall at Feltham in memory of one dead boy. Vulnerability is endemic among these young offenders.

What we also know about prison for young people is that 90 per cent of young males aged 14 to 16 sentenced to custody for less than one year are reconvicted within two years of being released. The overall rate for reconviction within two years of release of young offenders under 21 is 75 per cent. As the 1987 Government green paper *Punishment, Custody and the Community* said, "Even a short period of custody is quite likely to confirm [young offenders] as criminals". Sir Paul Condon, Commissioner of the Metropolitan Police, told Inner London magistrates in July 1997 that the traffic in Inner London courts had reduced because of the success of Operation Bumblebee in putting known burglars behind bars. He did not answer the question whether it will increase again when the burglars emerge from prison with little change to their attitudes or circumstances and new partners found for their crimes.

The peak age for males for known offending is now 18. After that it declines but, as far as is known, this is not because 19-year-olds suddenly begin to be afraid of going behind bars. It is because they gradually mature in every way; young men may settle down with a girlfriend (like Jason's older brother), even get a job. Those who have not been in prison are more likely to go straight in future. Those who reach prison are usually deeper into crime and prison gives the public only temporary respite from their activities. The 'incapacitation' argument depends on the rate at which they were offending before they were locked up and the rate at which they would offend if given an alternative punishment. Luke had not offended before so his detention in secure accommodation was solely a punishment for what he had done on one occasion.

Success rates for community programmes are hard to define. Do we mean by success total abandonment of crime? This is an ambitious target to achieve in a relatively short time when young people may have been offending for a considerable period. So is there a sliding scale while offences slow down or become less serious? Strange as it may seem, all programmes are not evaluated systematically. Pressure of work and the expense of computers to house and analyse the information are the excuses for this failure but rigorous evaluation should be made a priority for projects with young people and money for monitoring included in their budgets. It is good that one of the responsibilities of the new Youth Justice Board is to see the youth justice system has a computer system fit for the twenty-first century. However, the evidence that already exists suggests that young people who have attended well-structured community programmes do not reoffend as much, as badly or as quickly as those who are sentenced to custody.

A study published in 1995 by the University of Cambridge Institute of Criminology found that a year after completing intensive supervision programmes in the community young offenders had fewer personal problems likely to produce further criminality in the long term. In the short term, within 14 months of the end of their sentence, 81 per cent of those who had been in custody had been cautioned or reconvicted, compared with 71 per cent of those dealt with in the community. The young offenders on the intensive community projects saw their attendance as heavy punishment but nearly all of them rated the staff and projects as helpful, as did their parents. The omens for the future were better for them than for those who had been sent into custody.

The arguments against imprisoning all but the most dangerous, violent young offenders would have less urgency if the regime in young offenders institutions were more constructive. Sir Stephen Tumim, the former HM Chief Inspector of Prisons, says the aim of young offenders institutions should be to educate the young men who fill them. "The word punishment," he says, "doesn't come into it. The courts did that by depriving them of their liberty." There should be continuing education and training in skills for everybody in custody, even if they are there for short periods. There is also a strong case for giving those on longer sentences work experience and paying them for the work they do so that they have a nest-egg on release. One of the best features of the Blair government's plans for young offenders was the proposal for a proportion of the windfall tax to be used to finance jobs, education and training for them.

In 1999, because of lack of staff caused by lack of resources, young people on remand at Feltham young offenders institution, awaiting a trial or sentence, were locked in their cells for 22 hours a day. Such treatment, with its obvious dangers to the mental and physical health of the more vulnerable, surely breaks the United Nations Convention On the Rights of the Child, which has been ratified by Britain (as does the remand of young girls in adult prisons against which the High Court ruled in August 1997). These young people have not even been convicted—and the Audit Commission found that one-third of young people who have been remanded in custody do not receive a custodial sentence after they have been convicted. It is not just reform groups who protest. The 1999 report on Feltham by HM Inspectors was a damning indictment of the consequences of its lack of resources.

The regime is only a little better for those serving sentences. There are a number of workshops available for them at Feltham, for instance, which teach skills like painting, decorating and plumbing. The young men attend groups to address their offending behaviour and plans are made to structure their time inside and for their release, but according to the research I have quoted the work to change their attitudes and behaviour is not intensive enough to be effective. And access to education, the key to their future, is patchy. Custody is expensive but for it to have some rationale other than punishment it should cost even more.

It should be noted, too, that experiments in using a military model for young offender institutions have failed. The 'short, sharp shock' administered at detention centres first when William Whitelaw was Home Secretary and later under Leon Brittan did not have the beneficial effects its advocates forecast and in March 1998 the first US-style 'boot camp', initiated by Michael Howard, closed after only 12 months. It was found to be no more successful than other types of regime and places cost £31,000 per year, nearly twice the sum for ordinary young offender institutions. The closure of the Colchester venture went almost unnoticed in the press, unlike its opening.

The Home Secretary is considering putting the 25 young offender institutions into a separate unit of the Prison Service, with its own budget and staff. If there were sufficient funding, this would give an opportunity to change closed institutions into places where young offenders could begin to understand the implications of their offending and learn alternative skills for their future lives. The double nature of the new detention and training orders is also on the right lines. The aim is that when these orders are generally implemented young people will be prepared for their release from the beginning of their sentences and continue their training after release. But the fact remains that it is difficult in prison to prepare young people to change their behaviour on their release, to apply the lessons they have learnt inside to everyday life outside. And they will need more support in their home towns than at present exists.

At the moment the majority of those under the age of 18 in young offender institutions have not been involved in violence. The central question is whether any young offenders except those who are violent and dangerous should be incarcerated. The question has added urgency because the age for custody has been reduced. One of Jack Straw's early acts as Home Secretary in 1997 was to sign the contract for the Medway

Secure Training Centre to take up to 40 boys and girls aged between 12 and 14, to be managed at Cookham Wood in Kent by Rebound ECD (ECD stands for Education, Care and Discipline), a subsidiary of Group 4 which, with Tarmac, formed a consortium to build and run the centre. The same consortium of private companies won the contract for another STC planned to open in May 1999 at Onley in Northamptonshire. An American company, Wackenhut Corrections Corporation, and Seccor will run a third STC scheduled for autumn 1999 at Medomsley in County Durham. Two other regional sites for STCs have been designated.

Secure training centres were initiated by the Conservative government for children who had committed three offences that would be imprisonable for an adult—"three strikes and you're out"—and who in addition had either failed to comply with a supervision order or had reoffended while under supervision. There is no attempt to assess whether the previous supervision offered in the community was adequate or sufficiently intensive to deter the child from offending. Under the Crime and Disorder Act 1998 the Home Secretary also has a discretionary power to introduce detention and training orders for ten and eleven-year-olds.

The press at first called these secure training centres "child jails", no doubt thinking of them as suitable for the children it called "superpredators". When the Medway Secure Training Centre opened in April 1998, commentators were surprised to find that the regime was less harsh than they expected, with the emphasis on education. There is a high staffing ratio of one hundred adults (including catering staff) to 40 trainees. The children, called trainees, live in groups of five in house units, have single bedrooms, with toilet and shower en-suite, and have a brisk, well-structured timetable, with six hours a day in the classroom. Specialists take the education classes, one teacher and a classroom aide for four trainees, and an hour a day is spent on the crime avoidance programme in small discussion groups. There are good facilities for sport and the children learn practical domestic skills.

There was concern at the outset that the Home Office course for staff recruited to give the 24 hour care was centred on their role as custody officers. House masters and matrons at public and private schools, to which parents voluntarily send their children for a portion of the year, do not have as their starting point the physical containment of their pupils. It became clear, however, that every effort was being made to ensure a constructive regime, with a keyworker and a personal tutor for every child, emphasis on improving the children's ability to communicate and encouragement of visits by parents and guardians to review progress and make plans. Overnight accommodation was available for visitors coming from a distance.

Nevertheless, only two months after the centre opened, when there were only fifteen trainees, police with dogs were called in to control the children, showing how difficult it is to handle damaged and damaging children, thrown together in an institution with no ties to those who look after them. After only seven months a third of the staff, including the heads of education and care, had left, unable to cope with the pressures. Rigorous supervision in the community is promised for these children when they go home after being locked up in a Prison Service establishment for up to a year—sentences may be given for up to two years but half the sentence is completed in the community—but one of the difficulties the Medway Secure Training Centre identified at the outset was that local youth justice and youth offending teams usually did not have the resources to carry through suitable programmes. Some local education authorities refused to accept the children back into their schools from which they had been excluded. There was little support for the parents to help them control their hitherto uncontrollable children.

Common sense as well as humanity suggests it would be better to have spent the costs of secure training on intensive community programmes in the first place, for this generation of young offenders as well as to prevent future generations of offenders arising. Young Jason whom I interviewed needs more than a few hours tuition a week to fill his time and divert him from offending. For those few those children who are a serious threat to the public or themselves through their violence there should be specialist, therapeutic secure accommodation as near as possible to their homes.

So why do the public—and consequentially judges and magistrates—not accept that there should be better and cheaper alternatives in the community to teach as well as punish most young offenders? I believe they distrust the alternatives partly because they do not see them as a deprivation of liberty but principally because they do not know enough about them. If the present Home Secretary, Jack Straw, were to speak with as much fervour about the achievements of projects in the community as he does about punishment and curfews, perhaps he would convince the public that there are effective alternatives.

COMMUNITY PROJECTS

In my 1989 book about preventing juvenile offending, one of the six projects I described in detail was the Surrey Juvenile Offender Resource Centre. A decade ago its programme included most of the elements recognised today as being likely to work. First of all its aims were absolutely clear and each element of the programme it offered the 'heavy end' offenders reflected those aims. It took only young people who were in immediate danger of custody. Through the confidence it won for its work, between 1982 and 1987 the number of custodial orders for young people in the area was reduced from 16 per cent to 2.5 per cent of court disposals. The project was monitored by the specialist independent consultancy Social Information Systems. Fewer than half of those who attended reoffended within two years compared with the national rate of 80 per cent for reoffending after custody. 'Success' was not total but the complexity of the lives of the young people I interviewed recently for this book shows why it takes time to change the habit of offending.

The Surrey project was ahead of its time in the way it looked at the lives of the young offenders as a whole, working with many local agencies to teach them skills, get them jobs, slot them back into education or training and find them suitable, sheltered housing. A programme to tackle the offending behaviour was at the heart of each young person's package, with work on both an individual and group basis to foster awareness of the needs of others and the ability to resist peer pressure. The new disposal of reparation orders under the Crime and Disorder Act 1998 is akin to the supervised community service introduced in Surrey, for even their youngest offenders, to enable them to give something back to the community.

The current youth court disposal of a community service order is only available for those aged sixteen and over, partly because below that age young offenders do not often have sufficient skills to offer to the community but mainly because community service is arranged in a way that those who undertake it have to be well enough motivated to do the job without constant supervision. The young people in the Surrey programme were taught what to do and were supervised when doing their work. They tended old people's gardens, for example, and helped on National Trust and English Heritage renovation projects. One young man whose reports I saw did maintenance work in the graveyard of the church from which he had stolen: the punishment fitted the crime. This kind of direct and indirect recompense is now going to be possible everywhere through the introduction of reparation orders.

The project workers in Surrey made young people partners in shaping the plans, winning their commitment through their involvement. They also held regular, informal family meetings to keep members of the family in the picture and help them to see what they could offer, reinforcing the efforts of the project. Some families were offered family therapy. The young people on the pre-employment scheme were taught how to look for a job and interview techniques as well as skills which made them employable.

The accommodation scheme was particularly innovative, introduced in partnership with the local social services department, the area Probation Service and the housing department. They did not use foster parents but advertised for landlords and landladies on a commercial basis, asking for friendly lodgings for homeless teenagers. The young people received the support and counselling they needed (and the discipline) through their frequent contact with the project workers. In their digs they were given a key to the front door and expected to obey the rules of the household, taking breakfast and the evening meal with the family, a very different scenario from the isolation of living in a bed-and-breakfast hotel. In 1986-87, the first year of the scheme's operation, the project gave a secure base to 83 young people in this way. In the scope of its services, the Surrey project foreshadowed the kind of inter-agency work the 1998 Act wants to introduce through youth offending teams.

In 1999 perhaps the best publicised community project for serious young offenders was the Sherborne House Probation Centre in south-east London. Sherborne House takes young male offenders aged 16 to 20 from the Inner London Probation Service area as a requirement under their probation orders or, for the younger ones, under supervision orders with specified activities. Its achievements have been described in books (notably Roger Graef's *Living Dangerously*) and the media but are still not well enough known, even to judges and magistrates in London. Seventy per cent of the very serious offenders at the centre, often sent there as an alternative to custody, do not reoffend within a year of completing the programme. The young offenders have to attend four and a half days a week for ten weeks. The centre thus meets a key criterion for successful schemes: it gives intensive supervision. The programme balances essential elements: offending behaviour groups, life skills sessions, education and jobs guidance, training in workshops and reparation.

The workers at Sherborne House use imaginative means to get through to the offenders who rarely want to face up to the implications of what they have done. I saw the work of one session when the youths were asked to draw the incident for which they were last arrested in a strip cartoon of ten frames (Even those who write and spell badly can usually do a child's stick drawings for this exercise). Each person's strip was then discussed. Why did Kevin draw the victim he robbed the same size as himself when he was really smaller? What was he thinking before he accosted his victim, while he was taking the victim's watch and as he ran away? The offenders are also asked to write letters to their victims. Most apologise but some take time to lose their defiance. "You deserved it, you cunt", was one response I saw. It could not be sent to the victim but it did precipitate a lively discussion which made the young man think again. It would be interesting to see how much more successful Sherborne House would be if it had the funds for its courses to last six months, as recommended by research, rather than ten weeks.

Of the young people I interviewed, Mark showed the effectiveness of an element of reparation in the supervised activities arranged for him by the youth justice team in his area. He saw the point: "You can't give back something what you've done but at least you're giving something back. You're not just taking." He was partly motivated by the fact that he got half of the pay for his work: "I thought places like that would send you round and make you do it for nothing but they do give you something, like stipe [pay] you know, which is good." On balance I agree that it makes sense to allow young offenders to keep some of the money earned in this way. Working for themselves as well as others helps to remove the sense of frustration they often feel when they have admitted they did wrong. Altruism does not come easily to those not accustomed to thinking about others. The money they get for themselves increases the incentive to work hard. It gives them a sense of achievement, a feeling few of them have previously experienced. It is an effort to earn the money but once they have earned it they come to see how it can benefit others as well as themselves—and they grow to like that idea, too.

It is important for politicians and the public to realise that running any kind of reparation scheme is not cheap. It is easy to say that vandals should repair the damage they have done but they have to be taught how. Scrubbing off graffiti, as Michael Howard suggested when he was Home Secretary, seems a fair enough punishment for some but it involves the use of chemicals and has to be supervised. Even picking up litter has to be supervised. As long as there are funds to teach and supervise young people, then reparation is possible and desirable. I have no doubt that the new reparation orders will be welcomed and used extensively by youth court magistrates. It is, as the government has made clear, a disposal for when young people first appear in court for lesser crimes, and properly administered it should ensure that young people take responsibility for their offences and understand the point of the reparation, in the way Mark did.

Mark's project put the earnings of the young offenders into a pool to compensate their victims. There was no question of meeting the victim, deciding with the victim what the recompense should be or repairing specific damage. Such direct involvement of the victim with the offender is more complicated but it has been achieved under some mediation schemes. Both parties have to be carefully prepared, the purpose of the meeting understood and the meeting skilfully chaired. The young person must already have some insight into the effect of his offence and want to apologise and make amends.

It is certainly helpful for young people to have to take on board the fact that their victims are real people whom they have injured. Jason said, "I never think about the people when I do burglaries". Daniel went further: "I can't think about the people. I won't do it if I think about them. I don't care about that. It's their business." If Jason met someone he had burgled, maybe he would begin to think more about what he had done. It was like World War III, his mother said, if anyone touched anything of his. Maybe meeting a victim outside the family would help him to transfer his own sense of outraged ownership to others. If Daniel talked to someone at the building society he robbed, maybe he would begin to understand the terror that person felt when the youths leapt over the counter and not shrug it off as "their business".

It may be helpful for victims in some circumstances to see their aggressors rather than imagine them. If there is a continuing neighbourhood dispute or victim and offender know each other, it makes sense for a meeting to be arranged. However, it asks a lot of victims to meet those who have damaged their property or rummaged through their possessions and invaded their space. The last thing many victims of vandalism or burglary may want is to see their aggressors face-to-face. They may prefer to get on with their lives and hope the incident was a one-off occurrence (though many burglaries are not, unfortunately, single episodes—the thief who thinks he has found a good seam may return to mine it again). It must be the victim's decision whether or not to meet the offender.

"Restorative justice", as it is now called, is attractive for many reasons. It appeals to those concerned with the long-term reform of young offenders because it makes the young people acknowledge what they have done and see the connection between themselves and the victim. For both offender and victim there is an obvious element of fairness, a *quid pro quo* in paying back in kind, though young offenders and their parents will rarely have the means to compensate their victims fully in monetary terms. "An eye for an eye" is not only about vengeance. Finally, it is satisfying to the public to know "something is being done", something tangible and directly relevant to right the wrong.

Shortly before the Crime and Disorder Act 1998 created a national Youth Justice Board to oversee the quality of youth justice, National

Standards were drawn up by the Probation Service for youth justice teams. These were based on guidelines published in 1996 by a co-ordinating committee for the twelve boroughs of Inner London. They set out clearly the spectrum of services that should be available to tackle offending by young people, ranging from the provision of informative reports to the courts and facilities for those on bail, to autocrime projects (such as the one Tyrrell attended), access to drug advisory and rehabilitation services, guidance for careers and training for employment, advice on housing and benefits, educational services, opportunities for 'constructive leisure' and reparation or mediation schemes. Examples of components of the specified activity requirement of a supervision order were given, including work with groups and work with families.

The Inner London *Statements of Principles and Practice Standards* explained that the core services should be provided either by specialist youth justice teams or through partnership arrangements with other boroughs, other departments of the local authority or voluntary agencies. Everything suggested in these guidelines was admirable but collectively the total was only an ideal "wish" list. Up and down the country there were many youth justice teams offering young people on supervision orders elements of a package which could deflect them from further offending. Over 300 community programmes were listed in the second edition of a handbook produced by ISTD (the Institute for the Study and Treatment of Delinquency: now the Centre for Criminal Justice Studies). The trouble was that very few areas had all the elements available; and the situation was deteriorating because of restrictions on the resources local authorities could devote to youth justice. The motorcar project which served Tyrrell well was under constant fear of closure. It was only partially funded by the local authority where it was based. The staff had their salaries paid but they had to find the project's running costs from charities and trusts.

What has changed for the new youth offending teams (the "YOTs") being piloted in certain areas for 18 months from October 1998? These teams, which take the place of the local authority social workers and probation officers who were previously responsible for older young offenders in most areas, consist of a mix of social workers, probation officers, police, education and health personnel, bringing together a spectrum of experience to meet the spectrum of young people's needs. (It is to be hoped that representatives from housing departments will also be included.) At best, there will be the opportunity to look at a young person's needs in the round. A 16-year-old girl who haunts the London underground to pick the pockets of tourists requires guidance from all the named agencies if she is to change her life-style.

A welcome improvement is that the youth offending teams are enjoined to look beyond their local authority boundaries and to forge partnerships to provide facilities. Indeed, the task of piloting all the measures in the 1998 Act was given jointly to three West London boroughs and to Hampshire with the Isle of Wight, Southampton and Portsmouth. These authorities must work together to deliver their services, crossing professional boundaries within their individual youth offending teams and financial boundaries within their linked authorities. Pooled resources will mean more resources but will there be sufficient money in their kitties? The programmes needed for the Act's new action plan orders and for intervention by YOTs linked to final warnings by the police will stretch existing services. If the YOTs use voluntary organizations to provide some of the services, from youth work to parenting courses, they have to pay them.

The shortcomings that remain are not only in the range of services offered but crucially in the intensity and duration of the work. Most youth justice teams in 1998 did not have the staff to offer young people more than weekly contact, let alone daily programmes. The Audit Commission reported in *Misspent Youth* that 60 per cent of young offenders on supervision orders saw their supervisors only once a week and some less often—in contrast to the recommendation of research for at least two meetings a week or a total of over 100 hours of contact for persistent offenders. Where training in skills and education are concerned, the staff may try to find places for their charges on suitable external courses but these have to be paid for by a local authority with many calls on its purse, from protecting children at risk of abuse to caring for the increasing population of old and infirm people.

For once the findings of research and popular feeling converge in demanding that more of young offenders' time should be spent in supervised, constructive activity. The more serious the offending, the greater the need for intensive intervention over a number of months. This is especially important and only fair when supervision with specified activities is ordered as an alternative to custody. It is a considerable punishment and a real deprivation of liberty for these young people to have to attend courses as bidden, unused as they are to a regular life-style. They find it painful to examine their own behaviour and be made to think about their victims. The regime on community projects is tougher than the critics of community projects realise. But young offenders need to fill every day with constructive activities and address all the aspects of their lives in order to change.

The Youth Justice Board will set national standards and license local arrangements for community sentences and custodial institutions. It will achieve little unless it can ensure that youth offending teams have the resources to offer the requisite intensive and long-term supervision. At present the maximum number of days on specified activities a court can order is 90. Ninety days amount to only 18 weeks if there are sessions five days a week. Provided that there were the money to make additional training and supervision feasible, I would argue for legislation to increase the maximum number of days on specified activities under supervision orders.

BAIL IN THE COMMUNITY

Darren, aged 16, appears in the youth court accused of two burglaries, one of office premises, the other of a residential flat. He pleads not guilty to both allegations. He has one previous conviction for domestic burglary and others for theft from shops. He lives with his mother and is not employed or on a training course. The Crown prosecutor asks for him to be remanded into custody.

His lawyer says he has no history of absconding. He appeared in court whenever necessary for his previous cases so why should he not be granted bail, perhaps with conditions that he lives at home and does not go out at night? The Crown prosecutor replies that she is afraid he will commit further offences while waiting two months till his trial date because his mother will not be able to stop him going out at night. The first of the alleged offences took place at 2 a.m. He has a bad record and the public must be protected from his activities. She says he should be remanded in custody.

What the youth court magistrates will decide will very much depend on whether the local youth justice team can offer an effective "bail package" to keep Darren out of mischief day and night. Eighty-eight per cent of social services departments in 1997 offered youth courts some kind of bail support scheme to keep young offenders in the community while waiting for their cases to be resolved but few were comprehensive. The Audit Commission calculated in 1998 that £34 million could be saved if there were better bail remand schemes throughout England and Wales. The London Borough of Wandsworth's Bail Support Scheme costs about £100 a week for each young person compared with £600 a week for a place in a local authority children's home. Darren's youth justice workers may suggest that as a requirement of his bail Darren attends the youth justice centre for a couple of sessions each week and, if they have sufficient staff, that he reports there daily. They will try to slot him into activities at the local youth club and look with him at the possibility of college courses for the future to catch up on his education and give him training in skills.

But what about the crucial question of where he lives until his trial? The youth justice workers may argue that with day-time support it will be safe for him to live at home with a curfew forbidding him to go out between the hours of 9 p.m. and 8 a.m. What if the bench agrees with the Crown prosecutor that his mother will be powerless to stop him from breaking the curfew, despite him knowing he might be picked up by the police? What alternatives are there? The local authority will probably consider him too old and too unruly for a children's home where he would mix with younger, vulnerable children who are there because their parents for whatever reason cannot look after them.

What about secure accommodation? Those who run secure accommodation units are social workers, not prison officers, and within the locked establishment the young people are educated and kept occupied. But the cost of secure accommodation is up to £3,500 a week (This was paid until recently by the local authority whereas the Home Office paid for those remanded in young offenders institutions. Many local authorities were so short of funds that they could only pay for secure accommodation in exceptional cases.) In any case there are too few places available in secure accommodation to hold even vulnerable young offenders (which is why some 15-year-olds end up in prisons or other Prison Service establishments). And Darren does not meet the new criteria by which youth courts can remand the most vulnerable 15 and 16-year-olds to secure accommodation as opposed to custody.

The result is that although there is no violence in his record, in some areas the only way to keep him safe from further trouble while awaiting trial is to remand him to a young offender institution where, as we have seen, he may be locked up in his cell with no constructive activity for 22 hours a day.

Fortunately, there are some areas where local authorities do have the means to place young offenders safely in the community, to their benefit and at less expense to the community. In Brighton, for example, Darren would be eligible for RAILS, a remand and intensive lodgings scheme which places young people in families and plans day-time activities for them. The average time until a case is resolved is four to six weeks but some placements last up to six months, if the trial is for a grave matter in the Crown Court.

"It's a time when you can do something with them because of the threat of being locked up," says Sue, a single mother who has been a foster carer with RAILS for two years. The boys come to her resentful, especially if they have been given a curfew to stay in every evening, but they are also relieved that they are not in custody. Some of them are glad to have respite from a fraught situation at home and to be cared for by someone who does not have preconceptions about them. She

208 Children Who Break the Law

has fostered only one boy whose parents still lived together and many of the families were suffering what she calls "total breakdown". It takes a while for some of the young people to begin to talk about their situations but there has been only one boy with whom she did not "connect" after the first couple of weeks. She trained as a teacher and had worked on a youth training scheme but was new to offenders.

Sue responded to an advertisement by RAILS in the local paper. She says she had initial worries about managing the teenagers' behaviour—whether they would come in at night at the stipulated time—but never about any physical threat to herself or her small daughter. They like the presence of a little one. She describes her approach as "relatively laid-back" but she has clear house rules including no drugs and no smoking. "Nothing personal about the smoking", she tells them, "but I won't have it in the house because of Gwenny". Only one boy has had to leave—because she found a needle in his room. They have to get up in the morning because she goes to college and they have to go to bed at a reasonable time. She doesn't let them watch TV until 3 a.m. Somehow she manages to get them to make a move upstairs when she goes. They talk about their situation as and when the occasion arises, while cooking tea or watching television, about what happens next in the court process, about whether or not they want to go home, about going back to school or what kind of job they might try and train for. Both of them know this placement is not a long-term option which defines her role and gives the young person space to think about the future. Filling their day is the main problem for those not at school. The project does its best, she says, but some of them spend too much time just hanging round with their mates: "It's a vicious circle till they're motivated."

RAILS began in 1990 and now has about 50 referrals a year, mainly of young people in the East Sussex area aged 14 to 16 who are accused of serious offences and have been remanded by the youth court into local authority accommodation. There were in 1997 six families trained to undertake this demanding work. At the start of the placement there is an admission meeting attended by the young person, his or her parents, the foster carers and the relevant social workers. An agreement is drawn up, with everyone's expectations stated. The agreement is reviewed weekly with the young person. Arrangements are made about contact with the teenagers' families and care is taken to ease the transition at the end of the period of remand.

The foster families all attend a monthly meeting, partly for further training, partly for mutual support, and support is available for them round the clock from Carol Clarke who runs the scheme, the young person's key worker or a local authority duty social worker. Carol

Clarke like Sue emphasised to me that often it is the first time the young people have felt safe, living within consistent boundaries. She still has visits from a young man her own family fostered at the start of the scheme.

The foster families are paid about £250 a week for their responsibilities and for the young person's food and lodging. The total cost of a remand fostering place, including training and support for the foster parents and the project's overheads, is calculated to be about £400 a week, making it a bargain when compared even with a place in a local authority children's home, let alone any kind of custodial provision. The National Children's Bureau showed in 1995 that a switch to remand fostering from secure accommodation would make substantial savings. Secure unit managers in the NCB survey said that over a third of the children who were detained in their units could have been safely placed in the community in appropriate families. And what remand fostering offers in addition to value for money is a period of calm and individual attention for young people to begin to see that they can change the way they live.

It might well be asked why there are not remand fostering schemes in most areas for the likes of Darren. The idea is not new. In 1976 when I became editor of *Adoption & Fostering*, the quarterly journal of what was then the Association of British Adoption and Fostering Agencies (now BAAF), one of the first articles I published was by Nancy Hazel, a pioneering social worker in Kent, about the remand fostering scheme she had established there. The Dartington Social Research Unit commented in 1993 on one successful scheme:

> Contact with the Hampshire Scheme (Young Offender Community Support Scheme) brings a welcome reminder that ours is still a caring society. The NCH/Probation programme has uncovered a rich seam of people who are prepared to take in and shelter youngsters others have abandoned. For these young people to experience affectionate concern—in a life otherwise characterised by rejection—is enormously valuable.

The potential of remand fostering has been recognised since that time but a survey in 1993 by the National Foster Care Association found only 29 schemes in existence in fewer than a quarter of local authorities in England and Wales. One of the best pieces of news since the creation of the Youth Justice Board is the high priority and funding it is going to give to the creation of effective bail remand schemes throughout the country. It is to be hoped that most of them will be encouraged to offer remand fostering.

What about electronic tagging of young offenders which was recently approved for offenders under the age of 16 by the Blair government, taking over its predecessor's intentions? Would not an electronic tag round his ankle or wrist, connected to a monitoring unit installed in his home, have enabled Darren to live at home under a curfew since it would alert the police station if he ventured out of his mother's door at night? I can see little to justify the tagging of young offenders at present either on practical grounds or on principle. The research on the original pilot project for adults on bail found that despite the tags half those in the study broke some of their bail conditions. The Home Office Study on the first year of the trials found that the estimated cost of a curfew order with electronic monitoring was £675 a month compared with £202 a month for a probation order. Why not spend the money on paying for more time from skilled people who can help parents exert their authority and supervise young people more stringently?

The pilot use of tagging for juveniles in Greater Manchester, one of the three experimental areas, was delayed in 1997 until an acceptably small tag became available. The model used in Norfolk was seen as suitable for juveniles there. It is argued that—with a small enough tag—there is a case for using tagging to reinforce curfews as part of a package to put structure into a young offender's life, combined with supervision. But if supervision is intensive, tagging should be otiose.

The main objections to tagging are fundamental ones about the way children and young people should be treated in a civilised society and the way they learn to behave. What does it teach a young man about his relationship with his mother if only a mechanical alarm keeps him at home? Will he begin to respect her more? How will it affect his self-image, whether he is the kind of boy easily led by others or a macho leader? When the House of Lords debated the proposal in February 1997 Lord MacIntosh of Haringey pointed out that the tag would be still there, visible if the young person went to school, played sport or attended a training course. "The mind boggles," he said, "at the degree of humiliation to which children may be subjected by their fellows if they were carrying electronic tags." On the other hand, for those who cultivate a tough image the tag may be a trophy. It is unlikely that this kind of public shaming will help young people to change.

A New Tribunal

It is a paradox that in 1999 the youth court, despite the "welfare principle" under which it still operates, cannot arrange when a child appears in court on a minor charge the kind of pre-emptive package of intervention the police will be able to initiate through the final warnings they will give under the Crime and Disorder Act 1998. If a young person admits guilt and receives a reprimand, the police may refer him or her to the local youth offending team (the 'YOT') to make a preventive plan with the family to nip the offending in the bud and stop it from escalating.

Youth courts by contrast will not be able to make one of the new action plan orders, which have similar possibilities, until the young person's offending is "serious enough" to merit the restriction of liberty entailed by community sentence (i.e. a penalty in the community). Nor can they make supervision orders to put the young offender in regular contact with a social worker or probation officer who is enjoined, in the fine words of the Children and Young Persons Act 1933, to "advise, help and befriend" the young offender. As supervision places demands on the time of offenders, directs and restricts their activities, the youth court can only make a supervision order if such deprivation of liberty is appropriate. The needs of the offender are not relevant until the offending is 'serious'.

The law does not define levels of seriousness but generally speaking burglary, robbery, assault and stealing a car will always fall into the serious category whereas the court's attitude to theft from shops, attempts to steal, vandalism, minor vehicle offences, and being in possession of cannabis, will depend on the sums or amount involved and the circumstances of the offence. Until the introduction of secure training orders for 12 to 14-year-olds, the law countenanced "imprisoning" young people only if boys were 15 (girls 16) and only for those offences "which are so serious that only such a sentence can be justified." Custody used to be reserved for violent offenders but in recent years has increasingly been ordered for those involved in domestic burglary and car crimes.

The youth court cannot even ask for a report on the background and circumstances of a child or young person unless it has first decided that the offence is serious enough for a community penalty. The official name for reports is pre-sentence reports (or "PSRs") and they are exactly what their name indicates. They are tools to help the magistrates decide the sentence. But if the offence was not serious enough for a restriction of liberty, then will not be thinking about making a supervision order—and there will be no PSR.

To make a reparation order at the outset of offending and for minor offences, the magistrates have to have a report but that report gives details only of the proposed reparation and the young person's willingness to undertake the tasks. The youth court has no investigative powers on welfare grounds. Stealing from a corner shop, vandalising a park bench, may be one-off aberrations and not a symptom that a child is a member of a delinquent gang or out of control. But how is anyone to know that there is not a need for intervention or support unless someone sees the child and the family, contacts the school and asks? Was a boy of 12 off school just on the day of the offence or is he a regular truant? Is a 17-year-old girl charged with soliciting, who has bruises on her arms and a black eye, not in need of some intervention in her life? These are questions that have to go unasked and unanswered in the youth court if only a minor offence has been committed. The case may be picked up informally by social services— indeed, a perceptive chairman will suggest to a mother or young person that they might like to talk to the representative of social services before they leave the building—but there is no guaranteed or concerted action to try and divert the child or young person from crime.

So what can a youth court do with less serious offenders? Apart from the new reparation orders being piloted in some areas, it can fine them or their parents or make them pay compensation. A cynic would say that as most young offenders cannot find jobs, not even newspaper rounds, and as they mainly come from families living on state benefits, the quest to find the money or the loss of their pocket-money, if they receive pocket-money, may well precipitate more crime. Robert told me, in an aggrieved tone of voice, "That's what made me, that's what started me going out thieving, to get my pocket money back."

The court can at present also make a conditional discharge, although under the Crime and Disorder Act 1998 this option will not be available, other than in exceptional circumstances, for those who have within two years previously received final warnings from the police. A conditional discharge is in itself a form of "final warning". Offenders are not punished immediately for what they have done. If they commit no further offence of any kind in the period laid down, usually a year, they will not be punished at all. But if they get into any further trouble within the specified period, they will be punished for the earlier offence as well as the new one. If the court chairman explains clearly that they are not being let off but are being given a chance to prove themselves, this much maligned penalty may well be effective.

Strange to relate, there are no statistics comparable to those about the effect of cautions concerning the subsequent criminal careers of those conditionally discharged. We know that 70 per cent of children cautioned under the old system did not reoffend within two years but we do not know how many are deterred from offending while the threat of a penalty under a conditional discharge hangs over them. Such is the lamentable state of the statistics about juvenile offending that the numbers are not collected for those brought back to court and punished for their original offences. Until there is evidence that the conditional discharge is not effective, it is premature to suggest abolishing it or even curtailing its use as recommended by the government.

The new reparation order may be as simple as writing a letter of apology to the victim or it may entail doing work for the community, proportionate to the offence. The potential of this order is promising but, as has been said, its use will depend on what facilities and mediation skills are provided by the youth offending teams in different areas and I believe its impact would be greatly increased if it were combined with supervision.

At the moment we have a topsy-turvy system: in the name of justice supervision is not available to youth courts when it would be most effective, as soon as young people appear in court. If there has been previous intervention under the final warning system, that intervention may need to be reassessed and strengthened. If young people have been by-passed by the reprimand system because they would not admit to the police that they committed the offences of which they were accused, then the benefits of a programme to prevent further offending should be theirs from the start once the offence is proved.

Early intervention should be welcomed. It is a hangover from the old justice versus welfare debate to see all intervention on welfare grounds as an infringement of rights, disproportionate to the offences that have brought the child to court. However, it is crucial that children and families under the reprimand and final warning system do not admit guilt to offences as the easiest way out of their situation. It is also essential that any plans drawn up by youth offending teams are agreed with the young people and their families for them to be effective.

In total, I hesitate to give more than two cheers for the Crime and Disorder Act. Tinkering with the youth court's powers will not solve its underlying problems. The present youth justice system is not amenable to working out solutions with the parties concerned. I believe a radical overhaul of the constitution as well as the powers of the youth court is necessary for it to achieve a better balance between its judicial and welfare roles, for better protection of the interests of both the public and young people—and for the new statutory principal aim of youth justice, to prevent offences.

OTHER NATIONS' YOUTH COURTS

Most Western nations have a separate judicial system to deal with young offenders—indeed a separate system is one hallmark of a modern, democratic society—but the systems differ greatly. Here in the UK, Scotland has its own unique provisions for juveniles under the age of 16, as well as its own legal system.[1] The children's hearing system in Scotland decides what should happen to young offenders from the ages of eight to 16 without most of them ever appearing in a court of law.

When a child is accused of an offence in Scotland, the police or those making the complaint send the details to an independent public official, the reporter for the area. If the child and parents dispute the facts of the allegation, the matter goes for proof to the sheriff court, as do extremely serious cases like murder, arson and rape, the kind of cases that in England and Wales are heard and sentenced in the Crown Court under special "grave crimes" provisions (see p.192). Legal aid is available to the child in the sheriff court. But if the facts are accepted, as they are in the majority of cases, or once all but the most serious cases have been proved in the sheriff court, the reporter obtains reports about all the child's circumstances. The reporter then decides whether to conclude the case by giving the child a suitable warning, or to refer the family direct to social services for appropriate support and voluntary action, or to refer the case to a panel hearing as a compulsory order may be required.

The members of the panels for children's hearings are volunteers from the community, appointed for three to five years, and trained in the law, child development, the work of local agencies, and communication skills for the relative informality of the hearing. Many more people apply to become panel members than are required, attracted by the interest and importance of the work and perhaps also by the limitation of the commitment to a finite period.

The child or young person and parents sit at a table with the panel members and others who have relevant information or a relationship with the child, like teachers and social workers. The family may bring an adviser with them but legal aid is not available for lawyers. Everybody is expected to contribute to the discussion about what should happen next. The panel can discharge the case if it is satisfied that no intervention is necessary; it can request further reports; and it can impose a supervision requirement, with or without conditions to attend

---

[1] For an outline of the Scottish system, see *Introduction to the Scottish Children's Panel* by Alistair Kelly, formerly a reporter, Waterside Press, 1997.

projects which address offending behaviour or schemes for education and training. In England and Wales supervision orders are for a specific period of up to three years. In Scotland the orders are open-ended but have to be reviewed annually.

The differences from the system in England and Wales stem from the underlying philosophy. The best interests of the child are the main consideration in Scotland. The Kilbrandon Report, the outcome of a Royal Commission into Children and Young Persons in Scotland, which was published in 1964, led to the introduction of the children's hearing system in 1971. Kilbrandon found that the distinction between children who had offended and those who needed care and protection was more apparent than real, the overlap great between the 'deprived' and the 'depraved'. In addition, Kilbrandon supported the use of "social education" to help people understand and resolve difficulties.

About 60 per cent of referrals to reporters are of children who have committed offences, the rest of children who need protection from abuse, or whose families cannot control them or who are truanting from school. In 1994 it cost £183 for each case referred to the reporter in Strathclyde, Scotland's biggest local authority, and £880 for each panel hearing. By contrast it costs about £2,500 for the police in England and Wales to prosecute a young offender successfully. Crime rates in Scotland, despite the escalating drugs problem in some cities, are generally lower than in England and Wales. Many factors as well as the hearings system probably contribute to this fact but it is clear that a more welfare-orientated system protects the public as much if not more than the system in England and Wales.

Leaving aside the question of punishment, one of the most significant differences between the Scottish and English systems is the degree in which the child and parents are involved in negotiating the outcome of the case and what should happen to prevent a recurrence of offending. This feature is at the centre of the system called family group conferencing which began in New Zealand in 1989, spread to Australia in 1991 and is now used in some form in other parts of the world. Pilot projects have begun here in Kent, Hampshire and Thames Valley.

Family group conferences (FGCs) bring together in an informal setting, often after working hours or at weekends, the members of the young offender's family (grandparents, aunts and uncles as well as parents), other significant people in the child's life including those the child names as friends (teachers, youth workers, neighbours), and the victim or the victim's representative (In cases where there is no personal victim, shoplifting from a store, for example, the manager of the store will attend.) Social workers and others from local helping agencies are present to give information at the beginning of the meeting about resources available in the community for young people or their parents. Lawyers may be present. A professional co-ordinator makes the arrangements and chairs the proceedings. After a discussion about what happened and what the issues are now from everyone's point of view, the family is asked to draw up a plan of action to "make it right" for the victim and prevent future offending. The professionals record and subsequently monitor what has been agreed.

There is a strong element of reparation in the system. Half of victims in New Zealand say they are satisfied with the outcome and over 80 per cent of young people and families. It is thought that the families and young people are more committed to carrying out the plans because they, not the social workers, initiated them. They use the help that is offered better because they asked for it themselves and were not ordered to take it. It is important for the development of young people to acknowledge that what they did was wrong and that they now wish to make amends. But the key benefit is that the young people are not viewed in isolation from their families and the community to which they belong. They are responsible for having committed the offences but everyone connected with them contributed to their past and can influence their future. The theory is that they will want to please their family, those who care for them and for whom they care, and therefore be motivated to change.

"Reintegrative shaming" is the term used by Braithwaite in his 1989 book *Crime, Shame and Reintegration* to make the culprits understand what they have done and make it possible for them to show those who are closest to them and the victim that they mean to change —a very different kind of shaming from the public shaming involved in tagging young offenders or naming them in newspapers as has been supported as part of the communitarian approach.

Family group conferencing has its origins in Maori systems of community regulation. Our traditions have evolved very differently and it is debatable whether all families here are always sufficiently cohesive to work out plans together. Old quarrels and resentments could be renewed for families who do not meet regularly and it is not desirable to make scapegoats of particular children, labelling them as different and stigmatising them even if that is not the intention. But although there is no formal tradition here of families meeting to decide what to do about delinquent children, many families do operate a similar system in an informal way to solve their problems. Both Tyrrell's and Matthew's mothers called in the rest of the family to help them cope with bringing up their sons. Social workers in this country are accustomed to asking young people in need of care and protection to identify the significant people in their lives and families and to map their networks of support. The guidelines to the Children Act 1989 encourage the helping professions to look at what the extended family can offer before suggesting that children should be looked after by the local authority and family group conferencing is now being used in some areas in child protection work.

The pilot schemes for family group conferencing in Hampshire and the London Borough of Wandsworth have produced high degrees of satisfaction among participants. Mary Geaney, youth justice manager, Kent Social Services Intensive Support and Supervision Programme, says she thinks their scheme works because of the way it brings home to the young people the effect of their actions on the victim. A family group conference is held immediately after conviction. If victims do not wish to attend, members of the local branch of the nation-wide organisation Victim Support represent their interests. It is too early yet to know the effect on reoffending rates but the model used in New South Wales, Australia, has so far reduced recidivism by almost half. There are clearly elements in the system of family group conferencing which could be both helpful to young people and acceptable to the public in solving the immediate problem of what to do with young offenders.

The age at which criminal responsibility begins and the age at which young offenders graduate to the adult court varies throughout the West. In England and Wales the youth court deals with children and young people aged ten to 17 and under the Crime and Disorder Act 1998 children under ten may be made subject to child safety orders in the family proceedings court without the legal protection available to their elders. When young people are approaching 18 the youth court chairman will often warn them that if they continue offending they will soon be in the adult court where penalties are tougher and regard to their welfare lower in the scale of priorities.

The Scottish children's hearing panels are for children from eight to 16. In Germany, Italy, Austria and Hungary the age of criminal responsibility is 14; in Iceland, Denmark and Sweden 15; in Belgium and Luxembourg 18. In France the age of criminal responsibility is 13 but the same *juge des enfants*, children's judge, deals with offenders and children in care and protection cases. In Switzerland the age of criminal responsibility is only seven but there, as in other European countries and Scotland, the adjudicators put the co-operation of the parents at the front of their endeavours. As we have seen, there is a difference between empowering and ordering families to be effective.

A CATALYST FOR CHANGE

The headline in *The Independent* on the publication in 1996 of the Audit Commission Report *Misspent Youth* began "How £1 bn Public Money is Wasted", and continued, "Justice System for Juveniles Attacked as Shambles Despite Costing £1bn a Year." There is no doubt that despite the money spent, and despite the goodwill of all those involved in it, the present system of youth justice in England and Wales is flawed. It is not just that the pendulum has swung too far towards the principle of just deserts or that children in Youth Courts may be treated too much like adults in sole command of their destinies. The main problem is that the offence is viewed in isolation. It is assumed that offending is a discrete part of young people's lives which can simply be cut out on its own like a bruise in an apple.

The youth court I would like to see in England and Wales would be an effective catalyst for change. I say "catalyst for change" because it is clear from the knowledge we have of what works to reduce reoffending that there are no overnight solutions to stop children and young people offending. The youth court cannot wave a magic wand—or hurl a thunderbolt—to reform a young person instantly. This fact is acknowledged in other countries with systems which concentrate on showing young people alternative ways to behave and giving them the tools to lead ordinary, mainstream lives. The most attractive element of both the Scottish system and family group conferencing is the way they bring together interested parties, review the full context of young people's lives, and make children and parents participants in the decision-making.

It is tempting to suggest that England and Wales follows Scotland, cutting out the court process for most young offenders and having similar children's hearings which could make use of reparation orders and the methods of family group conferencing as well as supervision orders and voluntary arrangements. However, the Scottish system does not include adolescents aged 16 to 18, and when younger children deny charges, they are tried in the adult court which is not an appropriate tribunal. In addition, everyone agrees that clarity of aims is of great importance when working with young offenders. An appearance in a court of law does not fudge the issue that the child or young person has broken the law. The public thinks this point should be plain and it is generally acknowledged that accepting responsibility is a key element in moral development. Admission of guilt in court can be a stage on the way to maturity.

Would the answer be to transfer all proceedings concerning young people to the family proceedings court? In this court the welfare of the child is paramount. It would not be right to incorporate the concept of punishment into its ethos. Even the new child safety orders for children under the age of ten who have "committed an act which would have been an offence had they been aged ten" sit uncomfortably in this court.

The Youth Justice and Criminal Evidence Bill of 1999 proposes to put into operation, first through pilot schemes, the ideas the Home Office 1997 White Paper *No More Excuses* for referral orders. It is intended that these will be the standard sentence imposed by the youth court for first-time offenders. If the children have pleaded guilty, have no previous convictions and have never been bound over to keep the peace or be of good behaviour, they will be referred to a special youth offender panel which will draw up a contract with the young person to prevent reoffending. It will be the duty of youth offending teams to establish the panels which will consist of at least one member of their own team and two others. The young person will be accompanied by a parent or guardian and may bring one adviser (but legal aid will not be available for lawyers). The panel may, if it wishes, invite a victim to attend or any person the panel thinks may be "capable of having a good influence on the offender".

The "programme of behaviour" agreed, at the first meeting if possible, may include any kind of reparation, direct or indirect, including mediation sessions with the victim or affected people; a curfew to stay at home at specified hours; an undertaking to attend school, training or work; participation in specified activities (to look at their offending or their education or drug use or alcohol use); an order to stay away from certain people or places; and a general undertaking to comply with the programme arranged.

The contract under the referral order will last for a minimum of three months and a maximum of 12 months. Progress meetings may be arranged as necessary for changes in the contract. A final meeting of the panel, the young person and his or her parent or parents will decide if the conditions of the contract have been met or if the young person should be referred back to court for non-compliance. If they are referred back, the court may then either reiterate that the young person must complete the order or it may revoke the order and give an alternative punishment commensurate with the crime. If the young person reoffends during the course of the referral order, the youth court will decide whether to extend the referral order up to the maximum of a year or give an alternative punishment.

The items of the agreed programme will be recorded and it will be important to ensure—as in the home-school contracts I have advocated—that obligations are mutual, with the training and opportunities proffered by the responsible agencies set out as well as the young offender's next steps. The chairing of the panel meetings will be crucial with careful preparation by a skilled co-ordinator—those who chair the panels should be specially trained, as for family group conferences. Above all, the referral orders will only be effective in the long term if continuity is ensured, so that if necessary, there is voluntary liaison and support available and welcomed after the duration of the compulsory order.

The aims of the referral order are excellent. The order will use the principles of restoration (making amends for the harm done), reintegration (into the mainstream, law-abiding community) and responsibility (ensuring that the child understands the consequences of his or her own behaviour). It offers the chance of bringing together the important people in a child or young person's life with professionals to plan a better future. Best of all it will close the gap identified at the outset of this chapter between the final warning and constructive youth court action.

The new referral order has only one drawback: it is so limited. Why should the option of sitting round a table to agree a suitable penalty and preventive measures for the future, a "contract" with clear requirements, only be available once? Why should it not be available for those offenders who exercised their right to plead their innocence but were subsequently found guilty? And why should there be a different system for those who offend more seriously or more often and are therefore ordered supervision, usually entailing similar activities? The range of overlapping disposals in the youth court is now dauntingly complex and justice has to be understood if it is to be seen to be done.

My suggestion for a new youth tribunal would build on and extend the model proposed through the new referral orders. The precise composition of the panels at the time of going to press had not been made clear but a case could be made for including a magistrate, a member of the bench which made the order. Some would argue that the judicial role should be kept separate but youth court magistrates are to an extent involved in the planning of sentences under supervision orders when court reports are examined. It would be particularly helpful to have such a magistrate on the panel if, as I advocate, young people were referred to the panel after they have been found guilty in a trial. Too often at present the "brief facts", presented to those who sentence a young person once a report has been made, seem distant from the full facts heard by anyone present at the trial. Indeed, outsiders are understandably surprised that a different tribunal can give the sentence (One advantage of the judge and jury system in the Crown Court is that the judge has sat through the trial.)

There is also the point that the presence of such a magistrate might help to ensure that in the name of welfare the restriction of the young people's freedom was not disproportionate to the offence—a year's supervision for stealing a can of Coca-Cola, initially denied. In addition, it would be helpful for children and their families to feel that there are the same people in charge of their case and they are not having to repeat their story again and again to different people in authority.

Whether or not magistrates should be members of the youth offending panels (which in my view should deal with all except the very few violent offenders needing custody), I believe there should be changes in the selection and terms of service of youth court magistrates. First, they should all be selected by an independent body (in Inner London they are recommended by the Lord Chancellor's Advisory Committee) rather than elected from the existing pool of magistrates. This would ensure from the start a specific commitment to the special problems of preventing crime by young people (which is not to say that most of those at present elected to youth panels by their peers are not interested or knowledgeable). Second, all youth court magistrates should also sit in the family court so that they see the full picture of factors which can help to make young people criminals as well as deprived. They would also learn more there about resources in the community to help parents take control as well as to keep young people out of trouble. Third, youth court magistrates should be appointed for a finite period of up to ten years.

The Scottish experience has shown that there is no shortage of suitably qualified people to take on the responsibilities of membership of their children's hearings panels for a stated length of time and to attend meetings on a regular basis, sometimes out of office hours. Magistrates in England and Wales, once appointed, often stay on the bench till they retire at the age of 70. There is no doubt that as a magistrate you learn more every time you enter a court but more intensive training could be given before appointment to compensate for some of what is now learnt through experience and a shorter commitment might encourage more younger people and a wider spectrum of people to join the bench.

What about those young people who commit crimes so serious that custody is the only possible response to safeguard the public? If penalties in the community were better resourced and better known, on the lines I have advocated, they would be few in number but such young offenders would be sentenced by the youth court, as at present. However, secure training centres for 12 to 14-year-olds should be abolished both because they are ineffective and because imprisoning children is offensive in a civilised country.

Finally, there are those few young people charged with "grave crimes" like murder and rape and those accused of violent crimes for whom a longer period of custody than six to 12 months might be the only appropriate penalty to protect the public. I would adapt a suggestion of Annabella Scott, former Chairman of the Inner London youth panel, and others, that they should be tried and sentenced not in the Crown Court but before a designated Crown Court judge, called a children's judge and specially trained for the office, sitting with two lay magistrate colleagues in the venue of the youth court in special session. This last proposal would end the enormity and absurdity of public trials of young children in an adult forum as in the Bulger case. It would also be more appropriate for those comparatively few teenagers who are accused of committing serious acts of violence which may, to protect the public, necessitate detention and training in a secure institution.

I believe that such a simplified youth court system, working with young offender panels, would combine the best of the present youth court system, with its respect for the legal rights of young people, and the constructive approaches found in the Scottish and family group conferencing systems.

The success of this new way of dealing with young offenders would of course depend on there being sufficient skilled people and adequate resources in the community to work with young offenders in the ways we know are effective. Although some savings can be made by stopping wasteful and ineffective interventions, there is no escaping the fact that even under present government proposals to tackle offending by young people local authorities will have to spend more on all their services—education, health and housing as well as youth justice. I can only repeat that in the longer term suitable action to deter current offenders from reoffending will save taxpayers much more than it will cost them.

In themselves the extended panels should not be a great financial burden. We have seen that the costs of the Scottish system compare favourably with those of the English court system. The time spent by professionals at the panel hearings and by the co-ordinator in preparing for them would be a new cost but money would be saved by bringing all interested agencies together for concerted action instead of the duplication of effort that often occurs at present.

Would such a new system offer more immediate justice than the present system with its endemic delays? Yes, if the administrative delays down the line from police stations to the offices of the Crown

Prosecution Service are reduced and the role of specialist youth court lawyers clearly defined by the Law Society, as I have suggested.

Under a system which relies on such panels to agree disposals, would there be sufficient safeguards for children and their families against unwarranted intrusion in their lives, one of the principles on which the Children Act 1989 is built? I believe that this way justice would be done and also be seen to be done. Children and young people would still have lawyers in court if they disputed their guilt, and they would have a better opportunity to show their strengths and potential as well as their needs in the panel hearings to which they could bring advisers (The continuity provided by the presence of at least one magistrate monitoring the case would also ensure that the intervention was not disproportionately long.) Above all by making young people and their families partners in effecting change, the likelihood of such change taking place is greatly increased—and that, as we have seen, is what young people and their families really want, and what the public demands.

Dear Jack Straw

I am addressing this final chapter directly to you in the hope that because it is short you will read it yourself. One of the hazards of ministerial office is that everything you read has been sifted for you. You can't possibly peruse every relevant document, let alone all the books in your field.

The first part of this book is about people, not theories, people we often lose sight of when we talk about young offenders as a category or call them 'superpredators.' The lives of Tyrrell, Jason, Jacquie, Daniel, Luke and the others I interviewed, were my starting-point. It is the lives of individual children and young people like them as well as the public as a whole that your great office of Home Secretary protects and has the power to change.

As your time is limited, let's look first at what you are doing to be tough on crime, to protect the public, whilst remembering that you, too, have regard to the welfare of young offenders. You have steered through Parliament a Crime and Disorder Act to fulfil your manifesto pledges on young offenders, after a period of consultation. You are enacting further measures which affect the sentencing of young people in the Youth Justice and Criminal Evidence Bill.

Let's be positive first and applaud the overarching declaration of the Act that, "It will be the principal aim of the youth justice system to prevent offending by children and young persons." Fine words but does the Act empower "persons and bodies carrying out functions in relation to the youth justice system" to implement that aim?

What I like best about your approach so far is that you and your government recognise that your department cannot act effectively in isolation. For years the cause of justice and the futures of young people have suffered from the divisions between government departments in Whitehall, the Chinese walls between local authority departments in the town hall, and professional divisions on the ground. Peter is constantly paying Paul for services for young people in a Kafkaesque scenario. If a place at college would be the best chance for a young person who failed at school or was excluded from school, should there have to be a fight between education and social services about who pays the fees? Peter refusing to pay Paul was one reason why too many young people end up in custody, since custodial institutions were funded by the Home Office and local authorities could not afford more appropriate secure accommodation which they had to pay for (assuming that they could find vacancies in the first place). The idea of a joint purse is now established and the new Youth Justice Board, in creating a national strategy and setting National Standards, will put co-operation between agencies to the fore.

The new youth offending teams will bring together probation officers who used to supervise young people over the age of 16 (and were funded by your Home Office) and local authority youth justice workers from social services departments who dealt with younger offenders. In addition to representatives from the police, the teams will include the crucial education and health workers who will provide appropriate services after an assessment of the offender's needs, and agencies like housing will be brought in, too.

The problems of the young people I interviewed for this book, and the difficulties their parents faced, were numerous and interlinked. To protect the public from their offending in future it is not just a question of ensuring that young offenders learn to say "no" when they meet temptation, although they must acquire that skill. All these young people also need proper education, opportunities to use their leisure constructively, skills to earn a decent living, and jobs at the end of their training. Many of them also need somewhere suitable to live, supported in a way that is appropriate for their age. (I would like to see the use of bed-and-breakfast accommodation for young people under the age of 18 banned.) They would probably benefit, too, from the continuing advice and friendship of volunteer mentors from the community.

So far, so good. The trouble is that you have not supplied even the areas piloting the new measures sufficient resources to pay for the facilities on the ground which the youth offending teams identify as necessary. Take Jason, a 13-year-old I saw who was already deeply involved in offending, could not read properly and had only limited hours of education to occupy his time. Any YOT would obviously come to the conclusion after its assessment, as his local youth justice team did, that he needs full-time schooling and should be introduced to constructive out-of-school activities. He would possibly benefit from the attention of a mentor as well as sessions with his youth justice worker to look at the consequences of his behaviour.

But just like their predecessors the YOT members would not have the funds to pay for full-time special schooling, they might not find in their area suitable local youth clubs able to take Jason and they might not be able to secure funds to start a mentoring scheme in partnership with local business. Jason's parents might welcome more advice about how to handle him. I doubt if they would take kindly to being ordered to attend a parenting course when in their view they have done their best to work with people in authority since Jason was born, but in any case would the YOT be able to buy in the experts to run a course for them?

It is the bottom line which controls change today. Your Government bases its credibility on not spending its way out of difficulties, offering value for money, and refusing to put up taxes, just as the Conservatives did. Like Janus you are facing two ways. You want there to be alternatives in the community to divert young people from crime but you are not prepared to offer new money for them. Your contradictory situation is made worse because you are a victim of your own rhetoric. You are so careful to fall in with what you see as the public mood that you continue to spend money on extreme measures to contain in security away from home young people, and even quite young children, rather than strengthen projects in the community to reform and divert them from crime.

A few examples. You could show the Treasury how investment in the youth service would save public funds by keeping young people off the streets—it is pointless the government telling local education authorities to provide a youth service if they have no funds to do so. You could explain that it is cheaper as well as better to give local authorities the resources to train and fund foster parents to look after young people when they are on bail waiting for trials rather than to spend government money locking them up on remand in prisons. You could divert the funding for your new secure training centres for 12 to 14-year-olds to intensive projects in the community for this age group. And by shifting to community projects some of the huge sums spent on imprisoning non-violent older offenders you could give community projects the extra personnel and resources we know would make them more effective.

The government has trumpeted its mission to tackle social exclusion. Does locking up young burglars, vandals and car thieves help them to integrate into society, to feel the same as their more law-abiding peers? Will putting an electronic tag round the ankle of a 15-year-old make him feel more like other teenagers or make his family feel "normal"? What about "naming and shaming"? You haven't denounced this idea—far from it. Do you really think that encouraging judges and magistrates to allow the press to publish the names of serious young offenders will speed the process whereby delinquent teenagers will change their ways?

You believe you have already introduced a "formidable agenda of change" but I suggest that it only floats along the surface of what is needed and avoids discussion of the paradigm shift that is necessary in thinking about crime by young people. Through your new Acts you have introduced the possibility of early intervention to prevent further offending when children first come to the attention of the police and the courts but you have done little to ensure that there is the capacity in the community to take advantage of the opportunity and the youth court now has a confusing plethora of sentences it can impose. It remains an unsatisfactory forum for dealing with most children and their families.

You have excellent plans for the future to refer to a panel those who plead guilty to a first offence so that appropriate action may be taken, with everyone's agreement, to prevent further offending. But why so tentative? If a panel has advantages for preventing future offending by some, why should it not be right for all? I advocate in this book a sentencing panel for all young offenders up to the age of 18, except those guilty of the gravest crimes, which allows them and their families to help to work out ways they can change their lives. This kind of forum is the best one in which to explain and agree the concept of reparation which your Crime and Disorder Act introduces, to involve victims appropriately and to inculcate personal responsibility.

It is through the mediation of such panels that the aims of the parenting orders you have introduced would be best accomplished. I have argued against the compulsory nature of these orders but for 30 years I have advocated the cause of education for parenthood and argued that there should be courses on child development in personal development programmes in schools as well as more support for parents in the community. In discussion with panel members, with the focus on their child's offending, parents might well see the point of attending groups to help them with problems of discipline and handling difficult adolescents. They will not respond readily to being ordered to attend a course by a court and if they do attend, their expectations of there being an instant, magic way to control their children may be too high. It is perhaps unfair to bring in your personal experience but it is odd that you, as a parent whose son found himself in trouble, in whatever extenuating circumstances, see your experience as so different from that of most parents whose children err. Most parents, like you, want their children to be law-abiding. They resent being blamed for what their children do but are amenable to help.

The best news so far for arresting youth crime is your government's £540 million "Sure Start" programme, a programme for all agencies, starting with health visitors, to work with parents to promote "the physical, intellectual and social" development of their children. The Ministerial Group on the Family which you chair must see that funds continue to be committed to expanding the services for support in the early years. Health visitors reach all new families in a non-discriminatory, positive way, offering practical help and guidance when it is most wanted and most acceptable so that families do not fall early into a spiral of depression and inadequacy. More schemes are needed everywhere which include and empower parents, whether on the lines of Home-Start and NEWPIN, or literacy schemes and home-school partnerships. More nursery schools should replicate the features of the successful Perry Pre-School Programme including the involvement of parents. The concentration on supporting parents and enabling them to fulfil their responsibilities pays dividends in the long term: a quarter of those who end up in prison spent some of their early years in the care of the state.

What is needed now is a change of emphasis from endless, vengeful discussion about what to do with young offenders to passionate concern for preventing them from ever offending in the first place. As Home Secretary you could take the lead in changing the public perception of what works to stop young people offending by showing that it is only long-term measures that will get to the root of offending and prevent it. The trouble is that your rhetoric, Home Secretary, is stuck in the past. You are so busy reassuring the public that it is safe to walk the streets under New Labour that you sound like your Conservative predecessor Michael Howard. It is your job (and your opportunity if you want to go down in history as a Home Secretary who made a difference) to expose what I have called the defeatist fallacy. In the 1970s the view of an American academic, Martinson, that "nothing worked" with offenders filtered through criminologists to youth justice systems. When Martinson recanted and said "Sorry, I was mistaken", no-one heard him at first. It has taken until now for common sense and positive views to begin to surface. All you have to do is to tell people the truth: that we do know how to prevent youth crime.

You'll be surprised, I think, to see how welcome people will find this message. The general public is more responsive and intelligent than often portrayed. It may seem difficult to prevail over the tabloid view of life but it is your task—and should be your forte as a politician—to present and advocate the best approach to solving agreed problems.

You will capture the public mood if you paint a hopeful picture about what we can do. You will have to explain, of course, that results will not come overnight. But that is a concept I believe people are sophisticated enough to take on board, if it is presented clearly. Up till now academics have been unable to transmit the facts because they obfuscate them in jargon and politicians have been afraid to communicate them with the verve and force that is necessary. You could tell people with enthusiasm about the comparative success of community projects—and about how much more successful community projects would be with more young offenders if they had the resources to work with them longer. The public will not be surprised by the research findings that work with young offenders should be intensive—people have always wanted the days of young offenders to be filled constructively. They will also see the point of ensuring adequate training for those working in the field of youth justice. Most people would be shocked if they knew social workers, with their many and heavy responsibilities, have only a two-year basic training. Nor will they be surprised about the need to tackle as early as possible the problems that cumulatively lead to some young people spiralling out of control and into crime.

The depressing scenario now accepted is that crime is so prevalent in our society that it is endemic. As one of the mothers I interviewed said, "Everybody does it"—everyone seems to be on the make, we're all out for ourselves not for others. But there is another aspect of Britain today waiting to be revealed and ready to be encouraged: we are a nation of volunteers with a ready sympathy for just causes. Yes, you may respond, but that does not mean to say people want to pay for improvements in cash out of their own pockets. The Tories set the political agenda here by painting Labour as the spending party and you have accepted their diagnosis of the public mood, despite the fact that they were so resoundingly rejected by the electorate at the last election.

Your party's integrity is jeopardised by its pledge not to increase tax at all in the immediate future. 'Pay more now but less later', a penny on income tax as an investment for the future, are not slogans you are willing to promote. Why can't you start arguing now for new thinking, for considering long-term as well as short-term gains? You have tentatively taken the Liberal Democrats into partnership over constitutional reform. Why not look to their ideas for a way of paying for educational improvement which fits the new public mood? I am not arguing that people have altruistic genes. I am saying that people condemn human frailty out of fear for themselves but they would be willing to support a realistic way to build a safer society with better opportunities for all.

What I am asking is for you as Home Secretary to take the lead in creating a society in which we combine to fight crime by dealing with its causes and in which we keep those children and young people who have broken the law from re-offending by measures designed to include them in society, rather than by excluding them from it. Some libertarians might argue that the kind of social control I am advocating in the name of the community, offering 'support' to 'vulnerable' families, making education for parenthood compulsory in schools (with the implication that to bring a child into the world is not an uncomplicated right), 'putting pressure' on young offenders and families to 'agree' plans for their rehabilitation, is as authoritarian as anything we have had in the past. But any democratic society is based on acceptance of certain principles of which the Rule of Law is one.

It is time we had a Home Secretary who can show how policies relate to principle and who therefore does not go softly, softly on reform. I won't presume to ask you to do this on behalf of others, not even on behalf of the young people whose stories I have told in this book. I ask you to show your true colours, Home Secretary, to change your rhetoric and to change the government's tactics into an effective preventive strategy against offending by children and young people.

Yours very sincerely

Sarah Curtis, April 1999

Epilogue

When this book went to press, how were the eleven young people faring, 18 months after I interviewed them? The news was mixed.

Tyrrell was on remand in custody, accused of burglaries and stealing cars. He had continued living at the same children's home and at first he had kept on an even keel. However, he had not managed to complete a number of college courses he attempted, despite his ambitions. He had begun taking class A drugs (heroin). His social worker thought he had mental health problems but he was refusing to have a psychiatric assessment because both he and his mother preferred the label "bad" to "mad". A custodial sentence was expected.

Jacquie had been caught shoplifting again soon after I saw her but had nearly completed a year's probation without any more incidents. She was living with her aunt, had passed her driving test and was attending college regularly, so there were hopes that she would now succeed in the mainstream.

Jason had received a custodial sentence the moment he reached 15. His schooling had not been sorted out. Several fostering placements had failed. When a potentially suitable foster placement was found in a different local authority area, that authority had been unable to pay for his placement at a special school for children with emotional and behavioural difficulties. He was involved with others in a street robbery and resisted arrest when challenged in the course of attempting a burglary at 11 p.m. one night.

Daniel had been sentenced to five years' custody after another serious building society robbery.

Stephen was doing quite well after a couple of offences of possessing cannabis. He was working as a DJ in a club and trying to become a producer in the pop world. He had his own flat, the door of which, at the time I inquired about him, had been broken after a police raid. The police were looking for drugs but found none.

There were concerns about Mark's mental health. He had set up home with a young woman but was subsequently charged with violence against her. He was back at his mother's, not working and awaiting assessment for one of the few places at a full-time day centre in lieu of custody.

Both Josiah and Matthew had kept completely free of trouble. Josiah had got casual labouring work and Matthew was doing a college course, living on benefits in temporary accommodation found by the local authority.

The news about the twins was hopeful. Both had served custodial sentences since I saw them, though for old matters that had caught up with them. Robert was doing a City and Guilds course in car mechanics and Cliff had got an RSA diploma in youth work at the local college. They were living separately in council accommodation, both with girlfriends with whom they had "volatile" relationships. They had received an award from the Prince's Youth Business Trust to help them to train so that they could produce a business plan for setting up their own car business.

Luke had been in no further trouble and was doing well at school.

Bibliography

A New Three Rs for Young Offenders, 1997, NACRO.

Adcock Margaret and White Richard, editors, 1985, *Good-enough Parenting: A framework for assessment*, British Agencies for Adoption & Fostering (BAAF).

Allen Rob, 1996, *Children & Crime–Taking responsibility*, Institute for Public Policy Research (IPPR).

Asquith Stewart, editor, 1996, *Children and Young People in Conflict with the Law*, Jessica Kingsley.

Audit Commission, 1996, *Misspent Youth*.

Audit Commission, 1998, *Misspent Youth '98*.

Ball Mog, 1998, *The School, the Family and the Community*, Joseph Rowntree Foundation.

Bastiani John, 1995, *Taking a Few Risks: Learning from each other–teachers, parents and pupils*, RSA (Royal Society for the encouragement of Arts, Manufactures and Commerce).

Bottoms A *et al*, 1995, *Intensive Community Supervision for Young Offenders: Outcomes, process and cost*, Cambridge University Press.

Braithwaite J, 1989, *Crime, Shame and Reintegration*, Cambridge University Press.

Bright Jon, 1997, *Turning the Tide: Crime, community and prevention*, Demos.

Cavadino Paul, editor, 1996, *Children Who Kill*, British Juvenile and Family Courts Society/Waterside Press.

Crime, Community and Change: Taking action on the Kingsmead Estate in Hackney, 1996, NACRO.

Criminal Statistics England and Wales, HMSO.

Curtis Sarah, 1975, *Don't Rush Me! The comic-strip, sex education and a multi-racial society*, Community Relations Commission (now CRE).

Curtis Sarah, 1989, *Juvenile Offending: Prevention through Intermediate Treatment*, Batsford.

Devlin Angela, 1995, *Criminal Classes: Offenders at school*, Waterside Press.

Draft Guidance on Establishing Youth Offending Teams, 1998, Home Office.

Drakeford Mark, 1996, 'Parents of Young People in Trouble' in *The Howard Journal of Criminal Justice* vol. 35 no. 3, August 1996.

Etzioni Amitai, 1993, *The Spirit of Community*, Simon and Schuster, *The New Golden Rule: Community and Morality in a Democratic Society*, 1997, Profile Books.

Farrington D P, 1989, *Cambridge Study in Delinquent Development Long Term Follow Up: Final report to the Home Office*, Institute of Criminology, Cambridge University.

Farrington D, *Understanding and Preventing Youth Crime*, 1996, Joseph Rowntree Foundation.

FitzHugh Rafela, 1996, *Young Offenders Speak for Themselves*, Portobello Trust.

Getting to Grips with Crime: A new framework for local action–A consultation document, 1997, Home Office.

Gibson Bryan, editor, 1999, *Introduction to Youth Justice*, Waterside Press.

Gill Kevin, 1992, *Tackling Youth Crime–A practical guide*, Crime Concern.

Godfrey David, 1996, 'Lost in the Myths of Crime: The use of penal custody for male juveniles, 1969 to 1993', in *The Howard Journal* vol.35 no. 4 November 1996.

Goleman Daniel, 1995, *Emotional Intelligence*, Bantam Books.

Graef Roger, 1992, *Living Dangerously*, Harper Collins.

Graham John, 1998, *Fast-tracking of Persistent Young Offenders*, Home Office Research and Statistics Directorate, Research Findings No. 74.

Graham J and Bowling B, 1995, *Young People and Crime*, Home Office Research Study 145.

Graham J and Smith D I, 1994, *Diversion from Offending: The role of the Youth Service*, Crime Concern.

Graham J, 1988, *Schools, Disruptive Behaviour and Delinquency: A review of research*, Home Office Research Study 96.

Hagell Ann and Newburn Tim, 1994, *Persistent Young Offenders*, Policy Studies Institute (PSI).

Henricson Clem, 1995, *Parents Against Crime: A pilot project for the parents of juvenile offenders–an evaluation*, Exploring Parenthood.

HM Inspectorate of Prisons for England and Wales, 1997, *Young Prisoners: A thematic review*, Home Office.

Homeless and Hungry, 1992, Centrepoint.

Howard League, *Banged Up, Beating Up, Cutting Up: Report of the Howard League Commission of Inquiry into Violence in Penal Institutions for Teenagers under 18*, 1995; *The Howard League Troubleshooter Project: Lessons for policy and practice on 15-year-olds in prison*, 1996.

Hutton Will, *The State We're In*, 1995, *The State to Come*, 1997, Vintage.

Inner London Youth Justice Services, 1995, *Statements of Principle and Practice Standards*, NACRO.

Kelly Alistair, 1996, *Introduction to the Scottish Children's Panel*, Waterside Press.

Lansdown Gerison, 1995, *Taking Part–Children's participation in decision making*, Institute for Public Policy Research (IPPR).
Lewis, Inspector Edwin James, 1995, *Truancy: The partnership approach*, Police Research Group.
Martin Carol, editor, 1997 (2nd edition 1998), *The ISTD Handbook of Community Programmes for Young Offenders*, Waterside Press.
Martinson R, 1974, 'What works? Questions and answers about prison reform' in *The Public Interest* no. 35, and 'Martinson attacks his own earlier work' in *Criminal Justice Newsletter*, 9 December 1978.
McGuire James, editor, 1995, *What Works–Reducing offending*, Wiley.
Morris A, Giller H, Szed E and Geach H, 1980, *Justice for Children*, Macmillan.
Morrison Blake, 1997, *As If*, Granta Books.
NACRO briefing papers on 'The Crime and Disorder Bill' (1998), 'Getting Serious About Youth Crime' (1997), 'Exclusion from School' (1997), 'Families and Crime' (1997), 'Remand Fostering' (1996), 'What Should be Done About Persistent Young Offenders?' (1994).
National Protocol for Youth Justice Services: Statements of Principle for Local Services in England and Wales, 1996, ACC, AMA, ADSS, NACRO and ACOP.
No More Excuses–A new approach to tackling youth crime in England and Wales, 1997, Home Office Cm 3809.
O'Mahony David and Haines Kevin, 1996, *An Evaluation of the Introduction and Operation of the Youth Court*, Home Office Research Study 152.
Parental Responsibility, Youth Crime and the Criminal Law, 1997, Penal Affairs Consortium.
Pitts John, 1997, 'Crime Prevention in France and Britain' in *Criminal Justice* vol. 15 no. 4 November 1997.
Preventing Children Offending: A consultation document, 1997, Home Office.
Pugh G, De'Ath and Smith C, 1994, *Confident Parents, Confident Children: Policy and practice in parent education and support*, National Children's Bureau (NCB).
Pugh Gillian and De'Ath Erica, 1984, *The Needs of Parents*, NCB/Macmillan.
Raynor, Peter, 1997, 'Some Observations on Rehabilitation and Justice' in *The Howard Journal of Criminal Justice* vol. 36 no. 3 August 1997.
Roberts Helen and Sachdev Darshan, editors, 1996, *Young People's Social Attitudes–Having their say: the views of 12 to 19 year-olds*, Barnardo's.
Rutherford Andrew, 1995, *Growing Out of Crime*, Waterside Press.
Rutter M, Maughan B, Mortimore P and Ouston J, 1979, *Fifteen Thousand Hours: Secondary schools and their effects on children*, Open Books.
Smith C and Pugh G, 1996, *Learning to be a Parent*, Joseph Rowntree Foundation.
Smith C with Pugh G, 1995, *Learning to be a Parent–A survey of group-based parenting programmes*, Family Policy Studies Centre/Joseph Rowntree Foundation.
Standing Conference on Crime Prevention, 1991, *Safer Communities: The local delivery of crime prevention through the partnership approach*, Home Office.
Sutton Mike, 1996, *Implementing Prevention Schemes in a Multi-agency Setting: Aspects of process in the Safer Cities programme*, Home Office Research Study 160.
Sylva K, 1988, 'Does early intervention work?' in *Archives of Disease in Childhood* vol. 64.
Sylva K, 1994, 'The Impact of Early Learning on Children's Development' in Sir Christopher Ball, *Start Right: The importance of early learning*, RSA (Royal Society for the encouragement of Arts, Manufactures and Commerce.
Tackling Delays in the Youth Justice System, 1997, Home Office.
Tackling Youth Crime: A consultation paper, 1997, Home Office.
Tackling Youth Crime: Reforming youth justice, 1996, Labour Party 'Road to the Manifesto'.
Truancy and School Exclusion, 1997, HMSO Cm 3957.
Utting David, 1996, *Reducing Criminality Among Young People: A sample of relevant programmes in the United Kingdom*, Home Office Research Study 161.
Utting David, Bright Jon and Henricson Clem, 1993, *Crime and the Family*, Family Policy Studies Centre.
Utting Sir William, 1991, *Children in the Public Care: A review of residential care*, DHSS.
West D J, 1982, *Delinquency*, Heinemann.
Whitfield Dick, 1997, *Tackling the Tag: The electronic monitoring of offenders*, Waterside Press.
Wilson John, 1972, *Practical Methods of Moral Education*, Longman.

Index

fear of crime 10
Feltham Young Offender Institution 194 196 *et al*
final warning, see *warnings and reprimands*
Fitzharry's Secondary School, Oxfordshire 132
friends 94
fostering 181 208 (bail) 209
   National Foster Care Association 209

Geaney, Mary 217
Geese Theatre 160
Goleman, Daniel 159
Graef, Roger 201
grassing 62
"grave crimes" 192 207 214 222

Hackney/Kingsmead Estate 171 *et al* 177 185
handling stolen property, see *theft/handling*
Hammersmith and Fulham 177
Hanley, Stoke-on-Trent, initiative 136 167
Hazel, Nancy 209
health visitors 111
'Holiday Camps' 174
home-school projects 129
home-school contracts 219
Home-Start 111 115
Howard League 194
Howard, Michael 12 111 197 202 228
Hurd, Douglas 13

intermediate treatment (IT) 55 161 182 194
individual tuition 65 125 167
Inner London Probation Service (ILPS) 185 204
Inner London youth panel 222
introspection 150
ISTD (Centre for Crime and Justice Studies) 204
It'll Never be the Same 154
It's Your Life 152 154

just deserts 12
Juvenile Crime Prevention Strategy Group 168 170
Juvenile Offender Resource Centre, Surrey 160 199 200

Kate's Hill etc School, Dudley 130
Kensington and Chelsea/Lancaster West Estate etc 168 171 177
Kent Social Services Intensive Support and Supervision Programme 217
Kilbrandon Report 215
knowledge 150

Lambeth College 141
Law Society's Child Care Panel 188
Lawson, Lorraine 178
Lennox Lewis College, Hackney 142 *et al*
lifeskills 160
Living Dangerously 201
lodgings 201 207
Losers, Weepers 155

magistrates 179 190 202 221
Magistrates' Association 103
Manchester, Greater (tagging trials) 210

Medomsley, County Durham 198
   Wackenhut/Seccor 198
mentoring 178 180 *et al*
   London Mentoring Development Officer 182
Mill, John Stuart 158
Misspent Youth 89 90 170 180 187 189 193 204 218
morality 146 *et al*
   teacher training 152 *et al* 161 165
Morrison, Blake 146

NACRO 172
National Children's Bureau 209
National Parenting Development Centre 117
National Standards (Probation Service etc) 203 225
NEWPIN 111 119 *et al* 149 228
New Zealand 215
No More Excuses 219
Norfolk (tagging trials) 210
North West London, College of 141
Notting Hill Gate 168

Onley, Northamptonshire 198
Offending Behaviour, Skills and Strategems for Going Straight 161

Paddington Technical College 138
Paget, Sheila 170
parental perspective/responsibility/relationships etc 13 90 91 117 *et al* 229
   bind over 105 108/9
   Exploring Parenthood 111 117 *et al* 168
   parenting orders 108
   parents and schools 128
   'Parents in a Learning Society' 129 *et al*
Parsons, Carl 136
partnerships
   against crime 182
Patten, John 13 103 106
penalties 192
Perry Pre-school Programme 128 228
"persistent offenders" 190
police 136
preoccupation with self 150
press, portrayal of juvenile offenders 9 *et al* 90 193 198
Preventing Children Offending 108
prevention of crime/offending 11 14 117 et al 127 213 230
prison works 12
property-related crimes 89
Punishment, Custody and the Community 195

Queen's Park Rangers 183

race 98 184
RAILS, Brighton 207 208
Raleigh International 170 177
'Rat Boy' 9 10 101
Reducing Criminality Among Young People, etc 111
reintegrative shaming 216 et al
remand fostering 209 *et al*
reparation/order 200 202 204 212

Going Straight After Crime and Punishment
Compiled by Angela Devlin and Bob Turney
Foreword by Jack Straw, Home Secretary

Going Straight looks at a range of criminals who have changed their way of life. They include famous, notorious, creative and ordinary people who were prepared to talk about the turning point in their lives—the events which caused them to leave crime behind. Their candid explanations about how they rebuilt their lives—often full of remorse for their victims and determined to repay something to their communities—are challenging, illuminating and a cause for optimism.

'The compilers of this book are to be congratulated for this valuable perspective on crime and punishment' **The Rt Hon Jack Straw MP, Home Secretary**

'The launch of this book [at HMP Wandsworth] was quite simply the best I have attended. A stroke of genius by Waterside Press and a gathering I would characterise by the "John Marriott approach" . . . An absorbing book': **Dr Deborah Cheney**

ISBN 1 872 870 66 X. £18 plus £2 p&p. All royalties from *Going Straight* are being paid to UNLOCK, the National Association of Ex-Offenders

Until They Are Seven
The Origins of Women's Legal Rights
John Wroath

'In law a husband and wife are one: and that one is the husband': Blackstone. This was the law until well into the nineteenth century. *Until They Are Seven* looks at the historical background to the modern law concerning children. The result is an absorbing account of the origins of women's rights to their children and their property in which John Wroath recalls the brave efforts of Henrietta Greenhill and Caroline Norton which led to the Infant Custody Act 1839 and Matrimonial Causes Act 1857. The story is fascinating for its connection with several notable people of the time—including prime minister Lord Melbourne, playwright Richard Brinsley Sheridan and author Mary Shelley.

His Honour John Wroath is the former senior family judge for Hampshire and the Isle of Wight. 1998 ISBN 1 872 870 57 0. £12 plus £1.50 p&p

Children Who Kill Paul Cavadino (Ed.)
From the tragic Mary Bell and Jamie Bulger cases to events world-wide: An expert analysis. 'Highly recommended' *The Law.* 'A rich source of information' *British Journal of Social Work.* In association with the British Juvenile and Family Courts Society. 1996 ISBN 1 872 870 29 5. £16 plus £2 p&p

Introduction to Youth Justice
Winston Gordon, Philip Cuddy and Jonathan Black

Edited by Bryan Gibson

Introduction to Youth Justice deals with the major changes taking place in strategies for preventing youth crime and dealing with juveniles in and out of court.

This second edition is fully up-to-date, including

- the impact of the Crime and Disorder Act 1998
- the creation of youth offending teams or 'YOTs'
- the responsibilities of local authorities and other agencies
- police warnings and reprimands
- an authoritative outline of the youth court, its jurisdiction, procedures and enhanced sentencing powers.

This easy to read handbook provides a unrivalled source of information at a key time in the evolution of youth justice in England and Wales.

1999 176 pages ISBN 1 872 870 36 8. £13.50 plus £1.50 p&p

Introduction to the Magistrates' Court
Bryan Gibson

With the assistance of Winston Gordon and Andy Wesson

The **THIRD EDITION** of this popular handbook has been fully revised to take account of changes in law, procedure, practice and sentencing. It contains a fully up-to-date account of the jurisdiction, powers, procedures and practices of the magistrates' court, including a fresh additional section on evidence.

'An ideal introduction' *Law Society Gazette* (Review of the first edition).

1999 176 pages ISBN 1 872 870 68 6. £13.50 plus £1.50 p&p